EXPOSITORY STUDIES IN 2 CORINTHIANS

POWER OUT OF WEAKNESS

RAY C. STEDMAN

WORD BOOKS
PUBLISHER
WACO, TEXAS

Expository Studies in 2 Corinthians

Discovery Books are published by Word Books, Publisher, in cooperation with Discovery Foundation, Palo Alto, California.

ISBN 0–8499–2946–6
Library of Congress Catalog Card No. 82-050509

Printed in the United States of America

Contents

Preface

The second letter of Paul to the Corinthians is probably the least known of all his letters. First Corinthians is very well known, but many people consider 2 Corinthians to be such heavy reading that it has been called "Paul's unknown letter." It is too bad that we are so unfamiliar with it, because it represents the most personal, the most autobiographical letter from the apostle's pen. In 1 Corinthians we examined the church at Corinth. That letter is so valuable because the church today much resembles the church in Corinth; we live in "Corinthian" conditions now. But in 2 Corinthians we are looking at Paul; he is the one in focus as he lays himself open and reveals himself to the church. This, therefore, is a very personal letter from the heart of this mighty apostle. Here we see him more clearly, perhaps, than anywhere else in Scripture.

Titles by Ray C. Stedman in the "Discovery Books" Series:

Authentic Christianity (2 Corinthians 2:14–6:13)
Behind History (Parables of Matthew 13)
Death of a Nation (Book of Jeremiah)
Jesus Teaches on Prayer
The Queen and I (Book of Esther)
Riches in Christ (Ephesians 1–3)
The Servant Who Rules (Mark 1–8)
The Ruler Who Serves (Mark 9–16)
Spiritual Warfare (Ephesians 6:10–18)
Understanding Man (Genesis 2–3)
From Guilt to Glory (Romans) Vols. 1 and 2
Expository Studies in 1 John
Expository Studies in Job
Expository Studies in 1 Corinthians

1

Why Does It Hurt So Much?

Second Corinthians should, perhaps, be called Fourth Corinthians, because it is the last of four letters that Paul wrote to the church there. Two of these letters have not been preserved—that is why we only have 1 and 2 Corinthians—but they are not in the order that these titles suggest. Let us recapitulate a little of the background. Then one can refer back to this if any confusion about the chronology should arise. Paul founded the church in Corinth somewhere around 52 or 53 A.D. He stayed there for about a year and a half; then he went to Ephesus, where he remained for a few weeks. From there he made a quick trip to Jerusalem, returning again to Ephesus. While he was at Ephesus, he wrote a letter to the church at Corinth which is lost to us. It is referred to in 1 Corinthians 5:9, where Paul says he wrote to warn them about following a worldly life style. In response to that letter, the Corinthians wrote back with many questions. They sent their letter by the hands of three young men who are mentioned in 1 Corinthians. In reply to that letter, Paul wrote what we now call 1 Corinthians. In it he tried to answer their questions. We have looked at those answers in the volume on 1 Corinthians. He tried to exhort them and instruct them in how to walk in power and in peace; thus he sought to correct many problem areas in the church.

Evidently that letter did not accomplish all that Paul intended. There was a bad reaction to it, and in 2 Corinthians 2:1 we learn that he made a quick trip to Corinth. How long that took we do not know. Paul calls it a "painful" visit. He had come with a rather sharp rebuke to them, but again he did not accomplish his purpose. Again there was a great deal of negative reaction. So when he returned to Ephesus he sent another brief letter in the hands of Titus to Corinth to see if he could help them. This letter, too, is lost to us, unless it consisted of chapters 10–13 of 2 Corinthians. Titus was gone a long time, for transportation and communication were very slow and difficult in those days. Paul, waiting in Ephesus, grew very anxious to hear what was happening in the church there. He became so troubled that he left Ephesus and went to Troas and then up into Macedonia to meet Titus. There in Macedonia, probably in the city of Philippi, he and Titus came together. Titus brought him a much more encouraging word about the church, and in response to that, out of thanksgiving, Paul wrote what we now call the Second Corinthian letter, although it was really the fourth of a series of letters.

The opening greetings are somewhat similar to the first letter, but a little briefer and perhaps a bit more brusque:

> Paul, an apostle of Christ Jesus by the will of God, and Timothy our brother. To the church of God which is at Corinth, with all the saints who are in the whole of Achaia: Grace to you and peace from God our Father and the Lord Jesus Christ (2 Cor. 1:1, 2).

You will notice several emphases there. Chief among them is the fact that Paul says that he is not the representative of the churches but he is the Lord's apostle. His authority does not come from the church, or any members of the church, but from the Lord himself. This was a strong point with Paul. These days we hear teaching about how wrong Paul was in certain areas, that he cannot be trusted in parts of his writing, that he even said things we must reject today. We need to understand anew that the apostle himself said his authority came directly from the Lord. What he had learned and what he taught was taught to him by Jesus himself. "The Lord appeared to me," Paul says. "There were many visions and revelations from Christ," he says in effect, so that he did not learn his doctrine or anything he wrote from the other apostles. He learned it from the Lord directly. When you read Paul you are reading what Jesus said to him; therefore it comes with the full authority of the Lord Jesus himself.

Notice, too, that the letter is sent to more than the church at Corinth. It is sent to "all the saints who are in the whole of Achaia." Achaia was the ancient name for Greece as we know it today (except for Macedonia in the north). All the Grecian mainland, the Peloponnesus, the islands and so on, were part of Achaia. Therefore there were many churches to whom this letter was addressed, and we, even in the twentieth century, can rightly be included as one of them. As in all of Paul's letters, he offers them grace and peace. Now these are important words; they are more than a mere salutation. "Grace" is a word that gathers up all God is ready to do for us and give to us. All God's supply comes by grace. Therefore, anything God gives you—love, joy, peace, forgiveness, help, wisdom—is part of the supply of grace. The result of that supply in your life and mine is peace. When one's heart is resting and confident that God is at work, that person is calm within and is serene and untroubled of spirit. This is the way Christians are to live. The whole of the NT is addressed to that end. It is not only doctrine about how to go to heaven; it is also teaching on how to handle life, how to cope with pressures and stresses and how to face the difficulties and dangers of life. The constant gracious supply of God is to bring peace to our troubled hearts. We are to live at rest.

The God Who Strengthens

Now having said that, the apostle plunges right into his first subject—why Christians suffer:

> Blessed be the God and Father of our Lord Jesus Christ, the Father of mercies and God of all comfort, who comforts us in all our affliction, so that we may be able to comfort those who are in any affliction, with the comfort with which we ourselves are comforted by God. For as we share abundantly in Christ's sufferings, so through Christ we share abundantly in comfort also. If we are afflicted, it is for your comfort and salvation; and if we are comforted, it is for your comfort, which you experience when you patiently endure the same sufferings that we suffer. Our hope for you is unshaken; for we know that as you share in our sufferings, you will also share in our comfort (2 Cor. 1:3–7).

Two words, "affliction," and "comfort," stand out repeatedly in this passage; and the two belong together. Affliction is what we today would probably call pressure, or stress. It is what many of you, perhaps, feel when you think about going to work tomorrow. It is whatever ties knots in your stomach and makes you feel anxious or troubled about what lies ahead. It is what makes for hectic days and sleepless nights. It gnaws continually at your mind and threatens your well-being; it refuses to go away and leave you alone; it depresses you and darkens the future with forebodings of disaster. That is pressure, stress, and we all live with it. People were no different in the first century. They lived under pressure and stress just as we do. Paul experienced it as well, but along with it he experienced the comfort of God.

God's comfort is more than a little cheer or friendly word of encouragement. Paul does not mean that. The word basically means to "strengthen." What Paul experienced was the strengthening of God to give him a peaceful, restful spirit able to meet the pressure and the stress with which he lived. That is what Christianity is all about. In the Greek, "strengthen" is a word used also for the Holy Spirit. The KJV frequently calls him "The Comforter," but really it is "The Strengthener," the one who strengthens you. This is God's provision for affliction. It is amazing to me how many thousands of Christians dread their daily lives because they feel pressured, stressful, tied up in knots, and yet they never avail themselves of God's provision for that kind of pressure. These words are not addressed to us merely to be used for religious problems. They are to be used for any kind of stress, any kind of problems. God's comfort, God's strengthening, is available for whatever puts you under stress.

Thousands do not avail themselves of God's comfort, I believe, because they seem to behave like a person who is not a Christian at all—they try merely to escape their pressures. Or, if they are Christian, they pray that they will be rescued from their pressures, that the problems will be taken away. You can always tell how ill-taught Christians really are when they pray to have their problems taken away, or to be completely shielded from them. All their hopes are for escape somehow, and their reactions are either worry or a murmuring, complaining spirit of anger and fear. That is not true Christianity in action. Listen to Paul: "Blessed be the God and Father of our Lord Jesus Christ." He praises God for the circumstances of his life even though there were afflictions. He calls God the "Father of mercies and God of all comfort." He sees God's hand as having sent these very things into his life; therefore he never prays to have them removed so that he might escape from them. He sees them as opportunities for the release of the strength of God.

This suggests the first reason why Christians go through suffering. Recently, a lady said to me, "I know we are supposed to suffer as Christians, but why does it hurt so much?" Well, there are four reasons given in this passage.

First, it hurts because that is the way you discover what God can do. How are you ever going to find the comfort of God, the strengthening of God, if you are not under any pressure or stress? It takes this to discover what God can do. God will keep on sending stress until you understand this truth and begin to count on him to find from within the release that he provides. Do not try to run from it like everybody else is doing. Face up to it and do as Paul does by seeing these as opportunities to understand and experience anew the strengthening of God:

> For as we share abundantly in Christ's sufferings, so through Christ we share abundantly in comfort too (2 Cor. 1:5).

The strengthening is exactly equal to the pressure. That is a Christian life style; that is what every Christian ought to experience.

"Well," you say, "I know all about that. I've tried it many times and it doesn't work for me. It works for you; it works for all the others I talk to, but it won't work for me." I am always amazed at how many Christian exceptions go to church! I remember one minister who had a secretary who was always cheerful no matter how much she was going through. He said to her one day, "I wish I had your faith and optimism." She replied, "Well, you would if you'd read your Bible right." "What do you mean?" he asked. "I read it in Greek and in English." She said, "Well, you don't read it right, because Paul says, 'Glory in tribulation.' Now G-L-O-R-Y doesn't spell 'growl,' " she said. "When you get tribulations you growl, you complain all the time, but Scripture says glory in tribulations, welcome them as challenges, as opportunities, as occasions to discover the strengthening of God." The truly Christian reaction to troubles and pressures is to see them all as sent by a loving God who is still in control, who will limit them, as he promised, so they will not be more than you are able to bear. He has sent them deliberately to help you discover the inner strengthening that can keep your heart at peace, no matter what the pressure is. That is the first reason pressures are sent.

For Someone Else's Comfort

A second reason for suffering is found in verse 4:

> . . . so that we may be able to comfort those who are in any affliction, with the comfort with which we ourselves are comforted by God (2 Cor. 1:4).

I think the older you grow as a Christian the clearer this becomes. Your sufferings are not sent for you so much as they are for someone who is watching you and seeing how you handle the pressure you are going through. Older Christians easily forget that younger Christians are watching them all the time. When we give way to complaining and murmuring about our circumstances we are teaching these younger Christians (just as though we sat down with them and waggled our fingers at them) that God is faithless, that the Scriptures are not true, that we can get no adequate support for what we are going through. When sufferings are sent to us they are often sent so that others watching us will know they, too, can be sustained. This is what Paul says to this church. "When I suffer," he says, "it is for your comfort; it is that you might see what God can do, and what he can take me through he can take you through. Therefore, as you watch me you will see how to handle this." The lesson is set forth clearly:

> If we are afflicted, it is for your comfort and salvation; and if we are comforted, it is for your comfort, which you experience when you patiently endure (2 Cor. 1:6).

Patiently endure, trusting that God is in charge and he is taking you through this. He is not taking it away, he is taking you through it. So you patiently wait, rejoicing that the end is in sight; "this too shall pass." Someone once said his favorite scripture was, "And it came to pass." It did not come to stay, it came to pass. This, too, will pass, and you will be strengthened by it, therefore, patiently endure and discover the strength that God can give.

Paul then goes on to say their endurance was an encouragement to him:

> Our hope for you is unshaken; for we know that as you share in our sufferings, you will also share in our comfort (2 Cor. 1:7).

Sometimes I wish I could spare younger Christians their trials and pressures. I feel this way about my children. I would love to be able to deliver them from the pressure, from the test, but I know that I cannot, even as much as I want to, and it would not be good for them if I could. They need to experience the suffering so they can also experience the comfort. So Paul says to these Corinthians, "Our hope for you is unshaken. We've heard you are going through trials and difficulties and pressures and persecutions, but we're not disturbed. We know that if you share our sufferings you will also share our comfort, and the comfort is worth the suffering always." So he encourages them to go through this.

Notice, too, how we are encouraged to share with one another what we have gone through. Christians ought to share their problems, their struggles, their failures and their successes with each other, freely and openly, because this sharing is the very way we encourage one another. I was reading an article by Chuck Colson not long ago in which he said that he often asked himself why he had to go to prison as a result of Watergate. Legally, there was no reason why he should have been put in prison. Nevertheless, he ended up there and for a long time he struggled with this fact. Why did he have to suffer the humiliation, the shame, the disgrace and the discontent of prison? But then the answer began to come. While he was in prison he learned what prisoners go through. He saw these forgotten men and women of American society, the awful injustices they often face, the difficulty, even the impossibility of recovering themselves, and there was born in him a great sense of compassion and a desire to help. Since he has been released from prison he has devoted his whole life and ministry to going back in and helping these people. Now wonderful stories are beginning to come from prisons all over America of dramatic changes in human lives because Chuck Colson was sent to prison. That is why God sends us into difficulties at times. It is not always for our sake, but for someone else's sake. We have been brought along and matured to the point where we can take it and rejoice in it and handle it rightly. When we do, what a lesson we are giving to those who are following along behind.

I Can Do It by Myself

Now still a third reason for Christian affliction is given in verses 8 through 10:

> For we do not want you to be ignorant, brethren, of the affliction we experienced in Asia; for we were so utterly, unbearably crushed that we despaired of life itself. Why, we felt that we had received the sentence of death; but that was to make us rely not on ourselves but on God who raises the dead; he delivered us from so deadly a peril, and he is delivering us; on him we have set our hope that he will deliver us again (2 Cor. 1:8–10).

We do not know the details of this crushing time; some think Paul had a severe illness, and perhaps it was. Others, and I am among them, link this with the record in Acts 19 of the great riot which broke out in Ephesus, threatening the lives of the Christians in that city. At that time it appeared the whole Christian cause had collapsed in Ephesus and all Paul had labored on for years was falling apart. He must have gone through unusual emotional stress and physical threat during this time. He tells us that he was "utterly, unbearably crushed." Now that is the lowest ebb the human spirit can come to, the uttermost sense of despair. "Why," he said, "we felt that we had received the sentence of death." It was absolutely hopeless; he had given up; there was no way out. He could see himself losing his life at this point. But then he adds, "but that was to make us rely not on ourselves."

One of the major reasons God sends us suffering is to break the stubborn spirit of self-will within us. Our will insists on trying to work it all out by our own resources, to run to some other human resource, or in some way refuse to acknowledge that we need divine help. I find this in myself. I struggle sometimes. I do not want to pray about a certain matter because if I pray about it, it means I cannot handle it myself. Paul must have struggled the same way. This mighty apostle plainly and clearly understood the principles of how God operates. Still he had to go through a testing like this that he might again learn not to rely on himself. Read the story of Saul of Tarsus, that brilliant young Pharisee, and you see a self-reliant young man, confident that he has the world by the tail, that there is nothing he cannot do with his brilliant mind, his ability and logic, his strong, powerful personality. He felt he could handle anything, and again and again God had to break his self-confidence, to put him in circumstances he could not handle, that he might learn not to rely on himself, but "on God who raises the dead," the God for whom no cause is ever hopeless, who can bring life out of death.

That is, I think, the major reason for suffering. It is the pressure designed to destroy our determined stubbornness. But do you see how Paul comes to a knowledge of the true Christian life style? "God delivered us"—in the past; "he is delivering us"—in the present; "he will deliver us"—in the future. Paul has learned to trust God to take him through whatever life throws at him, no matter what it is. Now that is a Christian life style. It is time some of us Christians quit acting like the world around us, constantly complaining, murmuring and griping about everything that comes our way. We should see these as opportunities to display an alternative life style, to release in our lives a quiet power that will keep our hearts at peace, because we know our adequate God is handling the situation; he will take us safely through.

Pray for Each Other

Then a final reason for suffering is given in verse 11:

> You also must help us by prayer, so that many will give thanks on our behalf for the blessing granted us in answer to many prayers.

Once again, suffering is sent to show us that we are not individuals living all alone in life. We are members of a family, we are members of a Body, and we need each other. When you have a difficulty or a trial, share it with others so that they can pray with you, for many prayers will bring great deliverance. That is what this verse says. "In answer to many prayers" God will send a blessing which will awaken thanksgiving in many, many hearts. Paul says, therefore, "You must help us by prayer," so that there will be great thanksgiving for the great blessing that comes from many prayers. This is the reason for requests for prayer, for sharing our needs with one another, and for enlisting the aid of others in "praying us through" times of pressure, just as we ought to be ready to respond to those who are going through pressure with our prayers for them.

In these eleven verses, then, we see the way the Christian community ought to respond to stress and pressure, to difficulties and trials and disasters. God has sent them. God has allowed them to come as opportunities that we might learn again this amazing secret of inner strength, inner comfort, inner peace that can keep our hearts quiet, even though we are going through troubled times.

2

When You Are Misunderstood

It seems fair to say that in some area of our lives, we are always being misunderstood. What a commentary on life to notice how often our motives are misjudged, our actions misunderstood. We never seem to be free from the experience of having something taken in quite a different light than we intended it.

Here in chapter 1 of 2 Corinthians, we have a classic case of a misunderstanding that will help us in handling such matters. Paul here is sharing certain experiences which come from being a Christian in a pagan world. In the previous chapter, we saw how he spoke about the universal tendency toward pressure and stress and the afflictions of life. We saw how God has given us a source of strengthening so we can handle the pressure. Here we are looking at a misunderstanding that developed between Paul and the church at Corinth. We shall see his hungering for vindication and his desire to correct and straighten out the matter.

> For our boast is this, the testimony of our conscience that we have behaved in the world, and still more toward you, with holiness and godly sincerity, not by earthly wisdom but by the grace of God. For we write you nothing but what you can read and understand; I hope you will understand fully, as you have understood in part, that you can be proud of us as we can be of you, on the day of the Lord Jesus (2 Cor. 1:12–14).

Paul has not yet mentioned the problem which caused the misunderstanding (we will look at that later). But it is interesting that he starts out by making this plain to the Corinthians—his conscience is clear in the whole matter. He wants them to understand that this is not merely a defensive reaction on his part. His actions, no matter how the Corinthians may have seen them, are clear before God.

A Clear Conscience

When you are misunderstood, when somebody misjudges you, the first thing you have to ask yourself, as a Christian, is, "Is there anything about this that God condemns? Have I really done anything wrong? Does my conscience bother me about any part of this?" If it does, then your first step, of course, must be to confess it, to acknowledge it and admit that you have done something wrong. There may be many elements about the situation you are facing in which you feel justified. But there may be areas, at least, where you did something wrong. You may have lost your temper, you may have said some cruel or unkind things, you may have retaliated against someone. If that is the case, then this is where you have to start; you must have a clear conscience before you can go on. Much of the strife between people comes from their unwillingness to clear their consciences at the very beginning.

Notice how Paul does this. He sees no deviation from his normal pattern of behavior. As always, he seeks to be an open, transparent person who is not trying to hide anything, who is not resorting to guile or manipulation—what Paul calls, "fleshly wisdom." Apparently, he has done something to offend some of these Corinthians. He wants them to know that, as far as his standing before God is concerned, his conscience is clear.

Then he hopes to make them understand. That is what verse 13 means: "We write you nothing but what you can read and understand." He is going to try to clear this up. He hopes that they will be able to grasp it fully as he explains it to them, because he longs to restore a mutual sense of pride in one another. This is what believers ought to keep constantly striving for, a clearness of relationship with each other. It is important to notice that Paul makes a real effort to clear up this misunderstanding. Some people adopt the attitude, "Well, I am just going to forget it and hope the whole problem will disappear." But the trouble is that it usually does not disappear. Misunderstanding can be hidden in the heart; you may think you have dismissed it or forgotten it, but actually it is festering away, smoldering like a fire that refuses to go out. Sometimes, unexpectedly, it bursts into flames;

suddenly, you are angry at someone and you hardly realize why; but it is because something has been left unsettled. Everywhere in the Word of God we are taught that, as Christians, we must not let things lie unsettled. If we are upset about something or feel someone is upset at us, then we have to do something about it. That is what Jesus said in the Sermon on the Mount: "If you are offering your gift at the altar, and there remember that your brother has something against you, leave your gift there before the altar and go; first be reconciled to your brother, and then come and offer your gift" (Matt. 5:23, 24). Clear relationships are tremendously important. When they are neglected, strife, schism, division, hurt and pain in a church are the results.

Now Paul explains the problem that caused the misunderstanding:

> Because I was sure of this, I wanted to come to you first, so that you might have a double pleasure, I wanted to visit you on my way to Macedonia, and to come back to you from Macedonia and have you send me on my way to Judea. Was I vacillating when I wanted to do this? Do I make my plans like a worldly man, ready to say Yes and No at once? (2 Cor. 1:15).

The problem, obviously, was that one of Paul's travel plans had met obstacles; he had been forced to abandon "Plan A." It had involved leaving Ephesus, where he had been living, crossing the Aegean Sea directly to Corinth, and visiting them to help work out the problems they were having in the church. From there he had planned to travel by land up through northern Greece into Macedonia, to the cities of Thessalonica and Philippi, where he had planted churches, and to return again to Corinth, thus giving them what he calls here the "double pleasure" of his visit. He then had expected them to help him take ship from Corinth to Jerusalem to bring the gifts of the church to the poor starving saints there. This was his original plan, "Plan A," but he did not do it, as he tells us.

A Change of Plans

> I will visit you after passing through Macedonia, for I intend to pass through Macedonia, and perhaps I will stay with you or even spend the winter, so that you may speed me on my journey, wherever I go. For I do not want to see you now just in passing; I hope to spend some time with you, if the Lord permits. But I will stay in Ephesus until Pentecost, for a wide door for effective work has opened to me, and there are many adversaries (1 Cor. 16:5–9).

That was "Plan B." It involved Paul's going directly from Ephesus into Macedonia and working his way down the coast at last to Corinth; then, after his visit there, the Christians would help him on his way to Jerusalem and Judea. Now to us at this remote date, his change of plans seems an awfully silly thing to get upset about. After all, transportation was difficult and uncertain in those days. Communication was even more so; there was no way he could let them know of the change of plan. Yet it is apparent, from verse 17, that they were upset about this and their accusations were coming strong against him. (Titus had probably brought him word that there were some who had accused him of being fickle and changeable and unreliable. There was a group in Corinth who opposed Paul anyhow, and they were quick to seize on this as proof of their charges that he behaved just like everyone else, that he was an unreliable individual.)

Paul suggests, too, that some were actually saying he lived just like a worldling, a non-Christian, doing whatever was convenient, not bothering to try to keep his word in any way. It is always interesting to see how these letters, written in the first century, find such a remarkable correspondence to what goes on in our lives today. One of the major problems among Christians, especially younger Christians, is that they have not yet seen this truth: what ought to be characteristic of Christians is faithfulness to their commitments. If you say you are going to be somewhere, then either be there or let someone know why you cannot be there. It is amazing (and discouraging sometimes) to see how many Christians, even older Christians, will say they are going to do something, or be some place, and then never show up, never let anyone know, and show no sense of responsibility for fulfilling the promise and the commitment they made. Such conduct, Paul makes plain, is the characteristic of a "worldly man," of a non-Christian. It shows no sense of the faithfulness, the responsibility a Christian ought to have.

Yes or No

Paul now begins to explain what the true situation was. Unfortunately, his explanation is interrupted by one of those unhelpful chapter divisions we sometimes see; the passage actually falls into two major divisions: 18 through 22, and then 23 through verse 4 of Chapter 2. His first word is a wonderful statement of the divine provision for Spirit-led guidance:

> As surely as God is faithful, our word to you has not been Yes and No (2 Cor. 1:18).

Notice he does not say, "Yes *or* No." There is nothing wrong with saying "No" sometimes. One has to say "No" to many invitations to make a commitment. But if you say "Yes," then intend to fulfill it; that is what Paul is saying. Or if you say "No," then mean it. Jesus said this, didn't he? "Let your 'Yes' be 'Yes,' and your 'No,' 'No'; Anything beyond this comes from the evil one" (Matt 5:37, ML). As Christians we must learn to keep our word on these matters. What is wrong is to say "Yes" but mean "No." It is wrong to tell somebody you are going to be some place when you really have no intention of being there. It is wrong to say you will do something when you have no intention of doing so. Conversely, it is wrong to say you will not do something when you have every intention of doing it.

Paul goes on to explain where he is coming from:

> As surely as God is faithful, our word to you has not been Yes and No. For the Son of God, Jesus Christ, whom we preached among you, Silvanus and Timothy and I, was not Yes and No; but in him it is always Yes. For all the promises of God find their Yes in him. That is why we utter the Amen through him, to the glory of God. But it is God who establishes us with you in Christ, and has commissioned us; he has put his seal upon us and given us his Spirit in our hearts as a guarantee (2 Cor. 1:18–22).

Let us look at this for a moment, for it is a great theological statement. Paul is basically saying that no Christian can give a Yes *and* No commitment. That is contrary to the nature of a Christian, because it is contrary to the nature of God. God is not like that; he is faithful, Paul says. When God says "Yes," then it is an eternal "Yes." He will never take it back. When God says "No," he means "No." He never says "Yes" and means "No." Paul is saying that God's promises are always positive promises. Have you noticed that in the Scriptures? In Christ, it is always "Yes," Paul says. Whatever God promises, and you come to him in the name of Jesus and ask for, the answer is always "Yes." That is what he is saying, ultimately; it is "Yes," for God's promises are for blessing, not for cursing.

This is very clear in the great verse in John 3 where Jesus said, "For God sent the Son into the world, not to condemn the world, but that the world might be saved through him" (John 3:17). Now there will be condemnation, but that is not God's intent or purpose. The promises never offer condemnation; they deal with salvation; they are offered to us to deliver us. Jesus did not come to kill; he came to revive and to give life. "I am come," he said, "that they might have life, and that they might have it more abundantly" (John 10:10). God does not come to reject, but to restore. I have always loved that great word of the prophet Isaiah, where he is picturing God at work. He says he comes "to give beauty for ashes, the oil of joy for mourning, the garment of praise for the spirit of heaviness" (Isa. 61:3). That is the positive activity of God (Isa. 61:3).

When to Say "Amen"

Now, according to the statement here, all this is available to us in Christ. We actually begin to experience it when we say "Amen" to God's promise. This passage is rather obscure in the King James Version, where it says, "For all the promises of God in him (Christ) are yea, and in him Amen"—as though Christ is saying both the "yes" and the "Amen." But the Revised text makes it clear that it is God who, in Christ, says, "yes," and it is we who are to add the "Amen." That is why I love to preach in black churches. I get a lot of "Amens." It can be dull preaching to white people when they just sit and look at you. It is encouraging to get an "Amen" once in awhile, because it is a way of saying, "I agree. I believe that. I accept that. That is for me." What the text is saying here is that God gives you a promise in Christ. There are hundreds of them, and he offers you something in every one. You read one and you say, "That's for me, Lord. I want that." On this basis you obey the qualification or the commitment that the promise demands, and the promise begins to be real in your life. It is we who say the "Amen." God's positive supply actually appears when we obey from the depths of our being and say a resounding "Amen" to what he has said. The way to find God's blessing, then, is to respond to his promise by stepping out on what he says, taking it to yourself, and saying, "Lord, that is mine. Amen, I believe."

How to Say "Amen"

Paul adds that, by the presence of the Spirit in our lives, God has provided the means to understand and live by this promise. Paul adds that God has provided for our understanding of this promise by the presence of the Spirit in our lives. As you meditate on the promises of God, the Spirit of God is given to you to teach you what it means and how it applies to you. That is the work of the Spirit. He is not given to us so that we may have a good feeling now and then or to take us to heaven when we die, though he does all those things. He is given to us to open our minds to understand how the promises of God affect us and what God is saying to us in them. His teaching is always in line with grammatical rules and interpretative principles; the Spirit never denies that; he understands the rules of language, grammar, and so on, and it is helpful to us to know them. But nevertheless, it is ultimately the Spirit of God himself who brings a promise home to us and makes it alive to us, and who then offers to empower us to accept the gift.

Many times we are faced with a promise of God, but because we are sinful creatures we do not want to receive it. Many times I have had the experience of knowing that there was something God wanted me to do (or perhaps not to do), and I did not want to obey him. I knew there would be a promise of relief, or help, or blessing if I would do it, but every fiber of my rebellious flesh cried out against doing it; and I found it difficult to make myself do it. Well, that is where the Spirit comes in. A non-Christian would simply not do it. Non-Christians live by their feelings: "Whatever feels good I give myself to. Whatever does not feel good I do not want any part of." That is the way of the world, but a Christian is not to do that. He is to obey God. If he has difficulty doing so he is to rely upon the fact that the Spirit of God is in him to give him ability to act when He wills to act. When you choose to obey, the power to do so is always given by the Spirit of God. You can do what God wants. This is what Paul is bringing out here.

Let us now link this with the context. Why *did* Paul change his plan? That is what the Corinthians wanted to know. Why did he say he was going to come directly to Corinth, and would come twice to the city, but instead did not come directly—going by way of Macedonia—and came only once? Because the Spirit of God opened his eyes to see factors in the situation that made him change his mind. He could see that the great promises of blessing that God had for this church at Corinth would only be fulfilled if he did not come directly to Corinth, but instead went to Macedonia and waited for Titus there. So, convinced by the Spirit, in obedience to what he saw of the Spirit's teaching, and with a clear conscience, Paul changed his original plan and went to Macedonia instead of Corinth.

Report to the Boss

In verse 23 of chapter 1, on through verse 4 of chapter 2, he tells us the two things the Spirit showed him that made him change his mind. This is a practical passage on how the Spirit of God works to help us understand. Here is the first reason that Paul gives:

> But I call God to witness against me—it was to spare you that I refrained from coming to Corinth (2 Cor. 1:23).

That is reason number one. He did not come because he wanted to spare them.

> Not that we lord it over your faith; we work with you for your joy, for you stand firm in your faith (2 Cor. 1:24).

Moreover, he refrained from coming so that they would be free to act as the Lord directed, and not as Paul said. Now this is a very important principle, because here the apostle is challenging one of the widespread misunderstandings in the church in our day. Paul says, "Look, I am not your boss. If I had come to Corinth the way I had originally planned, after having already paid you a painful visit, it's very likely that my powerful personality, my strong will, my position as a respected apostle would have put such pressure upon you that you would have obeyed me—but without the conviction that I spoke for the Lord. So I did not come, in order that you might preserve freedom to do what God wants, not what I want." If he had come he would have given them the impression that he had authority over them. But that is not true, he says, "We are not lords over your faith. We are not your boss. We have no authority to tell you what to do or what to say or how to act, but rather" (and in a beautiful phrase he puts it), "we are helpers of your joy." That is wonderful, isn't it? Paul sees himself as a fellow worker, standing alongside them, helping them to understand what God wants so they would enter into the joy of the Lord. But he is not their boss.

One of the major problems the church is facing in our day is the widespread tendency to misunderstand the nature of authority and leadership within the church, to regard someone as the ultimate boss, getting directions and permission from him to do anything. If we Protestants are right when we say to the Catholics that God never intended to have one man, a pope, over the whole church, it is no improvement if we place one in every church.

Leaders in the church are not bosses. This is a common misconception. Many churches look to *the* pastor but you never see that term in Scripture. There are pastors, but never *the* pastor. Churches are not to look to the pastor for authority, for permission to exercise spiritual gifts. We do not have to ask our pastor whether we can teach in our home or not. We do not have to go to the pastor to get permission to use our spiritual gifts. The pastor does not give them to us. The Lord does and we are responsible to him for the exercise of those spiritual gifts, not to the pastor. The pastor is our helper; he is there to encourage us and to help us to understand what these gifts are, how to recognize them, but we are not responsible to him for exercising our gifts. He is responsible to his Lord to help us put them with others and to maintain unity within the church, but not to govern what ministry we have. That comes from the Lord himself. He is the head of the church, the body.

Hardly any principle or concept in the church is more misunderstood today than this particular concept. Peter says that elders are not to be "lords over God's heritage" (1 Peter 5:3). That is what Paul is referring to here. We are not lords, he says; we do not lord it over your faith. The word "heritage" in 1 Peter 5:3 (*kleros:* "inheritance") is the word from which we get our English word, "clergy." It is interesting, is it not, that Peter is telling the men whom we call "clergy" not to lord it over the real clergy, the laity. It is the *people* who are ministers of God. It is the *people* who are to carry on the work of the church and exercise its ministry out in the world, in every place. It is not the right of anybody to be boss in the church. As Jesus himself put it, "one is your Master, and all you are brothers." We are to help one another.

So the mighty apostle Paul himself clearly acknowledges this. He says, "That is why I did not come. I did not want to disturb that relationship. I did not want to preempt authority over you that belonged only to the Lord himself." As he himself put it in Romans 14:4, "Who are you to pass judgment on the servant of another? It is before his own master that he stands or falls. And he will be upheld, for the Master is able to make him stand." I love Phillips' rendition: "God is well able to transform men into servants that are satisfactory." Paul recognizes this.

No Desire to Wound

> For I made up my mind not to make you another painful visit. For if I cause you pain, who is there to make me glad but the one whom I have pained? And I wrote as I did, so that when I came I might not suffer pain from those who should have made me rejoice, for I felt sure of all of you, that my joy would be the joy of you all. For I wrote you out of much affliction and anguish of heart and with many tears, not to cause you pain but to let you know the abundant love that I have for you (2 Cor. 2:1–4).

The Spirit led him to see that he had already caused pain enough by his letters and painful visit. Paul is like a skillful surgeon. A surgeon must cut, but a good surgeon cuts only as much as is required. He derives no joy out of cutting people's bodies open beyond removal of the tumor or the cancer or whatever. As soon as that is done, and thoroughly done, he stops, because he does not like to create pain. That is what Paul is saying here. "I wrote to you a sharp and painful letter." (Whether this is 1 Corinthians or another lost letter is a debated point; I lean toward the latter view.) At any rate, Paul says, "I have already caused you much pain by what I wrote. The Spirit has shown me that if I came again I would just cause more pain; that might be quite unnecessary, so I did not come, because," as he puts it so beautifully, "I don't want to cause you pain. When you hurt, I hurt. Who is going to make me glad if I unnecessarily cause you to hurt? I wrote to you out of much affliction and anguish of heart and with many tears." What a beautiful picture of this great apostle writing with the tears flowing from his eyes. "I want you to see that behind the writing and the sharp rebukes there is no desire to hurt you, but a great heart of love, unwilling to let you miss the love and the joy of God. That is why I wrote."

This is a marvelous picture of the spirit in which we ought to handle misunderstandings. Not to hurt in return, not to retaliate, not to try to get even because someone has misunderstood us, but to explain it as plainly and simply and clearly as we can, always with the intention that, if there is anything hurtful to be said, it will be as minimal as possible, affirming our love and our concern for the individual involved. That is the way Paul did it.

3

When Discipline Ends

Thus far, Paul has addressed two problems in the church at Corinth: personal stress and misunderstanding. Now he turns our attention to the third concern: when discipline in a congregation should end.

> But if any one has caused pain, he has caused it not to me, but in some measure—not to put it too severely—to you all. For such a one this punishment by the majority is enough; so you should rather turn to forgive and comfort him, or he may be overwhelmed by excessive sorrow. So I beg you to reaffirm your love for him (2 Cor. 2:5–8).

The focus of this discipline is a matter of scholarly debate. Traditionally, it was linked with the problem of incest attacked in 1 Corinthians. But since Paul had both written again (in one of the lost letters) and paid them the "painful" visit (mentioned in 2 Cor. 2:1), it seems to many (and I include myself here) that the matter of incest had probably been handled, and another situation, perhaps a rebellion against the apostle's authority, is being resolved here. The point is that some form of discipline had been exercised; and now Paul is urging that, since the man had repented, it is time for a change of attitude toward him. This is a very helpful study on what a church ought to do when someone responds to discipline.

We have already seen in other passages that the Lord Jesus is the one who instituted a form of discipline within the church:

> If your brother sins against you, go and tell him his fault, between you and him alone (Matt. 18:15).

This is always the first step and will keep a congregation happier and more at peace than anything else I know. I have the joy of serving in a congregation like that. Few are aware of it—because this kind of thing is not publicized—but it is happening all the time in this congregation. Hardly a week goes by that someone does not act on that basis. Someone goes to a person he feels is out of line with what Scripture says and tells him his fault. Then usually, as Jesus went on to say, what should happen, happens:

> If he listens to you, you have gained your brother.

That is all that needs to be said about it.

But we are not to go to one another in areas where we merely feel irritated because someone is doing something differently than we would do it. We are to point out only those areas the Word of God has said are clearly wrong. Then, if there is resistance and unwillingness to face what is clearly wrongdoing, we are to take one or two others with us. Thus there may be witnesses to the discussion, just as Jesus said, with the hope that this will help the one concerned; the objective of discipline is not punishment, but recovery and restoration. If that approach is refused, then the third step is to tell it to the church, with the expectation that everybody in the congregation who knows the individual will go and plead with him to reconsider, to face the trouble and admit it, so that peace can be restored.

Evidently, that is the level to which this church had come. Whatever the problem, the man had resisted correction until it had to be told to all the church. (Paul is referring to that when he says, "For such a one this punishment by the majority is enough.") The church had acted and had been successful in carrying out this discipline.

Some may ask why such action is necessary. It is because, as Paul says:

> If any one has caused pain, he has not caused it only to me, but in some measure—not to put it too severely—to you all (2 Cor. 2:5).

Wrong actions are always hurtful, not only to a few people, but to everyone. Nothing is more deceiving than the attitude many people take today of, "Well, this is only between me and another person. No one else is being hurt by it." That is never true in a church. As John Donne has well reminded us, "No man is an island." While true of all humanity, in a church we are even more a family, and it is impossible for there to be strife and hurt and grievance between any two individuals that does not begin to spread and touch others as well.

I have been in churches where feuds had developed to the point that one family group would not speak to another. The whole church had been paralyzed spiritually; nothing was happening out in the community, no testimony of love and restoration was going on, and the church's effectiveness had ground to a halt. It happens many, many times: discipline must be carried out on a wider basis. In Corinth, it had already happened; it had already worked; this man had repented. He had admitted that what he had done was wrong, and had demonstrated it by what I like to call, "the mark of repentance." Paul urges them to comfort him that he may not be "overwhelmed by excessive sorrow."

The Mark of Repentance

This mark is the sense of sorrow, of remorse that you have been the instrument by which many have been damaged in their faith or in their feelings. We are often taught today that if you do something wrong, all you have to do is go and say to somebody, "Yes, I did that," and then expect forgiveness at once. Certainly we should forgive right away, yet the sign of true repentance is sorrow for hurt that's been caused. This is a quite different spirit than what we see at times today where people get angry if they are not forgiven instantly.

The mark of genuine repentance is that we do not really believe anybody ought to forgive us, that what we have done is hurtful, and we do not think we deserve forgiveness. Forgiveness is always freely extended to someone who does not feel he deserves it; and that is what is clear here. We can see this, if we look ahead to chapter 7, where Paul refers to this very incident again and the congregation's treatment of it:

> For even if I made you sorry with my letter I do not regret it (though I did regret it), for I see that that letter grieved you, though only for awhile. As it is, I rejoice, not because you were grieved, but because you were grieved into repenting; for you felt a godly grief, so that you suffered no loss through us. For godly grief produces a repentance that leads to salvation and brings no regret, but worldly grief produces death (2 Cor. 7:8–10).

Thus the mark of repentance is grief and sorrow over what is done. This man had come to that point; therefore it was time to end the discipline.

Of course, the purpose of the whole process of discipline at any stage is to bring somebody to recovery. The minute he achieves that it is time to end all the sanctions and degrees of pressure being applied, and begin to extend forgiveness and restoring love. That is what Paul pleads for in verse 8:

> So I beg you to reaffirm your love for him (2 Cor. 2:8).

Since correction is never to proceed from anger alone, but from love, the appropriate purpose is to reaffirm love. Paul suggests how that should be done when he says, "you should rather turn to forgive and comfort him lest he be overwhelmed by excessive sorrow."

The Process of Restoration: Facing It

Now, because this man had reached this place, Paul goes on to give us a statement of what restoration involves:

> For this is why I wrote, that I might test you and know whether you are obedient in everything. Any one whom you forgive, I also forgive. What I have forgiven, if I have forgiven anything, has been for your sake in the presence of Christ, to keep Satan from gaining the advantage over us; for we are not ignorant of his designs (2 Cor. 2:9–11).

There are three things of great importance in that paragraph which help us to understand how to bring people to restoration. The first one, as Paul clearly indicates, is to begin with a faithful confrontation. He says, "I wrote to you to see if you would obey"—not obey Paul as we have seen, but obey the Lord. It was not the apostle giving orders; he was only calling attention to what the Lord had said. Their obedience, therefore, was not to him but to the Lord. And it always is. No man has a right to give orders in the church, but only to call attention, as a brother, to the orders the Lord has already given. The Corinthians had obeyed; they had done what Matthew 18 required by telling it to the church.

That is always a painful and difficult thing to do. One of the reasons so many churches are rife with splits, divisions, and problems today is that their leadership seems to be made up of gutless wonders who have no moral courage and who are not willing themselves to act in obedience to what the Scripture says. When the church of which I am a part has had to take action of this sort, threats of lawsuits and of bodily harm were sometimes made against the eldership if we acted. We had to resist reproof by many people in the congregation who misjudged the situation, who thought it was wrong to act the way we did. It has sometimes taken courage to stand and obey the Word of God. But as Scripture says, "the effect of righteousness will be peace." If you will act rightly in love, and frontally with courage, the result is peace; such was happening in Corinth. The place to start, therefore, is with a faithful confrontation. And as in the church, so with our individual difficulties. If we have a difficulty with someone, we must do what the Lord says: "If your brother sins against you, go and tell him his fault, between you and him alone" (Matt. 18:15).

Forgetting It

But equally important is the readiness to forgive when a person has acknowledged that what he or she did was wrong or sees, with grief and sorrow, the hurt it caused. Then we are to instantly restore such a one, in the second step of restoration.

Here again the church often offends. One of the frequent causes for hurt and damage to individuals in the church today is an unwillingness to forgive things in the past that an individual has cleared up long ago. Take divorce, for instance. In many places where people have gone through a divorce, even with biblical grounds, it is treated as the unforgivable sin, worse than murder, adultery, or anything else. Those involved never come back to any level of acceptance or leadership. But that is wrong, and great damage is done because of it. If it is true that Paul himself had personally been insulted by the individual in question, notice how freely he extends forgiveness:

> Any one whom you forgive, I also forgive. What I have forgiven, if I have forgiven anything, has been for your sake in the presence of Christ (2 Cor. 2:10).

There are no hard feelings, no recriminations, no "well-I-can-forgive-but-I-can't-forget" attitude. Such reveals a lack of understanding of what forgiveness is. Forgiveness, basically, is a promise that you make; it is a promise you make to three different individuals. This is true always, in every case of forgiveness. First, it is a promise that you make to the individual who has offended you and now has repented, in which you are saying to him or her, "I will not let my attitude toward you be governed any longer by this offense. It has been put aside. My treatment of you from here on will be as though this had never happened." It is a promise you make never to bring it up again. In marriage many problems go on for years and years because we tend to go back and dig up all the past, an indication that it has never been forgiven. Some mates don't get hysterical, they get historical! That *is* the problem, and it *creates* a problem.

Second, it is a promise not to pass it on to anyone else. When a matter is forgiven it is to be forgotten. Now it may be that everyone knows it, because, as in this case in Corinth, it had been told to the whole church. But what it means is that no one throws it at the person again or holds it over his head or reminds him of it should any further difficulty occur. It is a promise to drop the matter, leave it in the past, and never bring it up to anyone again.

Third, and probably most important of all, it is a promise to yourself that when your memory goes back to the offense, as it will occasionally, you are not going to allow it to seize hold of your heart and make you angry all over again. The minute it comes back to remind you put it aside as something that belongs to the past; you are not going to dwell on it. It is a promise, therefore, to repeat your act of forgiveness, no matter how often the memory comes up. That is what forgiveness is; and Paul is ready to do this.

The reason, of course, is that Paul himself had been forgiven. People tell me sometimes, "Well, I just can't forgive in this case. The person said he was wrong, and has asked me to forgive him, but I just can't do it. It hurt me too much." Well, this is a revelation to me that the person has never realized how much he himself has been forgiven already. The basis for Christian forgiveness is always, "Forgive, because you have been forgiven." If you cannot forgive, it is because you have forgotten that you were forgiven. Paul says this to the Ephesians: "Be tenderhearted, forgiving one another, even as God for Christ's sake has forgiven you" (Eph. 4:32). That means we are not to be self-righteous and condemning, assuming the attitude, "Well, I could never do a thing like that." In the eyes of God you have already done worse, and been forgiven for it. The basis, therefore, for extending forgiveness to others is "Freely you have received, freely give" (Matt. 10:18).

Anticipating the Accuser

The third step in restoration, brought out in verse 11, is the need to keep Satan from gaining an advantage over us, for Paul says, "we are not ignorant of his designs." It is Satan who keeps bringing back to your mind the hurts of the past; he keeps interjecting them back into a situation. He is trying to get hold of you through the situation and wreak havoc with you and your loved ones. It is Satan who makes the leadership of a church quail at confronting some situation and say, "Oh, let's not get involved; let's forget it." That is Satan. He is seeking to gain an advantage over the whole congregation, to dilute their testimony and render them powerless in their effect on the community. He will bring it up again whether you like it or not; he will interject the same situation into circumstances in the future and you will have to face the same issue over and over again.

That is what Paul means when he says, "we are not ignorant of his designs." When an arsonist is loose you can expect fires; they are going to break out all over the place. We have an enemy who is like that, and when you have an enemy you can expect casualties. When you are engaged in warfare you can never decide that you will have no more casualties, because the enemy is there; he is the one who keeps it going. We often say in American history, "Eternal vigilance is the price of liberty." That is true in the spiritual realm as well. We are Christians in a battle. The enemy is constantly trying to take advantage of the situation. Only as we recognize this will we realize that the thing which defeats him is to extend full forgiveness when there are broken relationships among us. That is what keeps Satan from gaining an advantage over us. Elsewhere, Paul says, "Do not let the sun go down on your wrath. Settle this matter before nightfall, before you go to bed. Don't carry it over to the next day and thus give opportunity to the devil" (Eph. 4:26, 27). When we let it go on and on, unresolved, we are giving the devil an opportunity to get hold of everyone involved, to create more problems and eventually turn the whole church upside down.

The final element involved in restoration is always the spiritual awareness that we are in a battle, that we live in a crazy world under the control of a madman, so we cannot expect to settle it all once and for all. As an old movie once described it, "It's a Mad, Mad, Mad, Mad World" (I saw that title in Spanish on a marquee down in Latin America: "El Mundo es Loco, Loco, Loco, Loco"!). We deal with these problems in our own hearts; that is the way you turn off the attack of the enemy.

Some years ago I read about a mental hospital that had devised an effective test to know whether the patients were ready to go back into the marketplace again. The patients would be brought into a room where a water tap was flowing out on the floor, would be handed a mop, and be told to mop up the water. If they took the mop and just started mopping away, with the water still flowing, they would be put back in the hospital. But if they had the sense to go and turn off the tap first, and then mop up the water, the staff knew they were ready to go back into life.

There is no sense in trying to clear up a situation until we have turned off the devil's tap by forgiving that which has been acknowledged as wrong. If we persist in bringing it up over and over again, we are trying to mop up a situation where the water is still flowing. That is foolish; it cannot be done. That is why in many marriages, in many family relationships, and in some churches, these kinds of hurtful things go on and on for decades. Nobody has turned off the tap; nobody has forgiven one another and let it rest in the past, realizing that we all are in need of forgiveness continually. When forgiveness happens, then marvelous healing begins to take place. I could tell you story after story of how I have seen this happen. Whole congregations have been restored, whole family groups have been opened up when two angry people decide they will forgive at the smallest indication that injury has been acknowledged.

When Discipline Ends

Is there any more beautiful picture in all the Scriptures than the story Jesus told of the Prodigal Son? It is really the story of the old father waiting at home, watching the horizon and knowing that when his boy had reached the end and was ready to admit his wrongdoing, he would show up at the house again. At the first glimpse of his son on the horizon the old man runs down the road to meet him, his arms wide open. All the way home, the boy has been repeating his memorized statement: "I am no longer worthy to be called your son." But before he can utter a syllable, the old man has his arms around him and he is calling out for a celebration, to kill the fatted calf. Well, there was one who was not sorry, and that was the father. He was overjoyed, because he knew that his son would never have come back if he had not acknowledged his wrong. And he did not wait for the boy to admit that. He had already forgiven him. The very appearance of the lad on the horizon was enough to tell the father that his son was repentant, sorry for what he had done. And, "lest he be overwhelmed by excessive sorrow," the father forgave him from a full and free heart. Now that is God's picture of what he does with us.

4

Have You Got What It Takes?

I have often wondered how the apostle Paul would rate in ecclesiastical circles, whether he would be considered a success or not if he were carrying on his ministry today. It is hard to believe that a man who spent most of his time in jail, who never made enough salary to buy a home of his own, who never built a church building, never spoke on television, or even had a radio broadcast, who ran around so much that he had no permanent residence of his own, who frequently had to get a job to support himself, who admitted that he was a poor speaker and had a very unimpressive appearance, could ever be a successful pastor or minister. He just does not fit the accepted scheme of what makes for success in the ministry today. No wonder they had trouble with him in Corinth, and had difficulty believing that he was a real apostle.

That is what they were thinking when Paul wrote this letter, and that, perhaps, explains why chapter 3 begins with these words:

> Are we beginning to commend ourselves again? Or do we need, as some do, letters of recommendation to you, or from you? You yourselves are our letter of recommendation, written on your hearts, to be known and read by all men; and you show that you are a letter from Christ delivered by us, written not with ink but with the Spirit of the living God, not on tablets of stone but on tablets of human hearts (2 Cor. 3:1–3).

Convincing Credentials

It is amazing, unbelievable, that these people would ever think the apostle Paul needed a letter of recommendation when he came back to them. After all, he had led these people to Christ, and yet here they imply that the next time he came it would be good if he brought some letters from John, or Peter, or James, or one of the "real" apostles. Paul is asking them, "Do you really mean that? Don't you understand? *You* are our letter of recommendation. Christ has written it on your hearts. He didn't use paper, or engrave it on stones, as he did with Moses on Mount Sinai. He wrote it on your hearts, and the ink he used was the Holy Spirit. As for me, I'm nothing but the postman; I just delivered the letter. God did the work." Paul wants these Corinthians to understand that the changes which had occurred in their lives, the freedom they were experiencing, the deliverance from evil habits such as immorality, adultery, homosexuality, drunkenness, thievery—"such were some of you," he said—all happened because Christ had changed them.

When I read the New Testament I am always impressed at the scarcity—in the Book of Acts and in the letters of Paul—of words concerning the church and its ministry. Those early Christians did not go around, as we do today, talking about what the church can do for you, or about the value of becoming a member of a church. We talk about that in our day, but they did not even mention it because they understood that the church does not do anything for anybody. It is Christ who changes lives. It is Jesus who heals a hurting heart, or touches a lonely spirit, or restores someone burdened with a terrible sense of guilt for the wretchedness and evil of his past. It is the Lord who forgives and changes, and Paul states that very strongly here. He wants the Corinthians to understand that Christ has written this letter, not he, and they are the witnesses; their changed lives are all the testimony, all the recommendation, he needs that what he is doing is authentic Christianity.

If we applied that test to our churches across this country today I wonder how many would have a recommendation in the eyes of the community around? The ones who would read this letter were the whole watching world, "known and read of all men," Paul said; "everybody can see that Christ has done something to you." The only effective witness the church has in the world today is the change that Christ has made: the people you rub shoulders with, the tradesmen you do business with, the people you talk to in the normal course of your daily affairs ought to see that change. That is the point. There ought to be such visible evidence of God at work in you that people will say, "What is this? What's going on? I know your name is Bill, or Jane, or Mary, but somehow I get the feeling I'm talking to Jesus." That is what these early Christians exemplified.

This moves Paul to go on and answer the question he had asked in the preceding chapter. Christ, he said there, always leads us in triumph. He saw himself as the commanding general, marching in triumph through the streets of Rome, having won great victories everywhere he went. In another beautiful figure of speech, he said that his ministry was like a bottle of perfume, the fragrance of which was spreading all through the world—the sweetness and fragrance of Jesus Christ himself. So Paul's question was, "Who is sufficient for these things? Where do you get the ability to have *that* kind of impact upon those around you? Do you get it from a school? Is it a special course that you can take? Is it a seminar you can sign up for?"

The New Covenant

Now he comes to the answer:

> Such is the confidence (that is, the sufficiency) that we have through Christ toward God. Not that we are competent of ourselves to claim anything as coming from us; our competence is from God, who has made us competent to be ministers of a new covenant, not in a written code but in the Spirit; for the written code kills, but the Spirit gives life (2 Cor. 3:4–6).

This is an all-important subject. It is my deep conviction that this is the one truth above everything else in the Bible which God wants his people to learn. If I had to list the most important truth in the Word of God, aside from the deity of Christ, I would say it is this truth—the new covenant, the new provision for life that God has given his people. But the one thing I find most lacking in the church across the world today is the knowledge and understanding of this new way to live.

Paul is talking about confidence; and everyone in the world is trying to get confidence. Every time you turn on television, or listen to the radio, or pick up a magazine, you are bombarded with suggestions on how to become a self-sufficient, confident, capable, well-adjusted person, able to handle life. There are all kinds of approaches, and almost all work on the same basis. Confidence, we are told, has to come from yourself. You have to somehow find in yourself the power to achieve and to be a success. You can build this up through courses you can take and skills you can develop. That is how you will prove to be a successful individual. The world understands, quite properly, that you must have a degree of confidence. People who lack confidence, who are unsure of themselves, and insecure, go bumbling through life and never make a good impression on anyone and are always losing and failing. Therefore, the great aim is to build up a deep sense of confidence.

Paul realizes he needed confidence, too. There is nothing wrong with that. God knows we need to have a sense of ability. But the great question is, where does it come from? When Paul answers that question, he says, "It doesn't come from me. There is nothing coming from us; everything comes from God." Therefore he takes no credit for anything. Read through the writings of Paul (and it is true of Peter, James, John, and all the other apostles as well), and they are constantly denying that their ability, their power, ever comes from them. "Not I," Paul says, "but it is Christ who lives in me." "I labor, I toil with all the energy which *he* mightily inspires in me."

This new covenant is entirely different than anything the world knows anything about. The world would say that Paul was a success as an apostle because he did his dedicated best to mobilize all his resources and abilities to serve God with all his heart. But if you asked Paul, he would never say that. He would say that there was nothing coming from him. And he is not just being modest; he means it. "I don't make that kind of a contribution at all," he says, "everything is coming from God. The ability that is evident in my ministry, the changes that occur in people's lives because of what I am and where I go have nothing to do with my natural skills or ability. It's all coming from God at work in me." In the old covenant Paul did his best on behalf of God; in the new covenant God does *his* best through Paul. What a difference that is! That is the great truth we need to learn.

An Impressive Resumé

Now that is a rather amazing claim, for the world for twenty centuries has recognized that the apostle Paul was an unusually competent person. He had marvelous gifts. Perhaps he had the keenest mind of all time. Anyone who reads Paul admits that he had a powerful personality and a zeal which were simply remarkable.

He tells us in the letter to the Philippians that he had counted on four things for success. And they were remarkable things. First of all, there was his impeccable ancestry. He was born into the right family and he belonged to the right people. "I am a Hebrew of the Hebrews, born of the tribe of Benjamin, circumcised on the eighth day according to the Book." He could claim an ancestry that went all the way back to Abraham. The tremendous religious inheritance of the Jewish people was all his, he said. I know a lot of people who are counting on their ancestry for success. You can belong to a well-known family, and even though there may be a lot of personal weaknesses, even moral failures, evident in your own life, you can run for office and you will make it. Ancestry counts in this world, doesn't it?

As well as having an impeccable ancestry, Paul tells us also that he had a fantastic record of orthodoxy: "I am a Pharisee of the Pharisees." Now if any people ever gave themselves to careful, thoughtful, religious observance, it was the Pharisees. Scripture tells us that they tithed even the tiny little seeds they grew—cummin, mint, anise—and counted them out patiently, taking hours, so that they could give one out of ten to God. When they walked about on the sabbath day they meticulously took care never to spit on the ground because that made mud, and that was mortar, and that was working on the sabbath. So they carefully spat on rocks on that day. Paul says, "I was a Pharisee of the Pharisees, taking care that I did not break any rules."

More than that, he had a record of incredible activity. He was the most zealous young Pharisee of his day. At an early age it is possible he advanced to a tremendous position of prominence by being granted membership in the Sanhedrin, the ruling body of the Jews, even though he was but a young man. He was zealous in his career against the Christian church, "breathing out threatenings and slaughter," pursuing the cause night and day to stamp out the whole Christian community. And finally, he tells us that he had an unblamable morality. There was no charge you could level against him. His private life was just as clean as his public life. He was, before the law, blameless. So he counted on these: his keen mind, his brilliant record. He felt that he would be a success because of these things.

But as the record of Acts tells us, he had to learn through a very painful ten-year period that all this was absolutely worthless in getting God's work done. It would make an impressive performance record before the religious world of his day—as there are thousands today who are making impressive records, religiously, in the eyes of the churches in this country—but, as Paul had to learn, none of that was worth the snap of a finger in the eyes of God; it did not do God's work at all. If you want to change lives as Paul did, to upset whole communities, start people in new directions, give them liberty and freedom in the midst of guilt and oppression, you must learn what Paul learned, that it is nothing coming from you, but everything coming from God. God alone can do God's work. If there is no sense of dependence on him for that purpose, it is a wasted, useless effort.

Now that is cutting pretty deep, if we judge the current religious scene in terms of what Paul is saying here, isn't it? But he speaks of a *new* covenant. The old covenant is, "Here's a standard to achieve. Now do your very best to do it"—self-effort, to build up self-confidence. The new covenant is exactly the opposite. It says, "Just show up, present yourself. God will work through you; and what God demands, God himself will achieve, using you as the instrument of it. You will never get the credit for it; you can never say it was anything you did, or had, or were; it is God alone." That is why all through the Scriptures you find Christians denying that they were the explanation for what was accomplished, but that it was God himself at work. That is what Paul calls the new covenant; and God has made us competent to be ministers of it.

Now this is true of all Christians, not just apostles. We are all ministers of Christ; there is no special class set aside to be ministers. You too are called to be a minister of the new covenant, depending on God to be at work in you, not on your ability to do something for him. That is the truth revealed here.

A Prophecy Fulfilled

Jeremiah had described this new covenant in his prophecy long centuries before. He had said a day was coming when God would write his laws in people's hearts, not on tables of stone. It is the same law, but written in the heart, instead of presenting some external demand. God would live with them, they would be his people, he would be their God. They could draw upon his wisdom, his energy, his power and strength for any demand they had in their lives. He would instruct them by his Spirit, so that their eyes would be opened to see the real meaning of the things they learned. He would settle once and for all the question of their guilt. He would forgive their sins right at the very beginning; and they could rest upon God's constant washing and cleansing and forgiveness all through their lives. That is the new covenant as Jeremiah described it. It would change their whole motivation and outlook on life.

Perhaps with this very prophecy in mind, Paul now says something extremely important:

> . . . not in a written code but in the Spirit; for the written code kills, but the Spirit gives life (2 Cor. 3:6).

Have you found what a law, a demand, does to you? Have you ever realized how it hits you? Recently, a young man told me about an experience he had. He got up one morning and was thinking about his dad, about how much he meant to him, how he loved him, and how aware he was that morning of all the things his dad had done for him. His heart was filled with a sense of gratitude, and so he determined that after breakfast he would go out, without his dad having to say anything, and out of the sheer delight of pleasing him, mow the lawn and wash the car. He came down to breakfast, and just as he was about to leave the table, his dad said to him, "Son, before I get back today I would like to have you mow the lawn and wash the car. I really want you to do this. I don't want to come back this evening and find that you haven't done it." Then he left for work. This young man said, "It changed the whole picture. It just turned off all the incentive and motivation in my heart. I did it, but I had no further delight in it."

The outward law, making its demand upon us, awakens a sense of rebellion, as Paul describes in Romans 7. We all have it, we all dislike being told what to do. The external law invariably kills motivation. Many of us never seem to learn that lesson. We are constantly trying to order people around, make them do things out of pressure, little realizing that law is absolutely the kiss of death to all sense of desire and motivation within someone. This young man realized there was already a strong motivation, the most powerful of all, in his heart. He was all ready to mow the lawn and wash the car, and to delight in doing them, to feel a sense of joy in doing them, when it was a matter of gratitude for what his father's love and grace had meant to him.

This is almost an exact picture of what Paul is saying. The law, the demand of God in the Ten Commandments, a perfectly right and just demand of things we ought to do, nevertheless hits us always at the point of our rebellion. We don't like to be told that we have to do these things. But the new covenant is different. In it God has found a way into our hearts. Here he approaches us with the record of his love, of his willingness to die on our behalf, of his freedom to forgive us and to set us free from the guilt of our past, both the immediate past and the ancient past. Moreover, he makes us aware that he loves us, that we are approved of him, that he, in Christ, has already taken us into his family to stand dear to his heart, cherished by him. Having learned all that about us, then he tells us to serve him in whatever way our hearts delight in doing, and we go about it with an entirely different motivation.

A Splendor That Fades

To make this clear Paul gives us three contrasts. Though his language sounds a bit complicated, it is really very simple:

> Now if the dispensation of death, carved in letters on stone, came with such splendor that the Israelites could not look at Moses' face because of its brightness, fading as this was, will not the dispensation of the Spirit be attended with greater splendor? (2 Cor. 3:7, 8).

There is a kind of glory about the old covenant, an attractiveness, symbolized here by the brightness of Moses' face when he came down from the mountaintop with the tablets of law. But while God made Moses' face radiant, he also made the glory fade, because he wanted to teach something by that. It was a fading glory, a symbol of something that every one of us has experienced at one time or another. It is an attractive feeling to show how much we can do with what we have. Did you ever feel that? In sports, it's, "Give me a chance to show what I can do. Let me at it." In business every businessman feels the same thing. At every level of life someone can say, "I've been trained for that. I have the skills, I have the gifts. Let me show what I can do." We make a great impression. All to whose credit? Ours. We are the ones being glorified. Paul talks here about that feeling of attractiveness, of glory. But the record of history shows that everybody trying to live on that basis ends up a day late and a dollar short. It just never works. After awhile it all becomes dull, boring and routine, and death sets in. Paul is describing the ministry of death, the fading glory that does not last.

But when you discover the new principle, the principle of God-dependence, that in using your native skills, abilities, and training, God nevertheless will be at work, there is an excitement and a glory that is greater than the one you feel when you want to show off what you can do. It is not you, but God, who will accomplish things. That is a glory that surpasses.

In a second contrast, Paul says,

> For if there was splendor in the dispensation of condemnation (which condemned us, which brings guilt to us) (2 Cor. 3:9a).

Everybody who tries to live a life that is pleasing to God by self-effort always discovers that he never quite makes it because he never knows when he has done enough. A lady once said to me, "When I go to bed at night I often wonder if I had tried just a little harder maybe I could have done something that would have made God happy." But she never made it. Every night there was that feeling of "I didn't quite measure up today." That is the ministry of condemnation. It is the result of trying to do it on your own resources, by your own efforts. But Paul says,

> If there was a splendor in that dispensation of condemnation (if it had a glory about it), then the dispensation of righteousness must far exceed it in splendor (or glory, or attractiveness) (2 Cor. 3:9).

The Splendor That Lasts

Righteousness means being fully accepted, having a sense of being approved by God, of being honored and cherished by him. The nearest word I know to describe this is the word, "worth." God gives you a position of worth in his eyes. You don't have to earn it; you start with it. In the new covenant, God tells you, "I have loved you, I have forgiven you, I have cleansed you. You are my dearly beloved child. I intend to use you; you are part of my program; your life is significant. There is nothing more you can add to that. Now, on that basis, with the security of that acceptance, go back to your work." And you go with a sense of approval and security. Psychologists tell us that the only way we can function in the world today is with this sense of approval. If parents do not give their children a sense of security, they are torn apart by life, ravaged by whatever happens. And it is true of us as well. We need it all the time. We need this sense of being approved, accepted, loved, cherished. And this is what the new covenant gives to us.

Isn't that a greater glory than the anxiety of trying to earn your way into God's favor, feeling guilty because you never quite make it? This is so little understood in our land today that I know of churches where pastors feel their only good sermons are those which make the people go away feeling absolutely wretched and guilty. I know people who sit in a congregation and say, "Man, that's real preachin', pastor! I feel so bad; I feel so guilty. You really got to me today!" Good preaching? No, that is not where God starts. He starts with acceptance and security and love, and says, "Now, on that basis, operate."

Then, one final contrast to make clear the new covenant:

> Indeed, in this case, what once had splendor has come to have no splendor at all, because of the splendor that surpasses it. For if what faded away came with splendor, what is permanent must have much more splendor (much more glory about it) (2 Cor. 3:10).

Paul is talking about himself, looking back to the days when he counted on his background, his skill, his sharp mind and dedicated heart for success. He is saying, "I have come now to understand that God at work in me can do so much more than I could ever have done. I have come to understand that Christ's work in me is so much more effective than anything I could ask or think, that all the glory I once felt from my self-effort is nothing but a pile of manure (that is the term he uses in Philippians 3), compared with the glory of God at work in me. Self-effort has lost all its splendor. I don't try to psych myself up to accomplish something for God. I know that even in my feeblest weakness, God is able to work though me, and that is what I count on. What happens as a result is far more thrilling and satisfying to me than anything that ever happened before."

That is the true Christian life. That is what the world is waiting to see in our day. We are all called to be ministers of this new covenant. It is God who is making us able, not ourselves. If we understand that, life will never be the same again.

5

"Who Is Sufficient?"

In this chapter we begin what I think is one of the greatest passages in the New Testament. It actually begins in chapter 2, verse 14, and concludes with verse 2 of chapter 7. I believe it is the clearest explanation in all the Word of God of the secret of the apostle Paul's phenomenal ministry. I have discussed this section at length in my book *Authentic Christianity* because it has meant so much in my life, and because I have seen its impact on the lives of so many others. It is a splendid example of what genuine, true, authentic Christianity is. Yet, strangely enough, this great passage is but a parenthesis in the epistle—a digression on the apostle's part.

In Travail . . .

Waiting in Macedonia for Titus to return with news of the church at Corinth, Paul was feeling a great disturbance of mind, as we will see in a moment. Out of that disturbance grew this magnificent description of the power by which he labored and lived. It appears as a spontaneous outburst from the apostle's heart to counteract the sense of failure and despair he was feeling in his ministry at the time.

The background is found in verses 12 and 13 of chapter 2:

> When I came to Troas to preach the gospel of Christ, a door was opened for me in the Lord; but my mind could not rest because I did not find

my brother Titus there. So I took leave of them and went on to Macedonia.

These brief words gather up a tremendous experience in Paul's life. He had gone to Troas from Ephesus to preach the gospel of Christ. This was his great joy everywhere. Wherever he went he knew he would find people sunk in despair, filled with darkness, their lives governed by superstition and fear, people who, without realizing what they were doing, had fallen into terrible, hurtful things that were destroying them. It was Paul's great joy to come with the good news of Jesus Christ, the one who understood the hurts of men, the Deliverer, the Healer of hurts, the one who had the power to touch human lives and transform them. Paul longed to preach the gospel to all the earth if he could, because it was such a tremendous thing to see the power of God let loose among men to set them free.

So he came into the city of Troas for that purpose, and a great door was opened for him by the Lord; that is, there was a responsiveness to his message and great opportunity to proclaim it. Hundreds, even thousands, of people perhaps gathered in the marketplaces or wherever they could to hear the word of the apostle. A church was already there and the city was stirred as Paul came to preach. Yet he was unable to take full advantage of it. His heart was so troubled, his spirit so anxious for news of what was happening in Corinth, that he could not minister. He was restless of spirit and troubled of heart; and he had to leave.

I think he could see, as he waited there for weeks and perhaps months, that all his labors in Corinth were about to fall apart. He must have been gripped by a great sense of personal failure. In the visits he had made to Corinth, in the letters he had written, there seemed no way to work out this terrible problem eating at the life of this church, threatening to destroy the work he had done. In the midst of that sense of failure, pressure, and anxiety, he was given a great opportunity, but he could not lay hold of it. So he left Troas and went up into Macedonia instead, hoping to find Titus there to bring relief to his troubled mind.

Now I do not know if any of you have ever felt that way or not, but I have. I know what it means to be called on to preach and teach the Word of God at times when my heart was so filled with anxiety and distress that I did not know whether I could open my mouth or not. I understand what Paul felt, and I feel many of you do too, as he so honestly shares this with us.

. . . The Triumph

Yet the next verse is astounding:

> But thanks be to God, who in Christ always leads us in triumph, and through us spreads the fragrance of the knowledge of him everywhere (2 Cor. 2:14).

That is my favorite verse in all Scripture. What an outstanding expression of grateful thanksgiving for a powerful and effective ministry! And it stands right next to the verse in which he is confessing his failure and his weakness, his frustration and his despair. Now that is amazing, isn't it? Verses 14 through 16 give us a cry of grateful thanksgiving from the apostle's heart; verse 17 is a description from his own lips of his significant and effective ministry and yet they stand side by side with this admission of frustration.

Why this sudden reversal? Humanly speaking, the apostle's circumstances were dreary, dark and without encouragement. But spiritually, he says, on the basis of an understanding of how God works, he knew the circumstances were actually bright and glowing with great possibilities, and he was rejoicing. He calls it, "always led in triumph in Christ."

I think the Bible scholars are right when they say that Paul is thinking here, quite evidently, of the Roman Triumphs. It was a custom in the Roman Empire, when a conquering general returned from a successful campaign over one of the enemies of Rome that the Senate would grant him a Triumph. This would be equivalent to what we call a "ticker tape parade," such as New York City gives to honor a national hero. In the Roman Triumphs the conquering general would ride through the streets of Rome in his chariot, preceded by numbers of priests swinging pots of fragrant incense. Behind him would come the captives he had taken, being led to their execution in chains. Then there would come the generals of his army, the captains and the commanders of his forces. The streets would be filled with people shouting acclamations. Now that is what Paul says was going on at the same time he was feeling depressed, lonely, frustrated and discouraged in Macedonia. Is it not amazing that he would put those two things in juxtaposition?

The Fragrance of Christ

He further describes it as spreading the fragrance of Christ; the beautiful character of Jesus was becoming evident through this pressure on him:

> For we are the aroma of Christ to God among those who are being saved and among those who are perishing, to one a fragrance from death to death, to the other a fragrance from life to life. Who is sufficient for these things? (2 Cor. 2:15, 16)

In the Roman Triumph, to the prisoners bound in chains following the conquering general's chariot, the fragrance of the incense was an odor of death; but to those who were part of the army, and to the citizens of Rome who had been spared a threat to the city, that same fragrance was a fragrance unto life. Paul applies that to himself. He says that as he goes about preaching this good news that Jesus is alive and can free men and deliver them from their inner torments and pressures, a fragrance of the life of his Son rises up to God. Wherever Paul went, God could smell the sweetness and beauty of Jesus in what Paul was doing.

But more than that, it was also a fragrance of Christ to men. A fellow-pastor once told me of a funeral service he conducted for a man who had received the Lord not long before his accidental death. One small group there was upset by what he was saying about the freedom and the new life in Christ. They stood there, sullen and angry; and they wrote him letters about it afterward. To them that service was a fragrance of death unto death; they did not like it. But others were rejoicing in the hope and the freedom that Christ had given this man, despite a life of failure. To them that message was a fragrance of life unto life. At that point we are always dealing with blank, stark reality. This is what Paul is talking about. Wherever he went he said people were either helped on to freedom and life in Christ, or they were angered, their opposition hardened, and they were driven further unto death. But nobody took him for granted. He made an impact wherever he went. Paul describes his ministry in those terms.

What does this all mean? Surely it means that the world was unimpressed by the apostle Paul. When he traveled around the Roman Empire preaching this great message, he was never received by the Chamber of Commerce; no reporters followed him around giving verbatim reports of all that he was saying. Even in his own eyes he was not doing anything tremendous. He himself was feeling, as he says, frustrated and restless; a great sense of failure sometimes gripped him. But despite this, he knew that his success did not rest upon his feeble efforts to do something for God, but on his expectation that God was going to do something through him; he was at the very moment of his frustration being led in triumph by Jesus Christ; a great, widespread manifestation of the fragrance of Jesus Christ was going out; people were being set free, and his ministry was a success. So he cries out of the gratitude of his heart, "Thanks be to God, who in Christ always leads us in triumph."

If I did not believe in that great principle I would resign from the pastorate tomorrow morning. I once had the privilege of ministering for a week on the campus of a large university. For four days I taught the Word of God to 2,400 college students who sat quiet and responsive, listening to everything I was saying. It was a tremendous opportunity, but every morning I spoke from a very heavy heart. Like Paul in Romans 9, my conscience bore me witness in the Holy Spirit, that I had great sorrow and unceasing anguish in my heart. A family matter of deep personal urgency had burdened me with a very heavy heart, and the only thing that enabled me to keep going was confidence in what Paul is saying here. Despite the personal frustration and darkness that I was going through, I was also being led in triumph by Jesus Christ, knowing that out of my personal weakness would come a great manifestation of the strength of our Lord, spreading the fragrance of Christ.

A Different Victory

This is what is properly called the "victorious Christian life." We hear a lot about that today, and much of what we hear is unbiblical, in my judgment. Many seem to view "victorious life" as a thrill ride in an amusement park. At the "Pirates of the Caribbean" in Disneyland, for example, you get aboard a boat and go through a tunnel. Immediately you are assaulted by enemies; strange figures leap out of the darkness at you, brandishing huge knives and swords; pistols are discharged right in your face, cannons fire and cannonballs splash on either side of your boat, and it looks as though your life is in horrible danger. But you sit there, quietly unmoved, because you know that you will be led safely through all this, and nothing is ever going to get to you.

There are many people who have that view of the Christian life. They think because they are Christians, because they now happen to be a child of God, a son of the King, that they are going to be protected and kept from every pressure and danger of life, and nothing is ever going to get through to them. They quote many verses to support that view. But if that is the true "victorious life," then Paul did not know anything about it, because he went through terrible testings and great times of pressure. He will describe them for us in this very letter; they are almost unbelievable in their intensity and power to threaten and ruin his life. Yet he could cry out with great confidence and the triumphant spirit that rings throughout this whole passage, because he knew—according to the great principle which he had learned through much pain and anguish—that God was carrying out his purposes through the very weakness Paul experienced.

Some people see the "victorious life" as a constant, visible demonstration of such tremendous power that no obstacle can stand in their way. They expect to be like General Patton slashing his way across Europe in World War II, smashing all obstacles in his path, visibly triumphant over all his enemies. They expect to feel powerful, and to see the power of God let loose in such triumphant ways that all obstacles are visibly crushed. But again, if this describes victorious life, Paul knew nothing about it.

Instead, as we can judge from his life, the true victorious Christian life is a feeling of weakness, with only brief glimpses of success, seemingly going from one battle to another, from one conflict to another without ceasing, with little sense of personal triumph at the moment. And yet that triumph is occurring, and Paul is singing about it here. His life was making a powerful impact. It is clearly evident to us who live in this twentieth century that, apart from our Lord himself, probably no other human being ever has made such a fantastic impression on human history as the apostle Paul. He learned a secret that many Christians seemingly forget today. It is the secret of the impact of this mighty life.

Listen as he describes his ministry in this brief summary:

> For we are not, like so many, peddlers of God's word; but as men of sincerity, as commissioned by God, in the sight of God we speak in Christ (2 Cor. 2:17).

Notice the contrast there. "We are not like a lot of people," he says, "who are going around finding attractive little trinkets in the Word of God and peddling them like street salesmen, hawkers, making a good living from people's curiosity about some of the subjects the Word of God treats." They were doing that in the first century as they do today. The world is full of religious racketeers who are doing exactly what Paul called here, "peddling God's Word." Turn on the television, pick up a magazine, listen to the radio; you hear them on every side. They peddle tongues, or healing, or prophecy, or any number of things. While these have validity in themselves, these racketeers take the peripheral and secondary and make them central. The central truths of the Scriptures are neglected and a minor point stressed and that is all they write about, talk about, and think about. They hawk it as salesmen would a product in the economic world today. But Paul says, "We are not like that."

A second form of "peddling" wears a more respectable disguise. Certain people pose as Bible scholars, write learned discussions about various aspects or passages of scripture, and command high salaries for dispensing theological junk. It seems more easily peddled on college campuses than almost anywhere else. Yet all the while, the student body starves for closeness of relationship with adult leaders on the faculty. Christian college professors are charged before God to minister as shepherds to the young people who spend four years on their campus, but some among them shove aside or easily forget this responsibility. Speaking to such a situation, a colleague of mine once paraphrased with great impact a passage from Luke 17, where Jesus said, in effect, "Look, if you are going to mess with God's children you might well consider committing suicide first." That sobered those men and women, as it ought to sober us. Paul has nothing to do with this kind of a superficial, shallow approach to the Word of God.

A Different Ministry

His ministry, as he describes it, is fourfold. First, he is sincere; he practices what he preaches; he believes what he is saying. He does not preach cream and live skim milk. He is doing what he declares. And second, his ministry is purposeful. "We are commissioned by God," he says. "We are not sent into this world to enjoy ourselves and try and get through it and retire in a comfortable way. We have a goal to accomplish. We have been sent to do something." He declares in Colossians what it is: "that we may present every man mature in Christ. For this I toil, warning every man and teaching every man in all wisdom, striving with all the energy which he mightily inspires within me" (Col. 1:29). This is Paul's goal, and he never forgot it. That ought to be the goal of every Christian, to help one another grow up and become mature individuals, emotionally, spiritually, and in every way to forget our childish little ways, to turn away from that and grow up and be men and women in Christ.

Thirdly, he performs this ministry "in the sight of God." He is transparent in his personal life, with nothing to hide, nothing to keep from public view. The man or woman who lives in the sight of God is also open and transparent before men, for if God has forgiven and cleansed his faults what need he fear from men?

And finally, he did so "in Christ." Later on, he calls himself "an ambassador for Christ, as though God did beseech you *in Christ's stead,* be ye reconciled to God" (2 Cor. 5:20). He spoke with authority because he came as a representative of God himself to deliver a message the world desperately needed to hear.

It is hopeless to look to secular leadership to get us out of the mess we are in. If the church is not going to say to the world what God has sent it to say, there is no hope for this country or any other country today. It is truth we need. We need light in our darkness. That is what every one of us has been commissioned by God to declare—light in the midst of the darkness. Paul is not out to make a quick, soft living, raking in thousands of dollars by hawking some attractive truth in the Word of God; he is proclaiming the full truth of God so that people are truly delivered and set free.

What a ministry it was! No wonder that in the midst of it he raises this question, "Who is sufficient for these things?" When you think of what we are sent to do I am sure that question grips your heart. It does mine. Paul will answer that question in the third chapter, but he raises the question here because it is so obvious that no human resource is capable of this. Who can do this? What school can give you this capability? What course can you take? What human leader can you follow who will teach you how to function in these realms so that people are actually set free? "Who is sufficient for these things?"

Jesus himself raised the same question with his disciples. On one occasion he turned to the twelve and said to them, "Are you able to drink the cup that I am to drink and to be baptized with the baptism that I am baptized with?" In their ignorant futility they said, "Yes, sure, we are able," as many of us have unthinkingly said. But Jesus' words are very solemn. He said, "You shall drink indeed of my cup, and be baptized with the baptism that I am baptized with." He meant by this that there would be frustration, there would be fear, there would be loneliness and death in our experience, if we are going to see the power of God released in our lives.

The victorious Christian life is not one of continual victory, in the sense of overcoming all obstacles and feeling triumphant everywhere we go. No! It is one of anguish of heart at times, of deep inner doubts, of fighting with frustrations without and fears within, of being opposed oftentimes. But it is also a life which is confident that the God who is within us is able to work his work and do his will, that out of the fear, the frustration, and the failure, is coming triumph and victory and the fragrance of Jesus Christ. Have you come to that? That is what will change this world around us. God grant we will understand this as we go through this passage together.

6

Who Is That Masked Man?

Some of us older folks remember how we thrilled when we heard the call of, "Hi-ho, Silver!" to the beat of the William Tell overture, and the invariable question, "Who was that masked man anyway?" But in 2 Corinthians, Paul tells us who "The Masked Man" of the Bible is. It is Moses.

> Since we have such a hope, we are very bold, not like Moses, who put a veil over his face so that the Israelites might not see the end of the fading splendor (2 Cor. 3:12).

Clearly, the apostle is dealing with this veil as a symbol. God loves to teach with symbols; his favorite teaching method is to use a visual aid which he holds up before us to instruct us. Moses' "mask,' or veil, is a symbol of the old covenant, the law, the Ten Commandments, a certain standard of behavior. It also pictures our natural, typical response to the law—to try to obey it, either to the point of convincing ourselves that we have achieved it, or to the point of giving up and rebelling against it.

When Moses came down from the mountaintop, we learn that his face was shining, the symbol of the attraction, the glory, of trying to keep the law of God. Every one of us has felt that attraction at times. We know what it is like to feel that we have succeeded. Our blood quickens when we think we have met a given demand. Many people become very excited over that kind of thing today in the realms of music, sports, politics, and various other areas of human endeavor. All this is symbolized by the glory of Moses' face.

But it was a fading glory, Paul tells us. He himself has found something even more exciting. It is what he calls the "new covenant," a new way of living, provided by God in Christ. This gives us not only a right relationship with Christ right from the very beginning (not something we have earned, but something given to us), but also gives us the excitement of expecting God to work with us and through us so that when we do ordinary, normal things, God will be at work and great things will happen as a result. Now that is exciting.

I like the way one of the newer translations renders some of the verses just before this section, where the apostle is comparing these two covenants:

> Compare the giving of the rules with the reception of the Spirit. The presentation of the rules, which result in death, was so brilliant that the Israelites could not look directly upon Moses' face because of the glare of the presence of God. And yet the rules he received were destined to pass away. Won't the gift of the Spirit be more luminous? If the gift of rules which condemn a person was deemed marvelous, isn't the gift of a right relationship a greater marvel? As marvelous as receiving the rules has been, this gift is fading away because it is superseded by the reception of the Spirit. If what is abolished is marvelous, how much more marvelous is that which remains. (2 Cor. 3:7–11, *The Heart of Paul—A Relational Paraphrase of the New Testament.* Ben Campbell Johnson, Word, p. 88).

Because he has found this new basis for living far more exciting and more attractive than trying his best to keep the law, Paul says, "Since we have such a hope, we are very bold."

The mark of someone who has really trusted the new covenant is always boldness; he becomes confident. The root meaning behind this word is openness. He becomes right out front, out in the open, with nothing to hide, transparent. Because he is not counting on himself but is counting on God, he becomes confident and positive.

Death by Hiding

Paul contrasts this immediately with Moses, who put a veil over his face so that the Israelites might not see the end of the fading splendor. You can read that story back in chapter 34 of Exodus, where we are told that when Moses brought the Ten Commandments down from the mountain, his face was shining like the sun and the people actually fled from him. Moses called them back, and when he had finished giving them the words of God he put a veil over his face.

Paul tells us he did it so that they would not see the end of the fading glory. When Moses went back into the tent of meeting and met with God again, he took the veil off. When he would come out he would put the veil back on. But behind the veil the glory was fading and Moses kept the veil on because he did not want them to see the fading glory, the final result of trying to obey God with all your might.

What is that result? Paul has already described it for us in chapter 3. He calls it the "dispensation of death" (verse 7), "the dispensation of condemnation" (verse 9), and then in verse 11, "that which fades away." Trying your best to live up to what God wants will always bring you to this end, a sense of death. You will never measure up. Nobody ever does. You will never get the feeling, "Aha! at last I have done what God wants," because something inside of you will say, "Well, you may think so, but maybe God doesn't." So you will feel guilty, you will feel a sense of failure and shortcoming. Furthermore, Paul describes this condition as a sense of condemnation, that is, a sense of culpability, of failed responsibility. What you are left with is boredom, emptiness and a sense of futility.

This explains why many Christians, when they are honest, say, "You know, my Christian life is not very exciting. I find it rather boring, kind of empty." They confess to a feeling of waste and futility. That is a confirmation of what Paul is saying here, that when we think we can live up to what God demands of us it produces a sense of death and guilt and emptiness within us.

So this veil over Moses' face becomes a symbol for whatever hides the work of the law. Paul has been telling us the law has come to show us how useless it is to try hard to obey God. The law has come to make that real, to show us how absolutely futile is our trying. But a veil delays that feeling, allowing us to think we really are pleasing God and fulfilling his demands. The veil, therefore, puts off the sense of death, the clear realization of our inadequacy, which we need in order to receive the life that God is willing to give.

Perhaps Moses did not understand all this when he put on the veil. It is difficult for us to know what his motive may have been. Some commentators suggest he felt that if the people saw the glory fading away they would not pay any attention to the law and go on living as they wanted. Others have suggested that, perhaps, he was trying to preserve his own status symbol as a special mediator with God.

That is the position I have taken in my book, *Authentic Christianity*. I think that Moses, like many of us, was trying to preserve the reputation he had with the people and did not want them to see the glory begin to fade when he came out from God's presence—as many of us do not like people to see what is really going on inside of us. We want to preserve the image of a spiritual giant when actually we are far from it. Our family knows it, but we do not want our friends or anyone else to know. That may have been Moses' motive.

One thing is clear, however: it was not a bold or confident act on Moses' part. Paul contrasts his own boldness with Moses. What Moses did was born out of fear, out of compromise, an attempt to hide something that should have been seen. Paul makes this clear when he links Moses to the unbelief of the Jews in Paul's own day:

> But their minds were hardened; for to this day, when they read the old covenant, that same veil remains unlifted, because only through Christ is it taken away. Yes, to this day whenever Moses is read a veil lies over their minds; but when a man turns to the Lord the veil is removed (2 Cor. 3:14–16).

"I'll Do It If It Kills Me!"

The darkness, the blindness that lay over the minds of the Jews of his day, is the same nature as the veil that Moses put over his face. Obviously, the veil on Moses' face was a material veil made of cloth. Paul is not suggesting that the Jews walked around with cloth veils on their faces, but he is saying that the same thing the veil stood for with Moses was happening also to the Israelites of his own day: it hid the end of the fading glory, it veiled the terrible end of self-effort, the death that would result. It continues to conceal death to the Jews who read the old covenant, the Old Testament, even today. They do not see that the end of all their efforts to try to live a righteous life by human resources is going to end in death and condemnation, emptiness and a sense of futility and waste. But yet that is what happens.

Paul also calls it a "hardening"; he means it becomes a continual condition, a state of mind they enter into. In our day, 2000 years after Paul, this is still true. You can see it in Orthodox Judaism, much of Reformed Judaism, and certainly in Liberal Judaism; they are still trying to secure the approval of God on the basis of how they behave.

A good illustration of this is the following quotation from a letter a young man of my acquaintance received from a Jewish rabbi. This boy was of Jewish background but had become a Christian, and the rabbi was trying to defend Judaism:

> We Jews have rejected the Gentile Christian view. Judaism, as shaped by our rabbis in Palestine, conceived of the body (that is, our physical bodies) as a gift of God and to this day we regard the body as holy and wholesome, not a prison from which to escape. Any inclination by man to commit a wrongdoing, we hold, resides not in his body but in his heart or mind and this inclination can be overcome by a change of heart or mind. *Thus man, by himself, does possess, indeed, the power to atone for his own misdeeds.* And we Jews have in our Torah (the Old Testament) the guidance directing our hearts and minds to righteous living.

That, of course, is purely and simply the old covenant. The veil still lies over their minds so that they cannot see the end of the fading glory.

Now this is not an attack on Judaism, for Paul is not attacking Judaism. He is simply using Moses and Israel as an illustration of something that is true of the believers to whom he is writing and through them, to us as well. These people had become Christians, and by faith the Spirit of God had entered their human spirit and had established them into a relationship with Christ which could not be broken. In the spirit, at the deep level of human unconsciousness, they were linked to God already in an unbreakable relationship.

But the trouble was (and this is our trouble as well), in their soul, in their conscious experience of life, this veil was often over their minds. They still believed that if they tried hard enough they could keep themselves from evil and so live a life pleasing to God. That is the error that pervades churches all through this country and around the world today. It locks us into weakness, futility, condemnation and guilt and all the other phenomena so familiar in mediocre church life today.

Man-Sized Rules

What happens is this: once we become Christians we receive the gift of salvation by faith. We thank God for that, but then immediately we begin to set up rules of conduct. (We usually submit to someone else's for awhile, and then we begin to set up our own.) We determine what is wrong and what is right and set out to avoid the wrong and do the right.

Everybody has on his list certain things that are obviously wrong—murder, adultery, drunkenness, and so on. These are always on everybody's list because they are so clear in scripture. Then we begin to add others. Drinking, that is out; smoking, that is wrong; dancing, that is wrong; going to movies, theatre, whatever, all these are wrong.

There is no limit to where you can go in that direction. You can do like the Amish people and include wearing buttons as wrong; or using zippers, absolutely wrong; or playing instruments in a congregation, that is absolutely of the devil. There are groups who believe that once you have made your list, whatever it is, once you have your no-no's clear, then all you need to do to be approved of God is keep the list. Since they are external things, that by effort of will or mind you can keep from doing, you do have a possibility, it appears, of pleasing God.

Now you can either fail, because these demands are too unrealistic; give up entirely and throw the whole thing out; or, what is probably worse, succeed, and not do any of those things. You then begin to feel good about yourself because you have lived up to what you're persuaded God expects of you.

But you do not realize, because the veil is hiding the end of the fading glory, that when you think you have kept your list you begin to feel very proud of yourself. You do not openly admit that; you do not brag about how spiritual you are (you know that will get you into trouble), but inside there is a strong pride that begins to develop which will reveal itself outwardly.

When You Measure Up

The way it usually comes out is in some form of snobbery. You will look down on people. Most Christians suffer from this. For example, I look down on people who look down on people! That is prejudice. Certain types of people are acceptable and others you cannot stand. You cannot understand how anybody can put up with them—hippies, or blacks, or poor people—whatever.

You then begin to develop a critical spirit—others do not measure up. Where you feel you are strong you put down those who cannot make it in that area. There is nothing worse than a reformed drunkard, for instance. He makes everybody uncomfortable. You can become absolutely intolerant of others, impatient of lack of progress on their part. Or it comes out in the form of sarcasm, the way you talk about people, the names you give them. Archie Bunker is a clear manifestation of the bigotry that begins to emerge. And bigotry is a terrible sin.

The great problem is we are blind to these as sins. If we saw ourselves we would see that we are wretchedly self-righteous. But we really think

God approves of us. (We are like the Pharisees whom Jesus would scorch with his words because they were so wretchedly self-righteous.) And since we do not see these as sins, we never turn to the Lord about them. We think of them as minor peccadilloes that might be a little troublesome, but are not really sins. God is not very concerned about them because of the great record we have in his eyes. So we never confess them; we never acknowledge them as wrong to ourselves or anyone. We never turn to the Lord about them.

So, therefore, the blindness is never removed, because, as Paul says here, "when a man turns to the Lord the veil is removed." We cannot take it off any other way; there is no way we can show ourselves how self-righteous we are. We must turn to the Lord. That is the only way it is possible. Since we do not do this, we go on year after year hurting ourselves, hurting others, enjoying the momentary pleasure and sense of excitement we get from indulging these attitudes. But gradually there creeps into our life the end of the fading glory: the death, the darkness, the emptiness, the sense of futility, boredom, dullness, and "blahness" of that kind of Christianity. Paul is telling us to look right at it and see it for what it is.

But there is one great area of hope; and we get this in the next two verses:

> Now the Lord is the Spirit, and where the Spirit of the Lord is, there is freedom. And we all, with unveiled face, beholding the glory of the Lord, are being changed into his likeness from one degree of glory to another; for this comes from the Lord who is the Spirit (2 Cor. 3:17, 18).

The apostle reminds the Corinthians immediately that, though the veil is over their minds, the Lord is in their hearts, in their human spirits. Their hope of freedom comes from that great fact, for the One who is within them is God himself. Paul identifies him: "the Lord is the Spirit, and where the Spirit of the Lord is, there is freedom."

He is not confusing, of course, the personages of the Trinity. He does not mean that the Holy Spirit and Jesus the Lord are one and the same. He means that they are so identified in purpose and function that they seem to be the same; you can exchange one for the other. That is why "to walk in fellowship with Christ," and "to walk in the fullness of the Spirit" is to talk about the same thing. It is not two different experiences; it is the same. The Holy Spirit has come to reveal the Lord Jesus; therefore, what he does will not involve talking about himself but talking about the Lord. The Spirit-led life is one in which Jesus Christ is made visible and clear to our spiritual eyes.

Therefore, the one who is doing this is the Lord himself, "and where the Spirit of Christ is (the Spirit of the Lord is), there is freedom."

The Truth Does Make You Free!

Freedom is being out in the open; it is the boldness of having nothing to hide. The man who is free has no reputation to defend, no image to hide behind, nothing to preserve about himself. He can be himself.

Everywhere today we hear people longing to "be themselves." "I've got to be me," we hear, and there is nothing wrong with that, because God wants you to be you, too. The only thing wrong is the way we do it. We are taught in the world that the way to be "me" is to think about "my" advantage, "my" efforts, and to defend and demand them.

The Word of God teaches us quite another process. The way to be yourself, to have freedom, is not to be afraid to look at the evil in your heart and in your life, because you have another basis on which you can receive the acceptance and approval of God. It is a gift to you. It is faith, continually accepting anew the gift of righteousness, of already being pleasing to God, and on that basis serving him out of a heart of gratitude for what you already have.

Do you see the difference? You know you do not deserve it, but nevertheless, you have it. God's basis of deliverance is to give you the gift of full acceptance, of righteousness. You do not have to earn it at all, and your performance is not going to affect it. You already have it.

Glory That Never Fades

When you start looking at the One who is giving you this in your life, the Lord Jesus, and beholding him with all your veils taken away so you are not afraid to look at your own evil capacity, then a wonderful thing happens. Paul says,

> And we all, with unveiled face, beholding the glory of the Lord, are being changed into his likeness from one degree of glory to another (2 Cor. 3:18).

Without even knowing that you are doing it, just by rejoicing in what you have, and serving the Lord who gave it to you, you suddenly discover—and other people will discover—that you are becoming a loving person. The miracle, of course, is that love is the fulfilling of the law; the very demand that God made in the law, which you tried so hard to fulfill by your self-effort, will be fulfilled without you even realizing it when you begin to love out of the grace and the forgiveness of God.

A loving person is already fulfilling the law. He is compassionate, understanding, forgiving. He is firm when it comes to right and wrong; he knows how to speak the truth, but he does it in love. He is not constantly criticizing and judging others, because he understands the weakness with which we seek to obey these standards. Yet he is helpful; he tries to encourage people to rest upon the grace and forgiveness of God. Without realizing it, he suddenly discovers to his own amazement that he is becoming more like Jesus.

It is a process of growth. It does not happen in one great transformation when you are suddenly sanctified, or filled with the Spirit, or baptized. It happens as you keep your eyes on the glory of the Lord and not on the face of Moses; not on your self-effort, but on what he is always giving you. When you do, you discover the Spirit of God has been at work making gradual changes. You are becoming a loving person, easier to live with, more attractive, more compelling, your life is deepening, it is losing its shallowness; you are more understanding of things. That is the work of the Spirit. Notice what he says, "for this comes from the Lord who is the Spirit." It is not you who does it, it is he. He has the responsibility.

This accounts for what many of us have difficulty understanding. It is the work of the Spirit to remove the veil that keeps us from seeing ourselves and how futile it is to try to please God. There is another way of pleasing him: by accepting what he gives you. As long as you are trying hard you never can lay hold of what he is ready to give. Therefore, the work of the Spirit is to help you to see how futile your efforts at trying have become.

Moments of Truth

These are what we call "moments of truth." Did you ever have one? They are rather shocking. You think you have been going along, eating your Wheaties and doing OK, and suddenly you discover that you have been a very self-centered person, that what you thought was a perfectly acceptable life is filled with lovelessness, viciousness, and selfishness.

I have often told of the two young men who were students down at Duke University in North Carolina. They were invited to a masquerade party. They decided to go dressed in the costumes of the mascots of Duke University, the "Blue Devils," so they rented blue devil costumes.

Dressed in these, they started out for the party, and, without realizing it, they got mixed up and went by mistake into a church congregation at Prayer Meeting. When these people looked up from their prayers to see two blue devils walking down the aisle there was a great exodus, out the doors and out the windows, all except for one rather stout lady who got wedged in the front pew when she tried to turn around. She began to scream in terror, and these two young men, forgetting they were causing this problem, rushed forward to try to help her. When she saw them advancing on her she raised her hand, she rolled her eyes, and said, "Stop! Don't you come any further! I want you to know that I've been a member of this church for 25 years, but I've been on your side all the time!"

That is what the Spirit of God does with us. He suddenly makes us see whose side we have been on, and it is very upsetting. I have felt it many times. You suddenly see how futile it is to try to be good, but how wonderful it is to realize that by the gift of God you already are good in his sight. When you believe that, and out of sheer gratitude for that you begin to live and to do the things that fulfill the love that you feel in your heart, you suddenly discover that your behavior has changed as well, and that without being conscious of it you are becoming a loving person. That is what the new covenant is all about. That is the great glory of it.

7

Nothing But the Truth

Have you ever wondered why so many people do not believe the gospel when they first hear it, or even after they have heard it over a long period of time? Why do many who believe the gospel quit after they have been walking in the Christian way for some time? And why do some people whom you think will never believe it, suddenly believe? The first six verses of the fourth chapter of 2 Corinthians answer these questions.

The passage begins with a tremendous declaration by the Apostle Paul as to his own ministry:

> Therefore, having this ministry (the word means "this kind of a ministry") by the mercy of God, we do not lose heart (2 Cor. 4:1).

All through this passage he has repeated that theme—"We do not get discouraged"; "we do not feel like quitting"; "we are confident"; "we are encouraged." That note occurs again and again throughout the passage.

I meet many Christians who are getting discouraged today, some as seriously as the pastor who came to one of our seminars from a church in a different locality. He looked about him at what was regarded as a successful church with a good attendance and a clear financial situation, and every morning he felt a severe sense of failure and emptiness in what he was doing. Increasingly he felt that he was merely going through religious motions, that he was accomplishing nothing of any real and lasting value. He told us that so intense and deep was his depression that if it had not been for the shame he would have brought upon his family he would have taken his own life. The least he felt he could do was to quit the ministry.

Christians who feel ready to quit feel that they are not achieving anything. When you talk with them you discover that, basically, they do not see themselves, as Paul did, as being the instrument of God at work. They are focusing on what they are doing for God, or, in these discouraging times, what they are not doing for God. They do not seem to understand that the basis for the kind of ministry Paul had received is the new covenant, the new arrangement for living which God has provided in Christ.

In these next two verses the apostle gives us two great reasons why the new covenant does not allow discouragement. If you have struggled with this, I suggest you take this very seriously and think through why you feel discouraged at times. Do you understand this great principle which kept Paul from ever being discouraged, despite the many obstacles he ran up against?

The first reason is found in the first half of verse 2:

> We have renounced disgraceful, underhanded ways; we refuse to practice cunning or to tamper with God's word (2 Cor. 4:2a).

He says, "We have turned our backs on the ways and practices that bring discouragement." That is one reason he did not get discouraged.

I am always amazed at how up-to-date the Scriptures are. You would think that Paul had just been listening to some Christian radio broadcasts or television programs when he wrote this. Evidently there were people in his day, preaching in churches and evangelizing, who were practicing disgraceful, underhanded ways. They were relying on cunning approaches and even tampering with the Word of God. Paul says, "I have given all that up" (if he ever did it). "Seeing other people do this, I want nothing to do with it."

Deliberate Deceit

Notice particularly what these ways consist of, because this speaks to our own time. First, he says, "I have renounced disgraceful, underhanded ways," that is, the practice of deliberate deceit. Every now and then an article appears in the religious papers about some evangelist who hires converts to stand up in his meetings and confess Christ, or to come down front and give a testimony to being healed, to make the evangelist look like a success. That is sheer deceit.

You sometimes read of Sunday schools that bait and bribe people to come to church. Not long ago there was a report in the papers of a pastor who said that if he got a certain number of people out to Sunday school he would preach from his church belfry. He got the number he wanted so he went up in the belfry and preached his sermon. That is simply a form of bribery, getting people to come for some secondary, superficial reason.

I know of churches that give kids candy if they will get aboard their buses and come to Sunday school. Some even offer prizes, bicycles, and so on, to get kids out. They gain an appearance of success by relying upon wrong methods, deceitful things, disgraceful, underhanded ways. I have met preachers who have phony degrees, obtained for $10 or so from some diploma mill somewhere. They put letters after their name to impress people. But that is deceit. I know of missionaries who send reports home to their supporting churches about events that have no basis whatever in fact. They tell of things that never occurred, reporting achievements in the preaching of the gospel that never really happened, thus deliberately lying in the name of Christ. I know of Christians who tell someone else's experience as though it happened to them, and thus they lie in the name of Jesus. But Paul says, "I don't need any of those things anymore." Anyone who relies on that may gain an appearance of success, but sooner or later the bottom will fall out and they will be left with intense feelings of depression and failure and folly.

Paul says also he refuses to practice cunning. Now what does that mean? Well, it means to rely on some psychological trick played on people to get them to respond—some intense pressure tactic in a meeting, perhaps beautiful seductive music to get them to give way, or telling stories that bring tears to people's eyes, playing upon their emotions, this kind of thing. Paul says, "We don't need to use any of this. We don't rely upon that." In our day many seem given over to Christian showmanship, seeing who can put on the biggest spectacle to attract people, hiring a special band or getting trapeze artists to come and put on a show, and so on. Paul says that in the new covenant we do not rely on those kinds of things anymore.

Tampering and Twisting

Nor does he "tamper with God's word." Can you imagine anyone in the name of Jesus tampering with God's Word? Yet it happens all the time. Peter speaks of those who "twist the Scriptures." In 2 Peter 3:16 there is a reference to Paul's letters where he says:

> There are some things in them hard to understand, which the ignorant and unstable twist to their own destruction, as they do the other scriptures.

It is not difficult to do that. You can take a great biblical word and give it another meaning, and, using the same language, talk about something else entirely. The word "resurrection" has been disembowelled of its biblical content and made to mean something that it does not mean in the Bible. The word "Christ" is made to stand for a person or a being who does not exist in Scripture at all. People who hear one use that kind of language are fooled. That is twisting the Word of God; and it happens all the time in our day.

You find people who imply that the Bible is inferior to the discoveries of modern knowledge—present day scientific discoveries have proved it wrong and it is not to be trusted. That is tampering with the Word of God, because nothing in the Bible has ever been proved wrong by scientific discovery.

But the most common way of twisting the Scriptures is to resort to what is called "proof-texting." This means to come to the Bible with a preconceived idea of something you want to teach. Then you go through the Bible, picking out a few isolated passages here and there that sound like what you wanted to say. Then you list these so that when people hear you they say, "Well, that is biblically supported; he's got the Bible for that."

Every "Christian" cult that ever existed has done this. But unfortunately there are a number of widely respected Christian spokesmen, for the most part earnest and godly men, who do this very thing. Perhaps they are unconscious of what they are doing. They are using part of the Scripture to support what they say, thus tampering with the Word of God, and many people are being misled today by that kind of approach. Paul says, "I don't need that anymore. I don't rely upon those kinds of things. I refuse to practice psychological cunning on people or to tamper with the Word of God."

What, Then, Can We Say?

What does he do? Well, he tells us:

> . . . by the open statement of the truth we commend ourselves to every man's conscience in the sight of God (2 Cor. 4:26).

That is reason number 2 why Paul does not get discouraged. He does not have to think through some new gimmick which will get people out to hear the good news. He knows that truth is the most exciting and attractive thing in the world. He knows that when you come to people with the truth about themselves, about their lives, about the world in which they live—when you strip off the veils of illusion and the delusions by which man in any generation lives, and reveal the basic reality of what is there—you will get instant attention.

The test of any religion is not whether people like it or whether it is comfortable or whether it makes them feel good. The test, of course, is always, "Is it true? Does it fit reality? Does it explain what is going on in such a way that it conforms with the basic experience of every single individual?" The great thing about the good news is that it is the truth of God; it reveals the underlying reality of life. When you are talking about the Word of God you are talking about the way things really are.

A fellow-pastor and I had the privilege of going to a number of college and seminary campuses, speaking, by and large, to Christian young people. Yet in many of these places we found the students really did not think of the Bible as being a revelation of reality. They thought of it as some kind of religious flavoring to life, a kind of low calorie dessert which, if you like that sort of thing, is nice, but if not, you don't really need it. They thought that the real insights into life were found in the secular world.

On every one of those campuses we had the privilege of opening up the Book, teaching what it says in language that was, perhaps, fresh to them, but revealed what the Word of God is saying. Every time we received an instant reaction of fascinated interest. They sat quietly and listened as though they had never heard it before. They suddenly realized the Word of God spoke about them, about their sexuality and what it means, marriage and how it operates, how to handle the awful load of guilt, and what to do with fear and anxiety when they tie your stomach in knots.

That is reality. "The open statement of the truth" has fascinating power to attract people. It did when Jesus proclaimed it. Everywhere he went the multitudes hung on what he said, and yet they wondered. They said to themselves, "He doesn't teach like the Pharisees and the Scribes do, quoting all those authorities, and so on. Yet what he says rings a bell within us. Something inside says, 'That is right.' " The universal reaction to the preaching of Jesus came from "the *truth* as it is *in* Jesus."

Now that is what Paul proclaimed. He said, "When you do that, you don't need any gimmicks; you don't need any buildup; you don't need to bribe people and trick them to get them to come because they are expecting something else. Just take the wraps off what God has given and they will be tremendously attracted to it."

Furthermore, he says, "It speaks to the conscience, and not merely to the mind." Now I do not want you to misunderstand. Truth is addressed to the mind. God never sets aside human reason. He expects truth to be considered and weighed and evaluated by the mind. But behind that is the conscience, and a man's conscience can sometimes reach him when his mind is rejecting truth.

Paul knew that. He said we should not argue with people. That is why he warns Christians, "Don't get yourself involved in long controversies over words. They will get you nowhere. Don't get tied up with arguments, because you can't reach people that way. Tell them the truth. Depend on the fact that there is a voice inside them which God put there called 'the conscience,' that even when their minds reject what you say will keep saying to them, 'Ah, yes, but he is right, isn't he?' Sooner or later it will reach them."

C. S. Lewis, the great English defender of the faith, said that when he became a Christian he did so as an intellectual agnostic. When he came to Christ he came as though he were dragged, kicking and screaming, darting his eyes around in every direction, trying to escape. His mind was fighting it all the way, but his conscience had succumbed to the Word of God. The night he came to Christ he was the most reluctant convert in all of England. But he came, and he became one of the greatest defenders of the faith that the Christian gospel has ever had, outside of the apostle Paul, because his conscience was reached. Paul says in effect, "That's what I count on. I don't have to depend on me and my personality and my ability to persuade people. I go with a simple statement of the truth, and the conviction that God is able to reach the conscience even though the mind and the emotions may reject what I have to say."

Why Can't They See?

Well, you say, "If that is the case, then why don't more people believe this gospel?" That is the question they evidently asked Paul, which he is facing here at this point, because he goes on to say:

> And even if our gospel is veiled, it is veiled only to those who are perishing. In their case the god of this world has blinded the minds of the unbelievers,

> to keep them from seeing the light of the gospel of the glory of Christ, who is the likeness of God (2 Cor. 4:3, 4).

I want you to be careful how you read this because it is often misread. Some of the commentaries I read on this passage put it this way: Paul is responding to the question, "Why are people perishing?" and his answer is, "Because they are blinded by the devil." And then he asks, in effect, "Why are they blinded by the devil?" and his answer is, "Because they won't believe."

That is the way it is often understood. It means, if you take it this way, that the basic reason for people being lost is their refusal to believe, giving the devil an opportunity to blind them. But that is not what Paul says. It is the other way around. People are perishing because they do not believe; and they do not believe because they are blinded by the devil. The god of this age, the god behind the scenes of world events, the god whom the world unconsciously worships in everything they think and say and do, has brainwashed them. Therefore, they cannot understand what the good news is saying; that is why they do not believe it.

"I Don't Need Any Help!"

This is a great, revealing passage. Paul says the devil's tool is the veil. The devil is responsible for the unbelief of men, and men and women are helpless victims in the hands of the god of this age. This veil is the delusion that we are adequate to handle life by ourselves, that independent sense of pride which says, "I don't need any help; I can handle it by myself; I need no religious crutch; I don't need a savior." Put in the words of William Henley's famous poem, "Invictus," it is saying:

> It matters not how strait the gate,
> How charged with punishment the scroll,
> I am the master of my fate:
> I am the captain of my soul.

This is the veil which lies over the minds of people to keep them from seeing the death and condemnation that awaits at the end of the fading glory. The devil's purpose, Paul says here, is to keep men and women from seeing that Jesus Christ is the secret of being like God, of being godly in freedom and in loving others, ". . . to keep them from seeing the light of the gospel of the glory of Christ, who is the likeness of God."

Every Man's Desire

One of the great proofs that the Bible knows what it is talking about is its confirmation that everywhere, all over the earth, in any generation, in any culture or background, men long to be like God. They want to be in charge; they want to run things; they want to make final decisions about what happens to them; they want to control others and the events of their lives and they are frustrated and challenged if they cannot. They long to be like God.

There is nothing wrong with that. It is what God made us for. The dignity of humanity is that the intent of God from the very beginning was for us to manifest his qualities and his character. He has implanted that in the hearts of men and women everywhere in the world.

But our prideful arrogance assumes we can do this by ourselves, by our own efforts, by our own power, by our own abilities. We can run the universe. We don't need God. This is the lie, that veil, the devil uses to brainwash human beings everywhere to keep them from seeing that the only way they will ever be godlike is through Jesus. He is the secret of godliness. That word is a shortened form of the word, "godlikeness." A godly person is a godlike person, reflecting the character of God. The great fact the devil seeks to hide is this: Jesus Christ is that secret! Jesus said it: "I am the way, the truth, and the life. No one can come to the Father but by me."

So what hope is there that anyone who has been blinded by the devil will ever believe the good news? It looks hopeless, doesn't it? If a veil lies over their minds, and if the veil is removed only when they turn to the Lord, and yet in order to turn, men must see the glory of Christ that the veil obscures—what hope is there? It is very evident from this that men cannot remove the veil themselves. Only Christ can take it away. How then can men be saved? That is the question Paul is facing.

Who Can Help?

"Ah," he says, "that is where preaching comes in. That is why I have been sent."

> For what we preach is not ourselves, but Jesus Christ as Lord, with ourselves as your servants for Jesus' sake. For it is the God who said, "Let light shine out of darkness," who has shone in our hearts to give the light of the knowledge of the glory of God in the face of Christ (2 Cor. 4:5, 6).

This is a fantastic statement. We must carefully examine what it is saying. First, the apostle says, "Don't look to us for any help. We don't come preaching ourselves. We can't do a thing for you."

I was once listening to a man on the radio who was supposedly preaching the gospel. He closed his message by saying, "If you have faith in my prayers, then do such and such." That is not preaching Christ. That is preaching himself and it is a false gospel. You sometimes hear people say, "If you have faith in my ministry, do such and such" (especially send money), but that is not preaching the gospel.

Paul says, "We don't do that; what we preach is not ourselves. If you want to know where we fit in, here it is: we are your servants for Jesus' sake. We are not your masters; we do not own you; we are not your bosses; we do not come to tell you everything to do and give you orders and be a little pope in every church we come into. No, we are your servants. We have come to help you. We have come to minister to you, to labor among you, to teach and instruct you, but we are not here to boss you." The apostle is careful to make that plain.

On the other hand he wants them to understand, "You are not our masters either. We do not come to do what you tell us to do. We are your servants *for Christ's sake.* It is he who tells us to be your servant. He is our Master and our Lord." And then he turns their eyes to the One who can help.

Who Is Jesus?

> For what we preach is not ourselves, but Jesus Christ as Lord (2 Cor. 4:5).

That is the key. In the first century this was the fundamental declaration of the church: *Jesus is Lord.* Not "he is going to be Lord some day when he returns," but he *is* Lord. When he rose from the dead he said to his disciples, "All power is given unto me *in heaven and in earth.*" He is in control; he is in charge right now; he is running human history. All the events that occur in the world today take place because he has permitted them or has brought them into being. He is in charge; he is Lord, and the need of human hearts everywhere is to see that he is Lord.

Here are two of several verses which reveal clearly what the issue of salvation is:

> For whosoever shall call upon the name of the Lord shall be saved (Rom. 10:13).
>
> If you confess with your lips that Jesus is Lord . . . you will be saved (Rom. 10:9).

This is the key. It is not to call on Jesus as Savior. A lot of people are being told, "If you receive Jesus as your Savior, you will be saved." But nowhere in the Bible does it ever say that. He must be presented as Lord. He is Lord whether you know it or not, whether you receive him or not.

But when you bow to his Lordship, when you know that he is Lord and consent to his Lordship in your life, then he saves you. Lord is who he is; saving is what he does. When you realize, "you are not your own, you are bought with a price," and you agree to that, then he is not only your Lord, but he begins to deliver you, to save you from yourself and the world around.

On the basis of Lordship, then, Paul goes on to say that the moment a person sees that Jesus is Lord, God's creative power begins to operate in his life and light comes into his darkness; the veil is removed. Notice how he puts it:

> For it is the God who said, "Let light shine out of darkness," who has shone in our hearts . . . (2 Cor. 4:6).

Paul takes us back to creation, when the whole world lay in darkness. Nobody could do anything about it except God, who said, "Let there be light." Suddenly, out of the darkness, light sprang up in obedience to the creative word of the living God.

Paul says the same thing must happen before any man or woman ever becomes a Christian. God has to speak again that creative Word, "Let light shine out of darkness." When he does, the darkness disappears; the light shines into the heart, as it did with Paul on the Damascus road: "The light shone into the darkness of my deluded heart, and I saw that Jesus was Lord." He goes on to say, "the light of the knowledge of the glory of God is, therefore, seen in the face of Christ."

Truth Parted His Veil

Many years ago a man came to see me in response to a contact made by a member of our church. He had made friends with this man, a brilliant engineer with a tremendous mind, but a declared agnostic. They had talked many times, but he showed no openness at all to the gospel.

He had fallen into a severe depression, so intense and prolonged that he was fired from his job. But that only increased his depression. He was so morose and vegetablelike that his wife finally threatened to leave him, and his children all left home. He became so pathetic in his terrible depression that this Christian friend of his asked him if he would at least consent to come and talk with me.

So he showed up at my door and told me his story. He was so depressed it was difficult for him to talk; he showed no sign of any hope at all. I asked him the usual questions about what he believed, but he did not believe anything. He did not believe there was a God; he did not believe in Christ; he did not believe the Bible; he did not believe Jesus ever lived. I could find no ground of faith at all.

After trying to help him for an hour or two, I said to him, "I'm sorry. There is nothing I can do to help you. But I don't want to abandon you. I believe there is help for you. If you will come here every week I will meet with you and I will do two things for you. One, I'll read the Bible to you, and two, I'll pray for you. I don't know what will happen; that is all I can do, but if you are willing to do that I will do those two things."

To my amazement he consented. He kept coming week after week. I would read a portion of Scripture, and I would say to him, "Does that mean anything to you?" But he would say "No." Then I would pray for him, for his family, and for his home. By that time his wife had left him. He was living all alone in an apartment, unable to carry on at all, unable to work.

At least eight months went by, and we did this every week without fail. One day I said to him, "Isn't there anything I have read to you that means anything to you?" He replied, "Well, there is one thing. This morning I was thinking about it. You read the other day these words of Jesus in the Garden of Gethsemane, 'Nevertheless, not my will but thine be done.' That suddenly meant something to me."

Well, I didn't have the nerve to ask him what! It did not mean anything to me at that moment in relationship to him. But I said, "Mal, if that meant something to you, then let me ask you to do this: pray that prayer over and over again. Whenever you sense you need some help, when you are despairing, pray that prayer." He said he would.

So a few more weeks went by. I read other passages and nothing clicked. Then one day I read something, and he said, "Oh, yes. That's good, isn't it?" We took note of that and I asked him to memorize it and say it over and over. Then a couple of weeks later he found something else, and gradually there came a dawning light into his heart. Truth began to be real to him; he began to understand it. We prayed week after week, and as this light began to dawn it came on stronger and stronger. More and more of Scripture began to reach him, until the day came when he openly acknowledged that Jesus was Lord of his life and he surrendered to his will. Then he began to blossom and grow. He devoured the Word of God; he read it endlessly, hour after hour.

That was fifteen years ago, and I still get letters from him. He lives in Florida now; he joined a Christian group there. His family never did come back to him, but his letters are the most exuberant, radiant, and rejoicing of any I receive. He has nothing but praise and thanksgiving to the living God, the Creator himself, who took away the darkness by a creative Word, a fiat, who said of his darkness, "Let there be light." Seizing on the one gleam of light that Jesus is Lord, my friend was transformed at last.

Where do you find the light of the glory of God? In the face of Jesus Christ. And where do you find the face of Jesus? In the Scriptures. This book is all about Jesus. The gospels give you the record of his amazing life on earth; the epistles explain the implications of that life, his death and resurrection, and his present working for us; the Old Testament is full of anticipations of his character and his being. As you read the Bible and let the Spirit of God interpret it, the "face of Christ" comes clearer and clearer. That is how light comes into a darkened heart.

Are you walking in darkness? Well then, begin to seek the face of Christ. That is where the light shines. Not the Christ you hear about in all the popular presentations around us. There is nothing historic about the Jesus you meet in many of the presentations today. Oftentimes that is a false Christ.

But in the Scriptures you have the authentic Jesus, and in the fellowship of the people of God the character and the love of Jesus come through. In moments of communion and prayer you see the face of Christ. That is what turns off the darkness and brings the light into your life. You do not have to walk in darkness in this day and age when you can look at the face of Christ, for there is found "the light of the knowledge of the glory of God" for all to see.

8

Your Pot—His Power

Here in 2 Corinthians 4 we are examining one of the passages in the Bible that most clearly declares the process by which the power of God is released among men.

We long for, we pray for this power to be released among us; everyone wants that to happen. I am increasingly concerned, however, about the ignorance of Christians as to their true power. We are surrounded by evidences of decay in society, of increasing corruption, of the disintegration of personality, of increasing hurt and darkness and despair. But all the time I can hear Jesus saying to us, "*You* are the light of the world."

Paul has been describing his ministry in terms of direct combat with what he calls the "god of this age," the invisible being behind this darkness and corruption, the one who has, as he put it in the preceding passage, "blinded the minds of the unbelievers." But as Paul traveled about and declared that Jesus is Lord, then the light began to break out in the darkness of the world. That is God's process.

In verses 7 through 11 of chapter 4 there is a detailed description of how to exercise *the power of God;* and verses 12 through 15 describe how to display *the glory of God.* That is what life is all about. Christians are Christian in order to exercise the power of God and display the glory of God.

The Power of God

> But we have this treasure in earthen vessels, to show that the transcendent power belongs to God and not to us (2 Cor. 4:7).

First, God deliberately displays his mighty power through "earthen vessels." That term is not very complimentary. An earthen vessel is nothing but a clay pot, a beautifully descriptive term for basic humanity.

All of us are nothing but clay pots, although some have a little finer clay than others, perhaps. Clay can be made into beautiful, fragile chinaware, which, of course, cracks easily. Other pots may be more rough and rugged, made of adobe mud, baked in the sun (half-baked sometimes, perhaps). But this is our humanity. We are nothing but clay pots.

A pot, or a vessel, is made to hold something. Basic to our humanity is that we are not designed to operate on our own. We were made to hold someone, and that someone is God himself. The glory of humanity is that somehow God designed us to correspond to his deity; and his marvelous deity, with its fullness and wisdom and power somehow relates to and corresponds to and manifests itself through our humanity.

Paul is probably thinking of that Old Testament story of Gideon, who was called of God to deliver Israel from the Midian hosts who had come into the land. Gideon was nothing but an obscure member of one of the more remote tribes of Israel. He had no reputation, he regarded himself as inferior to everyone else, and yet God called him to deliver the nation. When 32,000 men gathered to help him, God cut the number down to 300. God told them to take earthen jars, common clay pots, put candles in them, and during the darkness of the night to circle the Midian camp. At the signal of the sound of the trumpets, they were to break the pots so that lights would spring up on every side. When they did that the Midian army was demoralized. They suddenly saw lights springing up all over the mountainside. Thinking they were ringed by an army, they panicked and began to kill each other.

That story has great significance for us, because it is really telling us that if we begin to live on the basis of the new covenant, acting and living as though Jesus is Lord, controlling everything in our life and the life of the whole world, we can demoralize the antagonists of Christianity and they will begin to attack one another. I have seen this happen. Christians often need not fight hard, pitched battles, for the battle is won by simply displaying the light that is in them.

Paul is saying that God's purpose in your life and mine is this: we are to live in such a way that people are actually baffled when they look at us. They will say, "I don't get it. I know this person. He (or she) is so ordinary; there is nothing outstanding there, but yet what happens as they go through life is so remarkable that I just don't understand it." They can see that the power is not coming from you; it is coming from God.

Weakness in Life

Paul goes on to describe the way it is going to appear:

> We are afflicted in every way, but not crushed; perplexed, but not driven to despair; persecuted, but not forsaken; struck down, but not destroyed (2 Cor. 4:8, 9).

I like the graphic way William Barclay translates these verses:

> We are sore pressed at every point, but not hemmed in; we are at our wit's end, but never at our hope's end; we are persecuted by men, but never abandoned by God; we are knocked down, but not knocked out.

Notice the weakness of the pot there, and the transcendence of the power. Transcendent means "beyond the ordinary." The power of God is not ordinary. It is different from every kind of power we know about, and so it is wrong to expect it to be dramatically visible. It is a quiet power that is released in quiet ways, and yet what it accomplishes is fabulous.

Here is the weakness of the pot: "We are sore pressed; we are at wit's end; we are persecuted; we are knocked down." On the other hand, here is the transcendent power: "We are not hemmed in; we are not at hope's end; we are never abandoned and we are never knocked out." That is the way God expects us to live.

The remarkable thing, and the place where we struggle, however, is that it takes both of these. It takes the weakness to have the strength, and that is what we do not like. We all want to see the power of God in our lives, but we want it to come out of untroubled, peaceful, calm circumstances. We want to move through life, protected from all the dangers and all the difficulties. We want to be like the "Pirates of the Caribbean" in Disneyland. We want to float through life in our little boats, gliding through all the difficulties. They will appear as though they are going to get us, but they never get close. We come safely out the other end with not a hair of our head mussed, with no real difficulty at all. But that is not what God has in mind. We are to have difficulties and afflictions and persecutions. We may expect to be "sore pressed," and "at wit's end," and "persecuted," and "knocked down, but never knocked out."

We are not even permitted to choose the scene of our own martyrdom. We cannot go through this list and say, "Well, I'll take a few afflictions, but I don't want to be knocked down." We get what God sends. Whatever he wills is what we must go through. Yet we will never be knocked out, that is the point.

Paul is saying that we are not sheltered from life's problems. I wish we could get that across to many today. It is difficult because the folk religion to which we are constantly exposed is telling us something else. It is telling us, "If you're a Christian, God will keep you from all dangers and troubles. Why, you won't even get sick if you're really a Christian; you'll have no physical illnesses; troubles will evaporate and never come to you."

This is absolutely wrong. Christians can get cancer, Christians can have financial collapse, Christians can go through difficulties, family separations, divorce, problems of every sort. In spite of all they may do, no matter how close to the Lord they walk, Christians can have these difficulties. Out of the troubles God wants us to demonstrate a different attitude, a different reaction than other people have. He wants us to manifest an obvious love and joy and peace in our lives that can never be explained in human terms, but can be explained only in terms of God at work in us.

That is not automatic, because I know many Christians who are afflicted and often crushed; they have perplexities that drive them to despair; they are persecuted and they feel abandoned; they are knocked down and often they are knocked out for weeks and years at a time. What makes the difference?

Dying to Live

Paul's answer is a marvelous description of the process of walking in victory:

> . . . always carrying in the body the death of Jesus, so that the life of Jesus may also be manifested in our bodies (2 Cor. 4:10).

Notice that the "life of Jesus" always flows from the "death of Jesus." We must have in our experience the death of Jesus in order to have the life of Jesus.

> For while we live we are always being given up to death for Jesus' sake, so that (in order that) the life of Jesus may be manifested in our mortal flesh (2 Cor. 4:11).

We all want, of course, the life of Jesus; every one of us wants to be like him. But the power of God is manifest when others see in us the character and the life of Jesus coming out of our pressures and trials.

I have always been amused and challenged by the verse in Colossians 1, where Paul prays that his friends in Colossae may be "strengthened with all power, according to God's glorious might." What are they going to use all this power for? It seems as though Paul ought to say, "So that you can go about doing great miracles; so that you can astonish people with the tremendous magnetism of your preaching and teaching, and be followed by great crowds, making a great impact."

But, of course, that is not what he says at all. He says, "I pray that you may be strengthened with all power, according to his glorious might, *unto all endurance and patience with joy.*" That is what takes power; that is where the life and the power of God are manifest. That is the life of Jesus: "endurance and patience with joy!"

Jesus' Secret

As we read through the Gospels, the Spirit of God brings to our mind's eye a beautiful and wonderful picture of the character of Jesus. We see his compassion of heart, his moral beauty, that attracted people everywhere he went. We note the serenity of his spirit, how he moves through every scene of anger and unrest with calmness and quietness. We see his disciplined will and his obvious joy in living. This is the "life of Jesus," and this is what we want, isn't it?

How do you get it? The secret, Paul says, is our consent to sharing the dying of Jesus, "always carrying in the body the dying of Jesus, in order that the life of Jesus may be manifested in our mortal flesh." What does he mean by the "dying of Jesus?" We know he does not mean that we have to go out and get ourselves nailed to a cross. That cross is a symbol of something very real in our experience.

What was Jesus like on the cross? He was not powerful and impressive and significant; he was not being applauded by the multitudes who listened to his every word. No, the cross was a place of physical weakness, of rejection by the proud and arrogant world around him. It was a place of obscurity, a place where he was willing to lose everything he had built, trusting God to bring it back and make it significant. Are you willing to give up all the things that make you look important to other people, to take the place of obscurity, if necessary, trusting God to use it however he will? That is the "dying of Jesus."

Human Potential

Today we are being assaulted on every side by the cult of human potential. Groups like est, Transactional Analysis, Transcendental Meditation and others are saying you need to find hidden resources in yourself that you can count on. You must develop these resources and then you will find yourself growing in confidence and ability to handle life. You can be at the top of the heap if you will send in a considerable sum of money and spend a weekend with them.

People on every side are believing that. And it appears to work. Many of them do find a new source of confidence, a new ability to function, to make a greater impression on others, but it all comes out at this point: the measure of their success is the degree to which they are recognized by someone else. Even Christianized versions of these cults take the words of Scripture and the songs and hymns of Christians and glaze them over and present them as a "Christian" way. But it is still the same old thing, working out to the glory of the individual, calling on him to rely upon his natural resources and abilities to succeed.

The true Christian gospel cuts right across this, labeling these resources as the very thing that the cross puts to death. We must come to the end of dependence on ourselves and rest upon the willingness of God to be at work in us, without any flash or demonstration, but changing our whole character, in loving and quiet ways, until it is like Jesus in the midst of rejection and lack of recognition. Are you willing to do that? If so, you too can have the life of Jesus.

Ready for Fame!

Here is where we struggle, isn't it? We want the power of God, but we want to get credit for it, too. If God does anything through us we want to be sure we get a write-up in *Christianity Today.* If anything happens in our midst, in our home, or in our family, we want it to be known that we spent a lot of hours in prayer over it, that we had counseled so-and-so in such-and-such a helpful way. We want to move in and get the credit every time. We want the life of Jesus, but we also want the satisfaction of our flesh. We want to be serene of spirit and gentle and compassionate of heart, but we also want the pleasure of telling people off when they are out of line. That is a great joy, isn't it?

It is amazing how we want to be free from anxiety, to have an untroubled, serene spirit about the future, but at the same time insist on the pleasure of worrying. We enjoy worrying; we feel so much more fulfilled if we have worried awhile, for we have done our share at least. We sometimes say to people, "If I don't worry, who will?" as though someone has to worry or nothing can be accomplished.

That is our real problem, isn't it? We want the kingdom of God, and we want our own personal rights as well. But you cannot have both. That is where the new covenant brings us, "always bearing about in the body the dying of Jesus in order that the life of Jesus may be manifest in our mortal flesh."

That is where verse 11 helps us, because God takes over. There Paul says, "while we live (not after we die, but while we live) we are always being given up to death for Jesus' sake." Verse 10 is a conscious choice we must make where we agree to give up our personal desire for recognition and significance, and so on in order to let God give it back to us in a right way. But verse 11 tells us God also places us in circumstances where we have to die whether we like it or not.

Have you been in those circumstances where no matter what you do you cannot seem to get any glory or credit for yourself? That is exactly where God wants you, because out of those times of inordinate pressure, times of hurt and despair and heartache and a sense of being wasted and not used, God is working his will. Others, perhaps, are being given life because of the death you are going through. Paul will speak more about that a little further on.

As I write these words, I am going through a "death" time and it does not feel good. It does not feel triumphant or victorious, but that is just the point. We are led in triumph by Christ, regardless of how we feel at the moment. It is his work that does it, not ours. Paul is calling us to this.

Sometimes the transcendent power within us is even recognized by the world. God, in a sense, forces the world at times to pay tribute to this kind of living. Martin Luther, even though he felt abandoned and helpless at the moment, dared to stand against all the secular and sacred power of the day for the truth of God; he finally became the most widely known and recognized man of his age, and has become one of the great names of history. A Mother Teresa can give herself to the slums of Calcutta, and with no longing or hope at all for recognition and honor, suddenly finds herself elected to receive the Nobel Prize. God can give honor if he wants to, but there must be the willingness to forego it for our own account.

The Glory of God

Paul next looks ahead to see what will happen in the church when this begins to happen among us:

> So death is at work in us, but life in you. Since we have the same spirit of faith as he had who wrote, "I believed, and so I spoke," we too believe, and so we speak . . . (2 Cor. 4:12).

He is quoting here from Psalm 116, where the psalmist declares by faith that the trials and the pressures he is going through are going to have some effect and impact in his surroundings. He cannot see it yet, but he says it is going to be true because God has said it.

Paul, too, says, "I don't see the life in you yet, but I know it is coming. We are going through the death; we are going through the pressure and the heartache, but it is going to have an impact on you. I know it is coming because that is the kind of God we serve."

> . . . knowing that he who raised the Lord Jesus will raise us also with Jesus and bring us with you into his presence.

Paul's confidence grows that this sharing is the very essence of life in the body of Christ. We share life with one another, and as you lose yourself in costly service, life becomes visible in someone else. We all know how this can happen, even in a family. Parents give themselves for years in order that their children might enjoy things. We can do this with one another in the body of Christ. We can endure the loneliness of prayer, and the faithfulness of upholding one another, the difficulty of counseling each other and see life come, as a result, in someone else.

Grateful for Glory

Paul concludes this with a wonderful picture of where it all comes out:

> For it is all for your sake, so that as grace extends to more and more people it may increase thanksgiving, to the glory of God (2 Cor. 4:15).

Notice where it ends, with increased thanksgiving. We are being told today that if we take certain praise expressions out of the Bible, "Praise the Lord," "Hallelujah," or "Praise Jesus," and in times of heartache say those over and over again, we can force God to deliver us from our trial; we manipulate him into it by using praise.

That is not what Paul is talking about. He is talking about people who have gone through great sorrow, deep hurt, real heartache, but in the midst of it they have looked to God for strength and have found his comfort. They have known and trusted his love, and the result has been there has been such an inner joy and peace and strengthening in the midst of the trial that they cannot help but give thanks to God that the whole thing came about.

Some years ago I clipped a letter from *Decision* magazine that was a wonderful testimony. I do not know whether it comes from a man or a woman, because only the initials of the writer were published; but it rings with triumphant thanksgiving:

> For a long time I had been bitter about life. It seemed to have dealt me a dirty blow, for since I was 12 years old I have been waiting for death to close in on me. It was at that time I learned I had muscular dystrophy. I fought hard against this disease and exercised hard, but to no avail. I only grew weaker. All I could see was what I had missed. My friends went away to college, then got married and started having families of their own. When I lay in bed at night thinking, despair would creep from the dark corners to haunt me. Life was meaningless.
>
> In March of last year my mother brought home from our public library Billy Graham's book *World Aflame.* I started reading it, and as I read I realized that I wanted God. I wanted there to be meaning to life. I wanted to receive this deep faith and peace. All I know is that now my life has changed and I now have joy in living. No longer is the universe chaotic. No longer does life have no goal. No longer is there no hope. There is instead "God who so loved the world that he gave his only Son that whoever believes in him should not perish but have eternal life."
>
> I continue to grow weaker. I am close to being totally helpless and am in pain most of the time, but sometimes I am so glad I am alive that it is hard to keep myself from bursting at the seams. I can see for the first time the beauty all around me, and I realize how very lucky I am. Despair is such a waste of time when there is joy; and lack of faith is such a waste of time when there is God.

This is the kind of thanksgiving that glorifies God. Out of the midst of the pain, the pressure, the heartache, and the perplexities there comes a joy, a strength, a faith, and a love that shows us the power is not coming from us, but from God. That is what impresses the world. May God help us to live like that.

2 Corinthians 4:16–5:5

9

Beyond the End

One of the great questions which all of us has to face—and all of us do face it even though it may be in the privacy of our own thoughts is, "What is waiting for me when I die?" There is a new, public interest in that subject today; books are coming out, explorations are being made, even scientific studies have been attempted in this field, though it is difficult to see how science can probe in this area at all. As we examine the answers being given, there are really only three categories of them.

No Exit

First, there are those who say that when you die nothing at all happens. You simply pass out of existence. Like a candle going out, your life gutters out into darkness; there is nothing left, no experience, no feeling, no reaction, no knowledge. Men, like animals, perish; they simply cease to exist, and that is the end of it.

Almost all who endorse an atheistic philosophy of life attempt to hold that view. The only trouble with it, of course, is its absolute despair. There is no hope for further meaningful development or experience. Human personality with all its possibilities and wonders is ended, and there is no hope at the end. The result, of course, of a life with no hope is the spreading of existential despair throughout our present existence. We see this widely on every hand.

This view of life has never been described in more eloquent terms, perhaps, than in these words from Lord Bertrand Russell:

> The life of Man is a long march through the night, surrounded by invisible foes, tortured by weariness and pain, towards a goal that few can hope to reach and where none tarry long. One by one, as they march, our comrades vanish from our sight, seized by the silent orders of omnipotent Death.
>
> Brief and powerless is Man's life; on him and all his race the slow, sure doom falls pitiless and dark. Blind to good and evil, reckless of destruction, omnipotent matter rolls on its relentless way; for Man, condemned today to lose his dearest, tomorrow himself to pass through the gate of darkness, it remains only to cherish, ere yet the blow falls, the lofty thoughts that ennoble his little day.

Those words reflect the despair that always grips the heart when anyone with that point of view contemplates the end of his earthly existence. Everything is "now," and people are urged to live for the present because there is no other life to come.

Grave Uncertainties

Then there is another category of answers, one which virtually says that when you come to the end of your life anything can happen. In fact there is such a wide range of answers, the possibilities are so broad that you, in effect, can pay your money and take your choice. The trouble with this view, of course, is that it is all based on wishful thinking, perhaps on demonic delusion, upon the uncertain and controversial experiences of people who claim to have died and returned to earth, or even upon old wives' myths and fables which have been around for generations. Countless reports are given today of the experiences of those who have left this life for awhile and then returned to relate their experiences.

How anyone could put any confidence in the testimony of someone whose mind is hardly in touch with reality at all and whose body is rapidly disintegrating is difficult for me to see. This category of answer always means there is no security, no certainty about the life to come. There may be such a life, but no one really knows; it is all based on dubious experiences. Such answers are so contradictory that it is clear these people do not know what they are talking about. In many cases, much of the so-called evidence is based upon what the Scriptures would call "deceitful spirits" who deliberately deceive men and women into thinking they have experienced life to come. But these are not real or genuine or based upon reality.

The One Who Knows

The third category, of course, is the Christian answer, the answer of the Word of God, based upon the teaching of the only man who, as far as history records, has ever clearly, openly, and ultimately conquered death. This man returned to the very ones he had taught before he died. He not only conquered death in others but ultimately conquered it in himself, and he has given us a great word of security and surety to rest upon. He sent his apostles to tell the good news that in Jesus Christ there is a certain future of glory and peace awaiting. For those without him, however, there lies a future of endless frustration, pain, and regret.

So in this passage from 2 Corinthians, beginning with verse 16 of chapter 4 and running through the opening verses of chapter 5, the apostle Paul lifts his eyes from the experience he is going through at the moment to the hope that lies beyond. He introduces it with that characteristic word we have seen all through this letter, the great cry of encouragement and hope:

> So we do not lose heart. Though our outer nature is wasting away, our inner nature is being renewed every day. For this slight momentary affliction is preparing for us an eternal weight of glory beyond all comparison, because we look not to the things that are seen but to the things that are unseen; for the things that are seen are transient, but the things that are unseen are eternal (2 Cor. 4:16–18).

Here is the great cry, "We do not lose hope." There is a reason for hope, not only coming from our present experience of the grace of God (as Paul has been describing it), but also as we look to the future. So we do not lose hope.

Wasting Away on the Outside

Then he gives three great reasons why he has such a hope in the hour of death:

> Though our outer nature is wasting away, our inner nature is being renewed every day (2 Cor. 4:16).

That gives him hope. It is true, he says, that the outward man is perishing. Now we need to clearly understand that there is a difference between the "outward" man and the "old" man which you read about in Scripture. The "old" man, of course, is what the Bible calls the "flesh," the evil moral nature we inherited from our fallen forefather, Adam, to which we died when we came into Christ. It is no longer "us." It is still present in us to tempt us, but as an alien with which we are no longer identified.

But the "outward" man whom Paul speaks of here is the body and the mind, which he says are slowly falling apart. (We can all give testimony to that. I have noticed that newspaper print gets smaller and smaller all the time. I cannot tell what is going on around me unless somebody reads aloud to me—which does not help much because they all talk in such a low voice. I have noticed, too, that people are younger than they used to be when I was their age, and people my own age are considerably older than I am. I ran into one of my college classmates the other day. He had changed so much he did not even recognize me!)

Renewed on the Inside

We simply have to face the fact that the outward man is deteriorating, growing weak and feeble, subject to much groaning and agony. "Well, that is what is happening to me, too," Paul says, "but I don't get discouraged, because the inner man is being renewed day by day." The "inner" man, of course, is the real "me." It is the human spirit inside that has its conscious expression in the soul. Thus the inner man is that combination of soul and spirit which marks mankind as different from the animals. Paul experiences this as being daily renewed.

The word he uses is, "made new," "made over afresh." He is speaking of the kind of inner stimulation of mind and spirit that keeps him triumphant, rejoicing, optimistic, faithful, trusting, expectant, as he lives day by day, even though the outward things, his body and his mind, are gradually falling apart. This renewal is the hope of the believer. Paul says this very fact testifies we are being inwardly prepared for something great to come.

In Romans 12 he describes this renewal as being "aglow with the Spirit." It is great to meet people who are aglow with the Spirit. Even though their physical man is undergoing great struggle and difficulty, their inner man is alive and encouraged, expectant in what God is doing. Do you meet the day that way? Have you learned to rise above the circumstances with the inner renewal of the spirit, by the Holy Spirit, that keeps you optimistic and rejoicing in the midst of the pressures and the problems of daily life?

Momentary Affliction

Now what is the basis for this kind of renewal? Paul gives us the second great reason for our hope for the future:

> For this slight momentary affliction is preparing for us an eternal weight of glory beyond all comparison (2 Cor. 4:17).

Every now and then you run into a verse of Scripture so full of possibilities, the language so rich, that you can ponder it and contemplate it for hours at a time. This is such a verse to me. What does "an eternal weight of glory beyond all comparison" mean? What could that be describing? The amazing thing is that Paul links it directly to the afflictions and the struggles of our present time. This has helped me a great deal, and I hope it helps you.

What he is really saying is, there is a direct tie between the affliction and the glory. The one is preparing for the other. We get this intimation in many passages of Scripture. In Romans 8:17 Paul says, "we suffer with him in order that we may also be glorified with him." In Ephesians there are similar references to the fact that if our time here has included affliction and trouble and hardship, as it does for every believer, it will therefore make even more sure the fact that there is a marvelous glory yet to come.

That means that no matter how great the trial may seem to us, two things are always true of it. One, compared with what is coming, it is relatively slight. That is what Paul says: "This 'slight' momentary affliction." Now if that was all you ever read of Paul you would be tempted to say, "Obviously he didn't have to go through what I have to go through. This Paul must have had an easy time of it. I sure would like to have been an apostle if all they had to go through was a 'slight momentary affliction.' He ought to live with my mother-in-law!"

But, of course, that is not all we know of Paul. In chapter 11 of this very letter he goes through a long list of his afflictions and there is nothing like it in the annals of literature. Nobody has ever gone through more than Paul, other than our Lord himself. He speaks of being beaten five times, of being beaten with a rod three times, of being thrown into jail many times, of enduring hunger, thirsting and fastings, of hardship, shipwreck, dangers and perils on every side. All this was part of his experience, yet he sums it all up in that wonderful way, "this slight momentary affliction." In Romans 8:18 he says, "the sufferings of this present time are not worthy to be compared with the glory which shall be revealed to us." Here again is mentioned that incomparable eternal weight of glory which is yet to come. It boggles the mind. It is beyond description.

The Weight of Glory

C. S. Lewis has a great message, which I hope you will read in its entirety, based upon this very passage. It is called *The Weight of Glory,* and in it is a passage that has always intrigued me. He says:

> We are to shine as the sun, we are to be given the Morning Star. I think I begin to see what it means. In one way, of course, God has given us the Morning Star already. You can go and enjoy the gift on many fine mornings if you get up early enough. What more, you may ask, do we want? Ah, but we want so much more—something the books on aesthetics take little notice of. But the poets and the mythologies know all about it. We do not want merely to see beauty, though, God knows, even that is bounty enough. We want something else which can hardly be put into words—to be united with the beauty we see, to pass into it, to receive it into ourselves, to bathe in it, to become part of it. (And then he adds these words:) The door on which we have all been knocking all our lives will open at last.*

Our present sufferings are preparing us for something so incomparable, so amazing, so marvelous that there are no words to describe it. That means that no trial, no pain, no isolation, no heartache, no loneliness, no weakness or failure, no sense of being put aside, is without significance. All of it is playing its part in accomplishing God's work in your life and the lives of others. It is building for us an incomparable weight of glory. I do not know what else to say about it.

Seen and Un-seen

How do we know that is true? The answer is in verse 18, where we have the third reason for our hope. Paul says,

> Because we look not to the things that are seen but to the things that are unseen; for the things that are seen are transient, but the things that are unseen are eternal.

It has always been difficult for men to believe that there are unseen realities, invisible to human eye and investigation, but nevertheless

* *The Weight of Glory* (New York: Macmillan Co., 1949).

very real and very important. Yet perhaps no generation ought to understand this more easily and with such certainty than we do today, because science is saying the same thing.

Science agrees with the Bible in telling us that behind the visible, material things we see and measure and taste and touch and feel are invisible forces inaccessible to our senses. Behind a visible piano with its material appearance of wood, science says there is nothing but motion by infinitesimal particles traveling at such tremendous speed they give the impression of being solid. The piano is made mostly of space, and if we knew how to do it we could throw a chair through it. There is so much space that neither would touch the other.

Our minds grasp that, but our emotions struggle with it because it seems to be contrary to our experience. But I hope by now we are learning not to trust experience. It is a very unsure guide. The things we see are passing, changing; they are ephemeral. All the events that happen in our life today will be as out-of-date tomorrow as yesterday's newspaper, all of them changed. They are like a movie; they are shadowy reflections of real things.

One Thing Reliable

What are the real things? Paul calls them, "the things that are unseen," the invisible forces at work of which the world is almost totally unaware. The Bible tells us what they are. There is the Word of God, the most unchangeable of all things, the divine utterance from the divine mouth that called into existence everything that is. God spoke and it *was,* and that Word can never be altered. "Heaven and earth will pass away but my words will not pass away," Jesus said. The Word is the one reliable thing in all the unreliable universe.

We understand by the Word of God that all things are held together by him. He is the Creator and the supporter of all things. Our eyes, therefore, must look beyond the visible to the invisible things. We learn that there are angels, both good and bad, working both for and against human beings. We are caught up in a great invisible conflict in which we are both under attack and supported by invisible hands. We labor and live in the midst of that battle so that, as Paul put it, "we wrestle not against flesh and blood, but against principalities, against powers, against the rulers of the darkness of this world, against spiritual wickedness in high places" (Eph. 6:12, KJV). They are the invisible forces that produce the events recorded day-by-day in the headlines of our newspaper. We must learn to read the newspaper with that in mind and understand what is going on behind the scenes of world events.

Ultimately, of course, there is God himself. Invisible to the human eye, is the Lord Jesus, Lord of earth and heaven and all the created universe, and though we do not see him, yet we love him and follow him. He is in control of history. As we approach the end of life these things become more and more significant to us.

When D. L. Moody, the great evangelist, was dying, his last words were, "Earth is receding. Heaven is approaching. This is my crowning day." That is the utterance of faith. That is looking at reality. Nothing is more encouraging to me than to realize that when I believe the Word of God I am becoming more and more realistic. This is what life is all about.

Now in the first several verses of chapter 5 we have a further description of the nature of our hope. Here we learn a little more detail about this "weight of glory beyond all comparison." The apostle describes it this way:

> For we know (Notice the word of certainty there. Not "we guess," "we hope," "we think," but we *know*) that if the earthly tent we live in is destroyed, we have a building from God, a house not made with hands, eternal in the heavens. Here indeed we groan, and long to put on our heavenly dwelling, so that by putting it on we may not be found naked. For while we are still in this tent, we sigh with anxiety; not that we would be unclothed, but that we would be further clothed, so that what is mortal may be swallowed up by life (2 Cor. 5:1–4).

What marvelous words! Here is a description of the present body of flesh and bones contrasted with the same body, risen and glorified by the activity of the Spirit of God. When you compare these words with those in 1 Corinthians 15 you can see that Paul is talking here about the resurrected body we shall receive when mortality is swallowed up by immortality.

A Sagging Tent

He uses the same terminology here. It is the body that is to be swallowed up by life. "In a moment, in the twinkling of an eye, we shall be changed," and this new body will be given to us. The present body, he says, is like a tent, a temporary experience. I once visited a family who were living in a tent while they were waiting for their home to be finished. It was very temporary; they were uncomfortable;

they could not wait for the real habitation to be completed so they could move in.

I sometimes feel like that in this tent of my earthly body. I am sure you do too. A tent is not very satisfying. The stakes begin to loosen, the poles begin to sag, the tent itself sags in various spots, the cold penetrates, and it is not very comfortable. Some of us feel that way as we grow older. But we are looking forward to the resurrection body, the permanent building which God had in mind when he made us in the beginning, the permanent dwelling place, designed by God without any human help, "a house not made with hands." Nothing human produces it or adds to it; nothing that the undertaker does while our body is being prepared for the grave adds a single thing to what God will do to produce the body of glory to come.

The point Paul makes is that it is already ours in eternity. "We have," he says. Notice the present tense: not, "We will have," but "*We have* a house not made with hands eternal in the heavens," already there, waiting for us to put on. "In this present one," he says, "we groan, we long" for something better. Don't you feel that way? How many of you have had to say, when you wanted to do something, "The spirit is willing but the flesh is weak"? We wish we could but we cannot, because our bodies will not let us. We long for something better.

"Further Clothed"

But Paul is very careful here. He says, "I don't want you to misunderstand. I don't want to simply die and float off to be with the Lord in a bodiless existence. I don't want to be disembodied." We don't want to be ghosts, spooks, haunting cemeteries to frighten people. Such expectations arise from the deceitful spirits. Many people are investigating today phenomena that have to do with haunted houses and all these other things. These are really the activities of demons. People who deal with these matters ought to be aware of that fact.

But the apostle says that this new body, the resurrected body, is an experience, not of being disembodied, but of being further embodied. He changes the idiom from the building to the body and says it is like being further clothed, so that it is *more* than we have at the moment. If you feel like you are clothed by being in a body, then in that body you will feel even more clothed, "further clothed." Then he uses this expression, "swallowed up by life," not by death. It is a further experience of fulfillment and satisfaction.

In the light of that, verse 5 is very reassuring, for Paul goes on to say,

> He who has prepared us for this very thing is God.

No one wants to float around in bodiless existence. The human spirit rejects and resists that idea. In effect, Paul says our actual experience will be this: "You will be further clothed upon at death as believers. You will have a new body. There is a weight of glory beyond all description and it will come instantly, for the One who has prepared us for this very thing is God."

People at this point ask, "How can this be? When our loved ones die we take them out and bury them or they are cremated. If you go out to the grave decades later you can dig it up and the body is still there. How could those people who died receive a resurrection body immediately when their bodies are still lying unresurrected in the grave?"

Many explanations have been offered for this, but there are basically three. One says, "We really are disembodied. When we die we go to be with the Lord in spirit, but our bodies are buried in the grave so we have to wait—incomplete—until the body is raised. It may take centuries, but we are just waiting around in bodiless existence." In the light of this passage that teaching cannot be accepted. Paul says he does not want to be disembodied, he does not expect to be and he who has prepared him for the very opposite is God himself.

Another theory suggests that when we die both our soul and our spirit go to sleep within the body with no sense of communication or experience. As in physical sleep, we wake up and do not know how long we have been asleep. Time is eclipsed, and we may sleep for centuries in the body. When we are wakened at the resurrection, it is as though nothing has happened in the meantime.

But this suggestion conflicts with the passages in Scripture that speak of being with the Lord immediately. "While we are at home in the body, we are absent from the Lord," Paul says in the very next verse: "to be absent from the body is to be at home with the Lord." In Philippians 1:23, he speaks of departing and "being with Christ; which is far better." Such passages speak of an immediate access, of being "at home with the Lord."

There are some who propose still a third alternative. They say that God gives us an intermediate, temporary body to use in eternity until our real one gets there—a kind of heavenly bathrobe we wait in while our real one is coming back from the cleaners. But once again there is not a vestige of Scripture to support an intermediate body.

What Paul means, of course, is that when we leave this body we also leave time. It is not easy to re-train our thinking along these lines, because we project time into eternity, assuming eternity is simply time going on forever, but it is not. Anyone who studies this subject carefully must distinguish sharply between the conditions of eternity and those of time. In *time* we are all locked into the same rigid sequence of events. We all experience 24-hour days because this earth rotates on its axis and nobody can speed it up. No one can choose to live 12-hour days while the rest make out with 24.

But in eternity there is no past or future; there is simply one great present moment. Therefore, the events we experience in eternity are never anything we have to *wait* for, they are always what we are *ready* for, what we are spiritually prepared for. This passage says that God has been spiritually preparing us for something, the coming of the Lord for his own, the return of Christ for his church, for each individual believer. The Scriptures clearly teach that when a believer dies, he experiences immediately the coming of the Lord for his own. Paul describes that event in 1 Thessalonians 4:16: "the Lord himself shall descend from heaven with a shout, with the voice of the archangel, and with the trump of God" KJV. With him will come all those who have been dead in Christ. Thus it will appear to those left alive on earth that the dead have been raised first when in actuality we are all raised together, "and so shall we ever be with the Lord." This experience awaits us immediately.

Verse 5 goes on to say that we have already tasted this in our spirit although not yet in the body, since the body is locked into time. It is unredeemed and unresurrected, but in the spirit, in the inner life, we have already tasted these eternal conditions. That is why Paul says:

> . . . (God) has given us the Spirit as a guarantee.

The daily experience of the Spirit's refreshing renewal, which Paul described earlier, is that guarantee. Something is happening to us. The old life is deteriorating, the outward man is falling apart, but the inner man is getting richer and greater and warmer and more loving. He is anticipating the future with increased expectation. That is a taste of glory.

I have always loved the writings of that dear seventeenth century Scottish Covenanter, Samuel Rutherford. His writings come down to us in the form of letters written while he was a prisoner for Christ's sake in Scotland. Some of those letters are expressive of wonderful faith. Ann Cousins went back through all of them and culled out certain phrases and idioms that he used and put them together in a song that was D. L. Moody's favorite.

> The sands of time are sinking,
> The dawn of heaven breaks,
> The summer morn we've sighed for,
> The fair sweet morn awakes.
> Dark, dark has been the midnight,
> But dayspring is at hand,
> And glory, glory dwelleth
> In Immanuel's land.
>
> Oh Christ he is the fountain,
> The deep sweet well of love,
> The streams on earth I've tasted
> More deep I'll drink above.
> There to an ocean fullness,
> His mercy does expand
> And glory, glory dwelleth
> In Immanuel's land.
>
> The bride eyes not her garment,
> But her dear bridegroom's face.
> I will not gaze at glory
> But on my King of grace.
> Not on the crown he giveth,
> But on his pierced hands.
> The Lamb is all the glory
> Of Immanuel's land.

It is a great hope. It is a hope to energize us in our present stress. If we have to go through struggle, we must always remember that the struggle, though it is God's choice for us now, is part of the immense privilege we have of sharing his sufferings, that we may also "reign with him" forever. What a hope!

2 Corinthians 5:6–17

10

What's There to Live For?

"What is there to live for?" That question fills many hearts today, both Christians and non-Christians alike. These are times of crisis, and many are troubled by the bleak look of the future. Teen-age suicide rates are rocketing as despair spreads. So many are asking the question, "What is there to live for?"

The hopelessness of our age and times has never been more eloquently stated, perhaps, than by that most eloquent of men, Malcolm Muggeridge, speaking at the Hoover Institute of Stanford University and reported in the *Los Angeles Times.* He summed up the end of Western civilization in these words:

> The final conclusion would seem to be that whereas other civilizations have been brought down by attacks of barbarians from without, ours had the unique distinction of training its own destroyers at its own educational institutions and providing them with facilities for propagating their destructive ideology far and wide, all at the public expense. Thus did Western man decide to abolish himself, creating his own boredom out of his own affluence, his own vulnerability out of his own strength, his own impotence out of his own erotomania, himself blowing the trumpet that brought the walls of his own city tumbling. And, having convinced himself that he was too numerous, labored with pill and scalpel and syringe to make himself fewer, until at last, having educated himself into imbecility and polluted and drugged himself into stupefaction, he keeled over, a weary, battered old brontosaurus, and became extinct.

Cause for Hope

The world of the first century looked similarly bleak, and there was no more reason for hope in the days of the apostles than in our own times. Yet when you turn to the pages of the New Testament you never see the reaction of despair. There is a note of triumph and of hope running through all these pages, although the circumstances of the New Testament Christians did not look any more hopeful than ours.

This passage from 2 Corinthians 5 is a wonderful answer to the question posed at the beginning of this chapter. Notice how Paul introduces it:

> So we are always of good courage, we know that while we are at home in the body we are away from the Lord, for we walk by faith, not by sight. We are of good courage . . . (2 Cor. 5:6–8).

"Always of good courage"; that note has been sounded again and again throughout this passage. In verse 1 of chapter 4 Paul says, "Having this ministry by the mercy of God, we do not lose heart," and in verse 16 of chapter 4 he says, "So we do not lose heart."

The key, of course, is the little word "so." *Because of* what he has been saying, he does not lose heart; he is of good courage. All through the account he has been talking about the power, activity and availability of God, the basis for Christian hope, the answer to flooding despair, the fact that God *is* doing something and can be counted on to act. That is where the renewing of hope in an individual must arise. God is going to act both in the future beyond death, and in the present, amidst the threatenings and the dangers of life as we know it.

Reasons for Courage

In this passage (chapter 5, verses 6–17) the apostle sees three very practical, helpful effects to us because of our relationship with God. The first he has already stated: "We are of good courage." Having this relationship, knowing this kind of a God, living in the midst of this kind of a life, we are, nevertheless, of good courage. He sees two reasons for it:

> For we walk by faith, not by sight. We are of good courage, and we would rather be away from the body and at home with the Lord (2 Cor. 5:7, 8).

The first reason is that we are in touch with the Lord by faith, not by sight. We do not see him, he does not come and sit down beside us and talk to us. He does not put his arm around our shoulders and encourage us, but nevertheless, we have his presence with us. That is the first great reason for renewed vigor and courage. No circumstance we go through ever means that we are abandoned and left to ourselves.

The Lord himself expressed this to the disciples in the Upper Room. That was a troubled moment; their lives were in danger, but he said, "Let not your hearts be troubled. Ye believe in God, believe also in me" (John 14:1 KJV). He promised, "Lo, I am with you alway, even unto the end of the world" (Matt. 28:20 KJV).

I hope, as Christians, we never forget this real and vital promise. It will sustain and encourage us no matter what our situation may be. We are not alone. He is with us. We walk by faith and not by sight. We have a full supply of love and peace and joy to keep us in the midst of anything. That is reason enough to say, "So we are always of good courage."

Home Ahead

But Paul sees another reason: "We would rather be away from the body and at home with the Lord." Looking on to the future, summing up the first five verses of this chapter, Paul sees the great weight of glory awaiting us, for which our present circumstances and trials are preparing us.

Looking ahead is always characteristic of Christians who understand the message of Christianity. Glory lies ahead of us, and the joys of it awaken anticipation and a sense of hopeful excitement. That energizes us in our endeavors today; it has an effect upon us now. As Paul put it in Romans 8:25, "We wait for it with patience." We are looking forward to being at home with the Lord.

Note that "at home" is used both for our life in the body and our coming presence with the Lord. What does it mean? You do not feel strange when you are "at home." You feel natural. You feel relaxed. You would feel very strained and unnatural if you did not have your body. You feel at home in it.

Using the same language, the apostle goes on to say that when you leave this earthly body and are given the body of glory awaiting you, you will be at home there, too. It will not be an experience of strain or difference, but of naturalness. Later on in this letter he speaks of being caught up into the third heaven, into the very presence of God. He says, in effect, "I didn't know whether I was in the body or out of it. I couldn't tell. I felt so much at home it didn't make any difference" (see 2 Cor. 12:2).

We are not headed toward something dreadful or so different that we need to be afraid. We will be at home with the Lord, in his very presence, seeing him no longer only by the Spirit within, but face to face. If it is true, as Peter puts it, that "Without having seen him you love him," how much more will we love him when we see him face to face? So we are strengthened to go through the difficulty of these days and to be of good courage because we are heading into light instead of darkness. That is the second result.

To Please the Lord With . . .

Then the apostle sees still another effect of our faith, in the next few verses:

> So whether we are at home or away, we make it our aim to please him (2 Cor. 5:9).

Whether "at home" (i.e., "with the Lord") or "away" (from the Lord, here in the body), either place, the purpose and aim of our lives is to please God. That eternal principle will not change when we leave this earth. The one real reason we have to be here on earth is to please God, to be a delight to him, to give his heart rejoicing as he watches us and works with us. As our children please us oftentimes, so we are to please the Lord. That is the sole purpose for living, Paul is saying here.

He declares precisely the two ways by which pleasing the Lord may be manifested. First, in the area of our motives:

> For we must all appear before the judgment seat of Christ, so that each one may receive good or evil, according to what he has done in the body (2 Cor. 5:10).

This is a frightening and misunderstood concept to many people. The apostle speaks of a "judgment seat," and that always strikes terror to our hearts. Many people, I am afraid, identify this with that sobering and imposing scene in Revelation 20 where all the dead, small and great, are standing before the Great White Throne of God. In an awesome moment of judgment "the books are opened." Lives are reviewed and eternal destinies are settled. It is a terribly impressive scene, and many think Paul refers to it here, too.

But if you read this passage that way you have totally missed the point. This is not a judgment to settle final destiny. This is a personal evaluation given to each individual by the Lord himself of what his life has really been like. It is as though you and the Lord walked together back through all the scenes of your life and he pointed out to you the real nature of what you did and what you said and what was behind it all.

. . . Our Motives Unveiled

The primary characteristic of the "judgment seat" is a disclosure of what has been hidden in the silent, inner reaches of our own hearts, not only to us, but also to others. The word used here is a very interesting one. It says, "We shall all appear." Literally, it is, "We shall all be manifested," "We shall all be unveiled," at the judgment seat of Christ, in the eyes of everyone. That is the point. Jesus spoke of this moment when he said, "Whatever is spoken in the secret places shall be shouted from the housetops." And it is described also in the First Corinthian letter, where Paul says, "Therefore, do not pronounce judgment before the time, before the Lord comes, who will bring to light the things now hidden in darkness and will disclose the purposes of the heart" (1 Cor. 4:5).

God's concern is not, as we often think, so much with *what* we do as with *why* we do it. There are, of course, some things we are never to do, certain clear-cut actions that are always sin. They are mentioned everywhere in the Scripture—murder, adultery, lying, stealing, and so on are always and invariably wrong, and to do them displeases the Lord.

But there are a great many actions, apparently right, that can still be displeasing to the Lord. If the reason you do them is to gain glory or fame for yourself or to get even with somebody else or to establish some wrong relationship God does not approve, they are wrong. Your motive is all-important. And more than that, as we have been learning from this passage, what you count on, your resource, is even *more* important to God. On what do you count for success—your ability, your education, your training, your background, something coming from you? Or do you count on the indwelling God who helps you to do the work and to carry it through to success, in his eyes if not in the eyes of men?

Hebrews tells us that "without faith it is impossible to please him (God)" (Heb. 11:6). Faith must be present in what we do or it is not pleasing to him. Paul understands this and wants that moment before the judgment seat of Christ to disclose nothing of shame to him, nothing he refused to face in life, but rather a moment of joy. The Lord will have the joy of showing him many things Paul thought were failures that were really successes. Things that he did that no one heard anything about will be brought to light and vividly displayed before others. So it is a time of disclosure, but it is also a time of evaluation when we learn for the first time who was right and what attitudes we should have had or should not have had. It is a helpful time of seeing the truth about ourselves.

. . . Our Motives Judged

If that frightens you I want to tell you this: There is something you can do about it now. Paul says, "If we judged ourselves truly, we should not be judged" (1 Cor. 11:31). The judgment seat of Christ, in this sense, has already started.

This is what the Lord does with me frequently. Does he do it with you? He is often, by his Spirit, pointing out to me that I had a wrong attitude or a wrong motive for doing something. Sometimes he reveals a right motive and confirms to me that I was doing the right thing with a right attitude; whether people accept it or not. That is the judgment seat of Christ going on now. If we will allow ourselves to face truth like that now we will not have to face it at the judgment seat of Christ. It will not be brought out there because it will already have been settled.

It is important that as we grow as Christians we allow the Lord to show us ourselves the way we really are. We should not fight back and refuse to acknowledge that he is right about things. The mark of spiritual progress is the increasing awareness of all the possibilities and potential for evil that lie in our hearts. That has been my case. The older I grow the more aware I am of how wrong I have been, how many people I have hurt unwittingly, and the increasing sense of the control that evil has had over me in my life and in my relationships.

Yet that does not make me despair because I know God has seen it all from the beginning. He has dealt with it and set it aside. That is no longer the basis of my relationship to him. He has given me the gift of righteousness. He loves me. He likes me. That is my present relationship to him, and this will be true at the judgment seat of Christ as well. It will be a time of disclosure, of evaluation, but also a time of encouragement where we will see and learn the real value of many things that we thought no one knew and which we ourselves often did not understand.

A pastor from San Antonio, Texas, told me about Hurricane Beulah which devastated that whole southern Texas area. Thousands of people were driven out of their homes, and the churches were opened to provide places of refuge for them. In this strongly Catholic city hundreds of the people housed in his Baptist church were Catholic. For many days, the people of the church cooked meals for the victims, transformed the pews into beds, provided recreation for them, worship services, and so on.

When the ordeal was over, the Catholic bishop, a godly man, came over to thank him. They had been friends for some years, and the bishop said, "I want to thank you and your people for what you have done for our people. I know that probably doesn't mean a lot—I'm just a man—but one of these days you're going to stand before the Lord himself. He will look at you with those beautiful eyes of his and say, 'Buckner, taking those refugees was a wonderful thing to do; I want to thank you for it.' That will mean something to you then," he said.

It is true, isn't it? The judgment seat of Christ is not only a time of honest evaluation, understanding the need for proper motives and proper dependence; it will be a time of encouragement as well: "and then shall every man receive a commendation from God."

. . . *Our Motives Rewarded*

Now you may be wondering, "What about the rewards here? I'm interested in those." I must confess I have had to review and revise some of my concepts along this line. When I was a young Christian I was taught that all of the crowns mentioned in Scripture—the crown of life, the crown of righteousness, the crown of glory, and so on—are the rewards one is given at the judgment seat.

I have come to see that this is not true. A crown is a symbol of God's gift to us of eternal life. Life in its various capacities or aspects is symbolized by crowns and they are always gifts. You can never earn a crown of glory, a crown of life, or a crown of righteousness. These symbols point toward the gift of eternal life which God gives us freely in Jesus Christ our Lord.

What, then, is increased or lost at the judgment seat of Christ? The answer is, opportunity to display the life that has been given to you. Our faithfulness here determines the degree to which we will manifest the glory of God. That differs according to the individual's faithfulness. In the parable of the talents Jesus said that those who used their talents, who seized their opportunities, depending on God and motivated rightly, would be given charge over five cities, and others charge over ten cities. What does he mean? He means that they will be given a greater opportunity, a greater area to display the nature of the life and the glory of God they have received as a gift.

That is what Paul means also when he speaks of "running the race" (Heb. 12:1), and "pressing on toward the mark for the prize" (Phil. 3:14). He beats his body to bring it into subjection, "lest . . . when I have preached to others, I myself should be a castaway" (1 Cor. 9:27, KJV). Or again, in 1 Corinthians 3:13, Paul is saying in effect, "Every man's work shall be tried, of what sort it is"—where it comes from, what is the motive behind it and what is the resource upon which it depended. Then if a man succeeds, "he shall be given a reward," a great opportunity to display that life; or, "he shall suffer loss," not having that opportunity. That is what the judgment seat of Christ determines.

. . . Our Motives Enacted

In the same vein Paul goes on to say we are to lead God-pleasing lives not only in our motives, but also in our faithful actions:

> Therefore, knowing the fear of the Lord, we persuade men; but what we are is known to God, and I hope it is known also to your conscience. We are not commending ourselves to you again but giving you cause to be proud of us, so that you may be able to answer those who pride themselves on a man's position and not on his heart. For if we are beside ourselves, it is for God; if we are in our right mind, it is for you (2 Cor. 5:11–13).

Fear of the Lord

Looking at his own life he says, "I am motivated to careful living by realizing there will be a full exposure of my motives." He calls that the "fear of the Lord." Not the fear of the Lord in the sense of trembling before God, but a respect for God, aware that he is a God of truth no one can turn aside—and can escape seeing the truth about himself. You cannot plead with God to escape this judgment. He is no respecter of persons. Knowing this Paul says, "That motivates me to be honest and faithful in the work he has given me to do, that of persuading men."

Do not read this as though Paul is saying, "I go around preaching hellfire and damnation so that people will come to Christ." That is not what he means by "knowing the fear of the Lord." It is **in his own life** that he faces the Lord with awe. In effect, he is saying, "Knowing that God will deal honestly, squarely and faithfully yet lovingly with me, I want every moment of my life to count. I do not want to waste my life. I do not want to spend it pretending to be something I am not. I want to be honest and open and genuine about all that I say and do." That is why he says, "Whatever I am is known to God, and I hope you can see it too."

Answers for Critics

"Furthermore," Paul says, "my actions are motivated with a desire to answer my critics. I labor in order that you might have an answer to give those who are criticizing me." Then he lists some of the things men were saying about him. Some were saying, "Oh, you know Paul. He's crazy. He's mad." They probably were referring to his account of his conversion on the Damascus road when a light suddenly shone and he saw the Lord. He told this story everywhere, and on hearing it people would say, "He's a dreamer. He's mad." Paul says, "If I'm mad, remember it is for God's sake. It is a madness that glorifies God. I see him and whatever I do is for him. Or, if I behave normally," he says, "that is for you, because that is what God has taught me to live for others." So his concern is that his actions be faithful and honest and open and properly motivated, and he will use the opportunities he has while he has the time.

The Ultimate Motive

The final motive to Paul, is living a life for others, motivated by love:

> For the Love of Christ controls us, because we are convinced that one has died for all; therefore all have died. And he died for all, that those who live might live no longer for themselves but for him who for their sake died and was raised (2 Cor. 5:14, 15).

"Controls" is from a word that means "constrains," "drives us out," "motivates us and then guides us, setting the limits to what we should and should not do." That, he says, comes from the sense that Christ loves him.

I do not know a greater and more powerful motivating factor than that. I am terrified sometimes at what God can do to me if I do not behave. That is a low motivation, but I confess it is there. But the thing that will get to me when nothing else will is to experience the love of Christ for me, that refreshment of spirit that I gain from the awareness that he loves me, is for me; he stands beside me and delights in me. That will move me as nothing else will. Paul here is experiencing an awareness that he is loved by God. There is nothing like it. It gives him a sense of security, a sense of self-worth, a good self-image. If you suffer from a bad image of yourself, then start thinking about what God says about you, how he loves you and how Christ loves you and has given himself for you. That will change everything.

Paul has learned that the death of Christ freed him from the need to live for himself. I do not know anything more relevant today than that statement. Everywhere I turn I hear people talking about what they need to "meet their needs." "I don't go here or I don't go there because it doesn't meet my needs." Now I want to tell you this: Jesus Christ died to set you free from that syndrome. You do not need people to meet these kinds of needs; he has already met them. If you have not learned that Christ meets your inner needs you will never get them met from any other source. No one *else* is able to meet them. If you lay that trip upon people you will suffer continual rejection because they know they cannot meet your needs.

"Christ died for all," means "all have died" so they might understand they live no longer for themselves. With *your* needs met by Christ, you can minister to the needs of others. "He died for all, that those who live might live no longer for themselves," no longer with their needs at the center of their life, trying to build everything around themselves, "but for him who for their sake died and was raised."

A New View

What will this do for you? First, it will make you *see* everybody else differently, and then it will make you *treat* them differently:

> From now on, therefore, we regard no one from a human point of view (2 Cor. 5:16a).

"Once," Paul says, "we were impressed with people who had power or money or fame. We followed them around, imitated them, dropped their names and wanted to be associated with them. Other people were obscure and we thought them of no value to us; we treated them like dirt," he says; "we had nothing to do with them. In fact, there was a time," he says, "when we treated Christ that way." This is the only reference in the whole New Testament that indicates that Paul may have personally heard Jesus. He says:

> . . . we once regarded Christ from a human point of view (2 Cor. 5:16b).

What did Paul think of Jesus? He thought he was a worthless rabble-rouser, a tub-thumping street preacher from a dirty little town in Galilee from which no one expected anything good. Because Jesus had no political standing, no family position, no training and no education, Paul assumed he was worthless. He tried his best to exterminate the religion that gathered about him because he regarded him as an imposter and a phony.

"But," he says, "no more. We've learned to look at people differently. We now see Christ for who he was, the Lord of Glory, the King of the Ages, the Prince of Life, God himself become a man." Paul's great Christological passages come to mind at this point. He says, "We don't regard him that way anymore, and we don't regard other people that way either. We see them for who they are, men and women made in the image of God but fallen from it. We see them as victims of the devil's lies, bound by the power of Satan. But they are important, significant people because God's image is in them and can be awakened to life again. We don't pay attention to their wealth or their status or their fame or anything else. Everybody, even the most obscure, the lowliest, the weakest among us is a possible child of God, made in the image of God and therefore tremendously significant."

A New Approach

I have come to see that this is the mark of someone who understands true Christianity. He is freed from bias and prejudice and playing up to people according to their status. He learns to be the same to everybody, no matter who they are. Therefore, Paul says, we are to approach people in a new way:

> Therefore, if any one is in Christ, he is a new creation; the old has passed away, behold, the new has come (2 Cor. 5:17).

What does he mean by that, in this context? He means simply there is always hope for everyone. No matter who he is, it is possible that he may be born again. No matter how violent he may be in opposition to the gospel, he can be changed. A creative God can reach the most hopeless, the darkest, the lowliest, the worst, the farthest away. And when they are reached you never need to give up hope for them because then they are part of a new creation. God has started a work that he is going to finish.

Often I tend to write people off. Do you do that? Recently I met an old acquaintance who had so offended and irritated me by his immaturity that I had long ago written him off. I thought he would never amount to anything as a Christian. But when I met him again, I was amazed at how he had grown. I thought nobody could change him. But God did, and he did it without any help from me at all!

I have learned that if you just wait you may not be able to do anything, but God can and he will. If you are in Christ you are a new creation. He has begun a good work in you and will not fail to perform it until the day of Christ. So there is always hope, even for me and for you. So we are to treat everybody differently because we no longer live for ourselves but for him who died and was raised again.

What a change that makes! What a reason to go on and live today. This is the finest hour to bear a Christian witness above all other hours in history. What a privilege it will be at the judgment seat of Christ to know that we stood for his name and loved in his name in the midst of the emptiness, death and darkness of a dying world.

11

The Word for This Hour

In the fifth chapter of 2 Corinthians, the apostle Paul has been painting a picture, a portrait of a Christian living in the midst of a dying world. A Christian is to be someone who radiates a great light of hope as he looks to the future. He knows a "weight of glory" awaits him, and that his present trials and difficulties are preparing him for that glory. He is to know that this "light affliction . . . is but for a moment (and is) working for us a far more exceeding and eternal weight of glory."

So a Christian living today ought to have a light in his eye as he looks toward the future, and he ought to have a flame in his heart, a passion born of the two tremendous motivating forces that we have already seen in this passage.

First, he should respect the fact that he cannot fool God; he cannot hide anything from him. One day all the hidden motives, all the inner secrets of his heart will be unveiled at the judgment seat of Christ, when he will see life exactly as God saw it. "Then shall we know even as also we are known." This fact motivates the apostle to guard what he was doing, to see that it was right, to be filled with right attitudes and right actions. "Therefore, knowing the fear of the Lord, we persuade men," he says.

Secondly, Paul says, "The love of Christ controls us." It constrains us; it drives us out. Christ loves Paul, has forgiven him and dwells in him and cherishes him, always supports and sustains him in whatever he is going through. He is never alone. This tremendous power motivates the apostle, as it ought to motivate us.

The third thing Paul has pictured here is the change of viewpoint that comes to a Christian. He says, "We do not look at people anymore from a 'human point of view.' We don't judge them by outward standards; we don't value them because they are wealthy or influential or famous. We see everyone as made in the image of God, but having lost the likeness of God." Yet people are able to be restored to that relationship. Any life, no matter how dissolute, wasted, empty or lonely can, by the touch of the divine life, be restored to usefulness, joy, peace and power, and be part of a new creation that God is working out.

We are to live like that. We are to have that in our thoughts every day. We are to be "renewed in our minds" by the Spirit of God; we must look at life this way because this is the way life really is.

Having said all that, the apostle goes on to describe the ministry God has given us. These words are among the most remarkable in the Scriptures. They are a description of the greatest, most powerful, most effective work going on in the world today. I do not hesitate to say that, yet this is a description of your ministry and mine; what Paul calls, "the ministry of reconciliation":

> All this is from God, who through Christ reconciled us to himself and gave us the ministry of reconciliation; that is, in Christ God was reconciling the world to himself, not counting their trespasses against them, and entrusting to us the message of reconciliation. So we are ambassadors for Christ, God making his appeal through us. We beseech you on behalf of Christ, be reconciled to God (2 Cor. 5:18–20).

We need to understand this "ministry of reconciliation" very carefully because this is *our* ministry. *Everyone* who knows Jesus Christ has been called by God to do this very thing. That is why he has left us here in the world. It is not merely Paul's ministry, or an apostle's, or even a pastor's ministry. It is *our* ministry. Notice how Paul uses the words "we" and "us" all through this passage. He shared it with those Christians of that early day in Corinth and he shares it with us today. This is what God has given us to do.

Origin of the Ministry

There are five things in this passage I would like to call to our attention. Notice, first, that this ministry comes to us from God himself; it originates with him:

> All this is from God, who through Christ reconciled us to himself and gave us the ministry of reconciliation (2 Cor. 5:18).

Now if this ministry comes from God, you and I are responsible to him to do this, not to anybody else. When Paul went around the Roman world he did not have to check in with the twelve apostles in Jerusalem to get permission to go into another country. They did not give him his commission; God did. He did not send them monthly reports on how he was doing. He had no board or authority over him, and neither do we in this regard.

As I travel around the country, in some churches I find that the pastor thinks it is his responsibility to control everything that goes on, all the ministry of the people, if they have any at all. They must get permission from him or from the board of the church to have a meeting in their home. Now it is certainly true that the knowledge of any ministry going on in a home ought to be shared with the staff of a church. They ought to be allowed to help, to give counsel, but no one is responsible for that ministry except God himself.

You do not have to get permission from the pastors or the elders of your church to have a ministry in your home, to reach out to your neighborhood. That is your responsibility before God. He gave you the home; he put you in the neighborhood; he asked you to reach out to those around you. He has given you the "ministry of reconciliation" so you do it as unto him. God sends us; he commissions us as he commissioned Paul. Moreover, Paul makes it clear that God reconciles us first, so that we do not go with something we know nothing about. We go with what we ourselves have experienced. That helps a lot. You are the world's greatest authority on what has happened to you. Nobody can tell you differently. When you go with the Word about how God has reconciled you and healed the breach, how he crossed the gap between you and him, and you find yourself now enfolded in his divine arms, supported by his divine grace and forgiven by his divine love, you can share that with someone else. That is the "message of reconciliation."

Addressed to the Estranged

Secondly, this powerful ministry reconciles the world:

> God was in Christ reconciling the world to himself, not counting their trespasses against them, and entrusting to us the message of reconciliation (2 Cor. 5:19).

Above all else, this is the message the world needs to know. The problem with people everywhere is they have no security, no sense of acceptance, no sense of worth. The universal problem of our day is one of poor self-image. Even the blustering people who try to pretend that they are self-sufficient know their bluster is a cover-up; they know they do not really feel that way. They are scared and frustrated oftentimes. They have to pretend that they are able to handle everything, but at the end of the day they know they were not.

The reason people feel that way is their sense of alienation, of estrangement from God. They live in a universe they obviously know does not belong to them. They did not make it; they do not run it. This whole world was running long before you and I showed up on it. People know that; therefore they feel uneasy. This estrangement and alienation is the supreme problem of our day. Any psychiatrist or psychologist will tell you that.

Paul is addressing just this problem. We are lost, we are alienated, we are cut off from the God who runs everything. This message strikes home to human hearts everywhere. It makes no difference what color your skin is, your background, or how you grew up. You can say this to a savage in the jungle; you can say it to a business man in the trade marts of San Francisco or Wall Street; you can say it to a craftsman, a plumber, a doctor, a lawyer. They all need this universal Word sent to the world.

The Message

Paul points out that this message will come in two forms. If it is really the right message from God, it does not come talking about the judgment of God over sin. When I graduated from seminary over thirty years ago, I came out convinced my job was to make men aware of their sin and the judgment of God upon evil. I was brought up in a theological generation that taught you have to scare people before they will become Christians.

Then I began to learn from verses like this. I saw how the apostles and the Lord himself delivered God's message. Almost universally, God's message says, "We do not need to talk about judgment. I've taken care of that." As Paul puts it here, "God was reconciling the world to himself, *not counting their trespasses against them*." I learned after a few years that all I need to do is go to people, taking for granted that, like me, they are hurting inside from their sins, and talk about a God who understands, who wants to relieve them from that hurt and has done something about it. He is not ready to throw them into hell; he opens his arms and invites them to come to a loving Father and be restored. He sees our hurt, our loneliness, our emptiness, our struggles and hungers to be something different than we are. He sees our sense of frustration that we cannot get it all together. He comes with a word of release that says, "I know that. I know you can't make it and I've done something about it. I've taken care of the whole problem of sin. Now let's just talk about relationship and make appeal to people to come."

Do not read this as though God is not concerned about human evil. Some people think that God is so loving he does not care whether they sin or not. He will just forget it all and they can come. But no, that is never the Word of the gospel. God takes sin seriously and sees it as a hurtful thing. This passage says very clearly (and reiterates it in verse 21) that God has done something at tremendous cost to remove this problem of sin. He cared so much about it he was willing to pay that cost.

The Messengers

The second way this message comes is by God sending people to be reconcilers. He sends you and me to be peacemakers; he has entrusted to *us* the message of reconciliation. That is why God put you in the neighborhood where you live, in order that you might be an island of light reaching out with the message of reconciliation.

It helps to know you do not have to go to your neighbors and friends and tell them all they are doing wrong. Most of them are living gross lives which offend us. We cannot help but feel disgusted. But some of the things we are doing offend them, too. We have to face that reality. We go to them and talk about the fact that, while we are no better than they, yet we are dealing with a God who has *done* something about our "gross-ness," who understands the problem and who deals with us in love and grace and forgiveness. That is a different message entirely.

Are All Saved?

So Paul goes on to point out, in verse 20, the third characteristic of the message: it requires a voluntary acceptance. It is not true that everybody is automatically saved. Some people teach today that God in Christ paid the debt of sin and, therefore, everybody is saved; they do not know it, but will find out when they die and all of a sudden wake up in glory. They will say, "We don't deserve to be here," and God will say, "Well, surprise! Christ paid for your sins and that is why you are here. Everybody makes it."

No, that is not true. Look at what verse 20 says:

> So we are ambassadors for Christ, God making his appeal through us. We beseech you (actually the word "you" should not be there. Paul is not addressing these Corinthians; they are already reconciled. He is telling them what he preaches to others.) We beseech on behalf of Christ, be reconciled to God (2 Cor. 5:20).

There would be no reason for that kind of a pleading entreaty on Paul's part were everybody automatically saved by the death of Christ. There is no universal salvation. It is as you receive this Word and accept it for yourself, as you come into a personal relationship with the Lord Jesus that the benefit of his death is applied to you. As it is when you were saved, so it is when your neighbors and friends receive it. That is why God sends us as ambassadors.

Why do nations send ambassadors? Because countries do not always relate to each other very well. Things need to be explained, to be approached with diplomacy and caution. An ambassador is a representative of a government, handling himself with such care and confidence that his government's message is conveyed in the most painless, least offensive way possible. Now that is dangerous. You can get yourself killed or taken captive as an ambassador in this world today.

Paul saw himself as an ambassador for Christ, pleading in the name of Christ, as though Christ himself was there, pleading with men to become reconciled to God, to accept this forgiveness that God was offering. "We beseech," he says, "we plead with men. We don't command them to be saved. We don't condemn them. We plead with them to turn and respond to a God of love."

The Bible paints no picture more beautiful than this one of God in his almighty power, the God who can do all things, who can carry out his will any time he chooses, nevertheless coming and pleading with guilty men and women to turn and be forgiven. Nothing is more descriptive of this than those words of Jesus as he wept over the City of Jerusalem: "O Jerusalem, Jerusalem, . . . how often would I have gathered your children together as a hen gathers her brood under her wings, and you would not!" (Matt. 23:37).

The Four Turn-Abouts

I find that often the case with us is that we face a possibility of rejection and we are afraid of this. Yet if we understand the message with which we come, it would make it so much easier. Years ago when I was in Dallas Seminary, I remember Dr. Lewis Sperry Chafer, the great founder of the Seminary, illustrating in class one day this message of reconciliation in a way that I have never forgotten.

He said that in the beginning when God created man in the Garden it was like this—and he put his hands together, palms inward, man and God face to face, in perfect fellowship with one another. Then came the Fall; man turned his back on God. Dr. Chafer turned one hand around so that it was clear that man had turned away from God. That is what Isaiah says, isn't it? "All we like sheep have gone astray. We have turned everyone to his own way." So because God is a God of justice, his justice required that he respond. He turned his back on man and man has been alienated from him ever since.

But in the work of the cross (and, of course, this was available to man before Christ appeared because the cross is an eternal event) God is reconciled to man. He turns back so that his face is toward man again, and now the message goes out to all men everywhere, "You turn around now and 'be reconciled to God.' " When that happens peace is restored. This is the "message of reconciliation." [illegible] are to go to men everywhere and say, "Be reconciled unto God."

The Result of the Message

The fourth characteristic of the message is that it achieves the "righteousness of God," the very thing that men want to have. Men want to be right with God. To understand this, reflect on how sensitive we are about whether people think we are right or not. Let somebody accuse you and what do you start doing? You start justifying yourself, don't you? And justifying is the word for righteousness in the Bible. You start saying, "Well, I did it because of this," or, "This is what I had in mind. I think I was right in doing that." We long to be right in other's eyes; everybody does.

How much deeper is our need to be right before God. And the way is set forth for us here:

> For our sake he made him (Christ) to be sin who knew no sin, so that in him we might become the righteousness of God (2 Cor. 5:21).

This is one of the most magnificent verses in the whole Bible. It is describing, of course, the mysterious transaction that took place upon the cross when Jesus, the sinless One, the One whose whole life was lived righteously, without failure, without fault, without evil—when the One who never did wrong was made to suffer for all the sins of you and me and the whole world. I do not understand it. He took our place, it says, and God agreed to it. It was something they planned between them. God sent his Son into the world to do that very thing and made him, on the cross, to be sin for us.

What that meant to him none of us can really imagine. Years ago when I was a new Christian I remember a song that was often sung in churches in those days, based upon the parable of the one lost sheep the shepherd went out to find. One verse in particular stuck in my mind:

> None of the ransomed ever knew
> How deep were the waters crossed,
> Nor how dark was the night
> Which the Lord went through,
> Ere he found his sheep that was lost.

No, we will never understand it. We will never know how much agony of heart and mind and spirit pressed upon Jesus, how the dark horrors of hell came upon his soul there on the cross.

But we *do* understand that God does not take sin lightly, that something had to be done to settle the problem of our evil. And it has been done: God has settled the problem of all our sins, every one of them, by placing them upon his Son. Jesus Christ has paid the full penalty which justice demands so that when we come to God he is not compromised by being good to us; his justice has been satisfied. His love, therefore, is free and released to be manifest to us. He accepts us in love and gives us, according to this verse, the righteousness of Christ himself. I do not understand that either, but I believe it. What a marvelous sense of acceptance and forgiveness and being loved that gives to me.

Now do not read that wrongly. It says, "So that in him we might become the righteousness of God." I know a lot of Christians who read that as though it means, "That gives me a chance to start trying to behave. If I work hard all my Christian life to be a good person, then I finally become 'the righteousness of God.' "

But he does not say that at all. Rightness is not something you are going to achieve, according to the way you behave. It is something you are, when you believe. You start your Christian life on that basis. When you believe in Jesus, you already have, instantly, the righteousness of Christ. You are righteous, you are forgiven, you are restored. That is the way God deals with us.

Because we have that righteousness already, we do not have to earn it. It is our delight to begin with it, to start acting righteous because we *are* righteous. I hope you understand this, because this is the "good news." It is no good news to come to a person and say, "Christ forgave all your sins up to now, but from now on you'd better watch it. You are going to have to pay for all those." No, no, that is not the gospel. The good news is all your sins are forgiven, all your life long, including those you have not even committed yet.

God knows your struggle. He has dealt with that. He is never going to retract his solution; he is never going to act in any different way toward you. Because the sin problem is settled he can come in alongside of you and help you learn how to act righteously on that basis. And he will—lifting you up, forgiving you, restoring you, strengthening you and staying right with you until this life is finally done.

So this is the glory of it. We learn here how a God of justice can come to a loveless, hard-hearted, self-righteous, selfish, hurting and hurtful sinner like you and me and not count his trespasses against him. That is the way he does it because "he who knew no sin was made sin for us that we might be made the righteousness of God in him."

That Christ May Profit You

The final word in this section (we must ignore a misleading chapter division here) is addressed to the believers in Corinth:

> Working together with him, then (this is a message now from God through Paul) we entreat you not to accept the grace of God in vain. For he says,
> "At the acceptable time I have listened to you, and helped you on the day of salvation." Behold, now is the acceptable time; behold, now is the day of salvation (2 Cor. 6:1, 2).

Do not accept the grace of God in vain, Paul says. What does he mean? Is it possible to "accept the grace of God in vain"? The grace of God is a general term which covers all that God has done for us in Christ. Paul is saying to people who are already reconciled, "Now, don't let that be in vain, empty, worthless, in your life." "Well," you say, "does that mean they can lose their salvation after they've got it?" No, Paul is not saying that at all. Such a question is clearly answered by many other passages.

He is saying that when you received Christ, he came to live within you to do two basic things. One, to show you the difference between right and wrong. (Some things you think are right are really wrong, and some of the things you think are wrong are really right. Christ has come to show you the difference.)

Second, to give you the power to *do* the right and to reject the wrong. That is what he has come for, and he intends to have you use this gift in every area of your life. If there are some areas where you do not pay any attention to him and do not apply or draw from him the strength you need to act, then in that area you *have* Christ, but it is as though you did not. He did not profit you anything. In that area of your life you have received "the grace of God in vain." Now God will help you, he is at work to change that, but until you agree with God in that area, Christ "shall profit you nothing," as Paul said to the Galatians (5:2, KJV).

When Does it Begin?

When do you do this? When are you to allow God's grace to profit you? There is only one word on God's clock: it is *now. Now* is the acceptable time. *Now* is the day of salvation. When are you going to start acting in love toward the people you live with? "Well," you say, "I've been planning to do it after the first of the year. I'm going to make a New Year's resolution."

No. God says, "*Now* is the accepted time." The devil's time is always tomorrow. That is why we never get around to drawing upon Christ for certain problem areas of our life. God's time is always today, now. When are you going to reach out to your neighbors and become friends with them so that you might have an opportunity to share with them the change in your life and heart? You do not have yesterday; it is gone. You may not get tomorrow. What you have is *now*; therefore, the Word of God always addresses us in this existential fashion. If you are going to act and you see something that needs to be done, do it now. Do not wait. Begin to live now. Enter into life now. That is God's time. Nothing else will avail.

As Paul contemplates this great message of a beseeching God reaching out to a dying, despairing world with a cure for all its troubles, pleading with man, he sees us as involved in the process with him. And his appeal to us is, "Don't wait. Do it now."

12

Sensible Fanaticism

Scripture tells us that as the apostle Paul traveled about the Roman Empire, he was frequently accused of being crazy. People heard the testimony of his remarkable experience on the Damascus Road, they saw how his dedication to life took away from him comforts and pleasures, and they said he was crazy. In fact, one Roman governor, Porcius Festus, said to his face one day, "Paul, you are mad; your great learning is turning you mad" (Acts 26:24). But the apostle did not seem to mind. Perhaps he remembered the occasion when the mother and brothers of Jesus came to take the Lord home because, they said, "He is beside himself. He is crazy."

We seem generously supplied today with a wide variety of kooks, weirdos and oddballs—steely-eyed fanatics with long forefingers, full of passionate speeches. Since many of them claim to be Christians, it raises the question of whether the early Christians really were like that. Do you have to be a fanatic to be a Christian?

Let us listen to the apostle Paul's description of his own life, and see how he describes his dedicated life:

> We put no obstacle in any one's way, so that no fault may be found with our ministry, but as servants of God we commend ourselves in every way: through great endurance, in afflictions, hardships, calamities, beatings, imprisonments, tumults, labors, watching, hunger; by purity, knowledge, forbearance, kindness, the Holy Spirit, genuine love, truthful speech, and the power of God; with the weapons of righteousness for the right hand and for the left; in honor and dishonor, in ill repute and good repute.

> We are treated as impostors, and yet are true; as unknown, and yet well known; as dying, and behold we live; as punished, and yet not killed; as sorrowful, yet always rejoicing; as poor, yet making many rich; as having nothing, and yet possessing everything (2 Cor. 6:3–10).

Is that fanaticism? If it is, I feel like the great English preacher, Charles Haddon Spurgeon, who, when he was told that Paul's conversion on the Damascus Road was really caused by a fit of epilepsy, said, "Oh, blessed epilepsy! Would that every man in London could experience epilepsy like that!" So if this is fanaticism, then I say, would that every one of us were fanatics like this!

What a magnificent description of a God-honoring life! What a marvelous pattern is held before us in order that we might respond to Paul's plea seen in the last chapter, "receive not the grace of God in vain." The "ministry of reconciliation" will look like this when it is lived out to the fullest. You and I may fall far short of a description like this. I feel I do. But though we may not equal in degree the way the apostle lived, we are all called to be like this, in kind at least.

Careful Caring

Paul begins his description by showing us how careful his ministry is before men:

> We put no obstacle in any one's way, so that no fault may be found with our ministry (2 Cor. 6:3).

It is important to be aware of what we look like to others, that we are careful not to allow anything in our lives to turn someone away from Christ. Paul lived continually with that objective in view, so that he says, "no fault may be found with our ministry."

Now people did find fault with him, and plenty of it. As we learn in this very section, he was accused of being a deceiver, a phony, a false apostle, of being filled with ambition, pride, and sarcasm. He was accused of many things. But none of them stuck, because his own conscience cleared him. He knew in his heart that these were false accusations, that he had "put no obstacle in any one's way," lest they should be hindered in coming to Christ. As this great apostle traveled about he took care to see that no offense remained in his life that would hinder someone else.

One of the saddest things in our day is the prominent Christian leader who allows offensive obstacles to wreck his reputation as a Christian and cast doubt and scorn on the Lord himself. We hear about these prominent people, but we must remember that every one of us is in the exact same place. People who know we are Christians are looking at us all the time to see how we behave. Paul lived in continual awareness that he was being examined by men. Therefore, he was very careful to see there was no fault found in his ministry.

Approved by God in . . .

The second category is his sense of approval before God:

> but as servants of God we commend ourselves in every way: through great endurance (2 Cor. 6:4).

Endurance is the key here. God, looking upon Paul's life, is pleased and glorified by the fact that no matter what happens to him he sticks with it. He endures; that is the point.

This word literally means to "stay under the pressure." We all feel pressure—pressure to give in here, to give up there, pressure to go along with something. But the mark of a Christian who has learned how to walk with God is that he stays under the pressure; he does not quit. The modern term, "hang in there," expresses exactly what this verse means—"Just hang in there and don't quit until you are triumphant."

There were certain pressures Paul goes on to list here, in groups of threes, which consist of three categories. First, there were

. . . Tough Circumstances,

afflictions, hardships, calamities.

Afflictions are the normal problems all men face. The literal word is "distresses." What distresses you, makes you unhappy, and irritates you? Are you afflicted right now? Are you under some pressure of circumstances that you do not like? Paul is talking about financial problems, in-law problems, disappointment of some sort, the threat of physical illness, whatever.

Then there were hardships. That is a word that really means "necessities," things you cannot help, things you did not ask for but you cannot get away from. Do you have some of those? It may be that a loved one has taken ill and you are his only surviving relative. You have the responsibility to help and you do not like it because it undercuts all your plans with a necessity laid upon you. Sometimes the physical ailments and handicaps you have are such necessities. There is nothing you can do about them; you have to live with them.

Fanny Crosby, that marvelous writer of many of our hymns, lived to be 95 years old and was blind all her life, but what a cheerful spirit she had, reflected in her great hymns. When she was 8 years old, she wrote,

> Oh, what a happy child I am
> Although I cannot see,
> I am determined that in this world
> Contented I will be.
> How many blessings I enjoy
> That other people don't.
> To weep and sigh because I'm blind
> I cannot and I won't.

On her grave in Bridgeport, Connecticut, there is a simple headstone with the name "Aunt Fanny," and these words,

> Blessed assurance, Jesus is mine.
> Oh, what a foretaste of glory divine.

That is dealing with necessities in a cheerful spirit, and Paul had learned the skill.

Then he speaks of calamities. The word is "narrow spaces," where life presses in on you and you do not see any way out at all. But in all of these Paul says he hung in there and thus glorified God. He did not quit; he stayed with it; he endured.

Not only were there tough circumstances, but there were

. . . *Tough Opposition,*

beatings, imprisonments, tumults.

Later on in this letter he tells us of five occasions when he had been beaten with 39 stripes. So there were 195 stripes he had already felt. Three times he had been beaten with rods, sticks at least one inch or more thick, laid on his back. He had been stoned once in the city of Lystra and left for dead. All this he had already endured, but he had hung in there despite that. I feel inadequate when I read an account like this. I think one good whipping would wipe me out, but Paul had suffered many of these beatings.

Then there were imprisonments. According to Clement of Rome, who wrote just a few years after Paul died, Paul had been in prison seven different times in his life, although we only have three of those times recorded in the Scriptures. That is a hard thing for the spirit to bear—an active, vigorous man like this locked up and shut in. But it did not make him quit. He hung in there.

There were also tumults, mobs, Paul says. There is nothing more frightening than the feeling that you are about to be set upon by a mob. I have not been attacked by one, but I have been close to it at times. It is a frightening thing to feel that you are going to be attacked by overwhelming numbers and that no one can help you. Paul faced those situations.

. . . Tough Commitments

Then there were certain commitments that he had already undertaken. He calls them,

labors, watchings, hungers;

These are things he chose for himself. His work of preaching and of making tents at night so he could feed himself and those who were with him, often meant long nights of sleeplessness and missed meals because he was paying his expenses by his labors. He did not have to do this but he chose to because it was part of his deep drive of commitment to get the good news out. So in these three categories—tough circumstances, tough opposition, and tough commitments—he faced continual conditions of pressure.

Yet he never quit. This is the thing that challenges us in these easygoing days of ours. I find so many want to quit, to throw in the towel, to give up when God sends them into tough circumstances. But Paul did not. That is what was God-pleasing and God-honoring about his experiences. This is what made him "approved" by God.

To Manifest Character

Not only did he face these conditions, but in the midst of them there was a certain character that he displayed:

> by purity, knowledge, forbearance, kindness, the Holy Spirit, genuine love, truthful speech, and the power of God.

There are two divisions here, each containing four parts. The first four are consistent qualities of the apostle's life.

First, there was purity. Isn't it surprising that he puts this first? Yet it is pertinent to us, because Paul lived in days of widespread immorality, just like ours. He had to travel and live in the midst of a people given over to the pursuit of sexual immorality, yet he says he was careful to see that his mind and his thoughts were pure. It indicates that there was no giving way to hanky-panky whenever he went into a strange city by himself. He never said to himself, "Now's the chance to do some of the things I have been wanting to do but was afraid somebody might hear about." No, wherever he went he was guarded and kept by the conviction that he was related to and possessed by the Holy One. Therefore, he kept his mind pure and his thoughts correct and he judged the temptations to evil in his life.

The second quality was knowledge. That is very important. What enabled him, in a sense, to be pure was the fact that he constantly "renewed his mind," as he puts it in Romans 12. His mind was renewed by the Holy Spirit as he reminded himself of the way God looks at life.

How do you keep yourself pure and how do you face life as a Christian in this day and age? The only answer is that you deliberately remind yourself of what the Word of God teaches about life. You have to renew your mind every morning so that you look at yourself and life and those around you as God sees them. It is a deliberate effort not to drift along as the world does, reflecting all the attitudes of those around you. It is deliberately choosing to think rightly about life.

Then there was forbearance. That simply means longsuffering, patience, and particularly patience with other people. It is always interesting how people get to us, how hard it is to keep putting up with them, forgiving them, and ignoring some of their irritating ways.

I often think of that remark of Mel Trotter, the great evangelist, who used to say, "There are a lot of people I know who are wonderful Christians. I know they are going to go to heaven some day, and oh! how I wish they would hurry up!" Do you know people like that? Paul had to face them, too, and he had to learn to be patient with them. We all want to be patient, don't we? But we want it given to us right now, and that is what is difficult.

Then there is kindness. That means thoughtfulness, courtesy, warmth in our words and in our tone of voice—no coldness, no sharp, cutting sarcasm. These four things characterized the apostle: purity, knowledge, forbearance, kindness. Those are the qualities he worked at manifesting in his life.

The Resources to Rely On

Now in the next four Paul goes deeper, showing the resources he relied on in order to be like that. First in the list is the Holy Spirit.

When you became a Christian, God gave you the Holy Spirit to live in you, and he came to stay with you. In John 14 we are told that when the Spirit of truth comes he will "be with you forever." He will never leave you or forsake you. He is your constant companion through life, to be your helper, your strengthener, your comforter, your guide.

Paul relied on the Holy Spirit more than anything else. You cannot continually manifest this kind of a character unless you are resting upon that kind of a resource, and this is why he puts him first.

Linked to that is "genuine love." In an earlier passage Paul says, "the love of Christ constraineth us" (2 Cor. 5:14, KJV). Jesus was his resource, not only by the Holy Spirit, but also as Lord of Lords and King of Kings, as the One "who opens and no one shall shut, who shuts and no one opens" (Rev. 3:7), as the One who was the companion of the disciples through all the troubles and trials of their years with him.

He is with us, too. If you read the record of the great saints, they always proclaim that what held them steady and kept them under the pressure was the continual sense of companionship with the Lord Jesus and the love of Christ for them. This is what enabled them to reflect that same love to others.

The third resource, what is translated here as "truthful speech," really should be "the Word of truth," i.e., the Scriptures, the knowledge of how God sees life. You cannot live without studying your Bible. It tells you what the world is really like, what you are up against, and what you are facing in the pressures and dangers and joys around you. Paul spent a great deal of time absorbing the truth of the Scriptures.

Finally, there was the power of God. Even in the simple things he did, Paul saw that God was at work. God would make them have impact far beyond what could ordinarily be expected. This is always the secret of a God-honored life. It has tremendous power to change people, power coming from God working with us, resurrection power going beyond anything we can anticipate.

. . . *in Warfare*

The third area of his approval before God is the conflict that he wages:

> with the weapons of righteousness for the right hand and for the left; in honor and dishonor, in ill repute and good repute (2 Cor. 6:7, 8).

Later, in chapter 10, Paul will speak of these weapons of righteousness, saying they are not ordinary human plans and programs. He confronted the social injustices of his day as we must confront those of our own: racial strife, the drug traffic, the erosion of morals, the breakdown of the home, the rise of crime, the terrible danger from international warfare.

What must we do about these things? Paul says he came at them with "weapons of righteousness for the right hand and for the left." There is some disagreement as to what that means. While some commentators feel Paul is contrasting offensive (right hand) and defensive (left hand) warfare, I believe he is referring to our public conflict (the right hand) and the private conflict (the left).

Whatever its precise sense may have been, he was aware that he was in a sharp spiritual combat; and he did not employ ordinary pressure tactics and legislative corrections. Though these have their place, he used prayer, faith, love and righteous behavior as the weapons by which he attacked the problems around him. And he did it "in honor and dishonor," that is, whether he was popular or unpopular.

Paul says it does not make any difference. In all this he says his life is pleasing to God because it is by faith. He did not count on himself; he was not trying to make a big display before others; he had no personal ambitions. It was God at work in him.

Confounding the World

Then he closes with this wonderful series of contrasts. I do not even need to comment on them, they are so self-evident:

> We are treated as impostors, and yet are true.

Some were calling him a false apostle because he was not one of the twelve.

> as unknown, and yet well known;

Once there was a time when everybody had heard of Saul of Tarsus. He was an up-and-coming young Pharisee who was making a name for himself. But that is all gone now. Nobody ever hears of Paul the apostle. No television cameras follow him around; no reporters write up all his meetings. He is unknown, and yet known in heaven, known throughout the universe.

> as dying, and behold we live;

How many times people must have spread the word, "Well, poor Paul is gone. They killed him over there in Lystra." But to everybody's amazement he shows up again. He keeps returning, keeps reappearing on the scene despite all the dangers and trials he faced.

> as punished, and yet not killed;

That is a record of God's chastening upon him. There were times when, as a loving father, God chastened the apostle, as he chastens us. Yet Paul says, "He doesn't wipe me out. He loves me. Though I am chastened I am not eliminated."

> as sorrowful, yet always rejoicing; as poor, yet making many rich; as having nothing, and yet possessing everything (2 Cor. 6:8–10).

What a magnificent life! I know you feel, as I do, that we don't measure up too well in this regard. But the thing that glorifies God, whatever it is we are up against, no matter how tough it may be, is hanging in there, depending on him to see us through, to win the crown and win the prize. We are all in that race.

I want to close with these words from A. W. Tozer, that rugged old prophet from Chicago. He says:

> A real Christian is an odd number anyway. He feels supreme love for one whom he has never seen; talks familiarly every day to someone he cannot see; expects to go to heaven on the virtue of another; empties himself in order to be full; admits he is wrong so he can be declared right; goes down in order to get up; is strongest when he is weakest; richest when he is poorest; and happiest when he feels the worst. He dies so he can live; forsakes in order to have; gives away so he can keep; sees the invisible, hears the inaudible, and knows that which passes knowledge. The man who has met God is not looking for anything; he has found it. He is not searching for light, for upon him the light has already shined. His certainty may seem bigoted, but his assurance is that of one who knows by experience. His religion is not hearsay. He is not a copy, not a facsimile. He is an original from the hand of the Holy Spirit.*

That is the life that wins, the "ministry of reconciliation" in action. May God grant that we will see this as we are called to minister in this day and hour. There is no apostle Paul in the twentieth century. There is but you and me, and our lives lived out in these times. Yet the same witness and the same testimony is to be ours before a lost world.

---

* *That Incredible Christian* (Wheaton: Tyndale, 1978), p. 11.

13

Watch Out for These

One of the most abused verses in the whole New Testament is 2 Corinthians 6:17. Many people fear and avoid it; others use it as a kind of club to clobber anyone who violates any of the common taboos of fundamentalist Christianity:

> Therefore, come out from them, and be separate from them, says the Lord, and touch nothing unclean;

When I was a young Christian this verse was widely used by Christians to justify a kind of evangelical monasticism, a total isolation from the world. But it was so artificial and mechanical, the opposite occurred; a form of worldliness came into the church that poisoned its life and paralyzed its testimony. Much of the youth revolt a decade ago resulted from this sterility. But if we examine this verse in its context, such a distortion will be corrected.

Note especially the loving atmosphere in which this exhortation is set. This is part of Paul's description of what he has called the "ministry of reconciliation," the ministry that belongs to every single believer, without exception. We are all called to be "ambassadors for Christ," beseeching men to be reconciled unto God, reminding them that God is not imputing their trespasses against them. He is not angry with them because of their sins; he is beseeching them to turn to him that he might heal them and restore them in his love.

Paul described this ministry in the closing verses of chapter 5, illustrating it in a moving description of his own life. Now he confronts the obstacles that invariably defeat us if we are not careful to obey this injunction.

There are two of these obstacles in this passage, *restricted affections* and *defiling compromises.* Let us look first at this problem of

Restricted Affections

> Our mouth is open to you, Corinthians; our heart is wide. You are not restricted by us, but you are restricted in your own affections. In return—I speak as to children—widen your hearts also (2 Cor. 6:11).

Paul loved these people in Corinth, and he manifested that love in various ways toward them. He demonstrated it here by two special things. "Our mouth is open to you," he says. He communicated with them; he told them what was going on in his own life; he shared with them his feelings, his struggles, his failures, his pressures, his problems.

That is always a mark of love. To open up to someone is to love him. Contrariwise, to close up and not communicate is to violate love. As I travel around the country, I find this is probably the number one problem in churches today. Christians actually think it is right for them to be closed in on themselves, to be private persons, unwilling to communicate who they are and how they feel and where they are in their lives.

That, of course, is the way of the world. The world teaches us to be private, to let no one see who we are. But we need to understand that when we become Christians there is the one thing we must not do. We must learn to open up to one another.

That Paul loved these Corinthians is shown by the unmistakable marks of love: "our mouth is open . . . our heart is wide." The open mouth is a symbol of full communication. He has opened himself to them; he has hidden nothing. Now he wants them to love him back in the same way—not for his benefit but for theirs.

"Our heart is wide," he says. He means there is no favoritism; he included the whole congregation, not merely loving the nice people among them. He loved them all—the difficult ones, the ones who were struggling, the hard-to-get-along-with ones. He demanded that no one meet a certain qualification before he loved them. He accepted them as people. Though he knew their struggles, weaknesses, failures and resistance, still he loved them.

The problem was that they were not loving him in return. The problem in churches, families and marriages is the failure to understand the reciprocal nature of love. Love is a two-way street. It always is; it is inherently so. Love requires a response. Paul was loving them, but they were not loving him back. They were closed; they were unresponsive; they were coldly self-contained. And the result? Paul puts it in one word: they were "restricted."

They were limited, bound, tied up by themselves; they were imprisoned within the narrow boundaries of their own selfish lives. As a result, they could not experience the richness of life. Many individuals today are Christians, but their lives are cold and barren. They are lonely oftentimes. They are bored; they find life hardly worth the living. They have to struggle to get up in the mornings, to make themselves go on.

Why? Paul puts his finger right on the problem. It is not that they are not being loved. People reach out to them and try to touch them and help them, but they are not responding, and love that is not reciprocated is frozen dead in its tracks.

To be loved is to be given an opportunity to step into a new and wonderful and greater experience of life. When you love a child you free him. He relaxes, he begins to experience himself. We have all felt this. So, to be loved is to be given an opportunity to step into freedom, *if* you respond. The fulfillment of that opportunity depends on you. You are given the opportunity by the one who loves you, but you lay hold of it by loving him back.

That is why Paul pleads here with these Corinthians: "Oh! Corinthians, widen your hearts unto us. You are not restricted by us. You are restricted by yourselves, in your own affections. If you really want to experience the richness of love, then love back when you are loved."

This is one of the most important lessons we can ever learn in life. Love must respond. When you are loved what do you do? Do you love back or do you say, "Oh, what a wonderful feeling! I hope they will keep that up"? Do you expect it all to come to you without a reciprocal response from you? No, that is impossible. Love must respond.

C. S. Lewis had a wonderful comment, which is helpful at this point:

> To love at all is to be vulnerable. [That, of course, is what keeps us from loving back. We are afraid we are going to risk something, and we do. He goes on:] Love anything and your heart will continually be wrung, and possibly be broken. If you want to make sure of keeping it intact you must give your heart to no one, not even to an animal. Wrap it carefully

> around with hobbies and little luxuries; avoid all entanglements; lock it up safe in the casket or coffin of your own selfishness. But in that casket—safe, dark, motionless, airless—it will change. It will not be broken, it will become unbreakable, impenetrable, irredeemable. The only place outside heaven where you can be perfectly safe from all the dangers and perturbations of love is hell.*

People who do not learn to love back when they are loved, live in a little hell of their own making. So Paul ends with this loving, fatherly appeal: "In return—I speak as to children—widen your hearts also." If they begin to love back, that will enable them to share themselves, to open up, to communicate how they feel, to begin to respond with affection as well. They will begin to live.

In many congregations, Christians are cold, tied up in themselves. They sit in services and do not even speak to those around them. Sometimes this frigidity is even encouraged as a kind of reverence, supposedly, but God is not interested. He is interested in people who are open and responsive to one another.

This coldness is what turns young people off. They come to our services and the people are so cold and formal that they are repelled. When congregations learn to be open, responsive, warm, loving and reaching out it is always exciting. Young people are attracted to that and they will come.

It is a great feeling to be loved, and we want it to increase, but we ought to understand that it cannot increase until we respond. God loves us and is constantly displaying that love in a thousand and one ways, but we do not feel that love until we respond to what we already have. Until we begin to talk to him and tell him how we feel and express our gratitude and thanksgiving, we cannot grow and increase in his enriching love.

Do you see now why Jesus said, "The greatest commandment of all is 'Thou shalt love the Lord, Thy God, with all thy heart, and with all thy soul, and with all thy mind, and with all thy strength' "? God has already loved us and displayed it in providential care, supplying food and shelter and clothing and family concern and friends and all the richness of life. In our salvation he has provided the lifting of the awful sense of guilt and rejection and has exchanged a sense of worth for our feelings of unworthiness. He has given us a sense of belonging to a family, of having a purpose for life. He has given us a challenge, a new power and a new relationship. All those are gifts of

---

* *The Four Loves* (New York: Harcourt, Brace, Jovanovich, 1960).

love, and as we respond more and more we experience more of the same.

This is what concerns Paul here. So he urges the Corinthians, "Open up, communicate, show acceptance. It is basic to all else." That is problem number one. If you do not respond to love, then do not wonder if your life remains cold, barren, lonely, empty and meaningless. When you are loved, deliberately love back and life will begin to expand.

Defiling Compromises

Now Paul addresses the second great obstacle to the ministry of the reconciliation:

> Do not be mismated with unbelievers. For what partnership have righteousness and iniquity? Or what fellowship has light with darkness? What accord has Christ with Belial? Or what has a believer in common with an unbeliever? What agreement has the temple of God with idols? For we are the temple of the living God; as God said, "I will live in them and move among them, and I will be their God, and they shall be my people" (2 Cor. 6:14–16).

A defiling compromise is any involvement with an unbeliever that limits us and keeps us from being what we ought to be. Paul puts it here, "Do not be mismated with unbelievers." ("Mismated" is literally the term, "unequally yoked," as the King James Version puts it.)

Do you know what a yoke is? We are all familiar with the covered wagons of the last century in which our forefathers crossed the plains. Usually they were drawn by yokes of oxen. A yoke is a wooden frame or bar with loops at either end, fitted around the necks of two animals which tied them together and forced them to function as one. That is what Paul speaks of here. He is thinking of Deuteronomy 22, where the law says, "Do not yoke together an ox and an ass." That may seem strange to us, but God was concerned that they not tie together two animals of a different nature.

I have never seen an ox and an ass yoked together, but when I was traveling in the Middle East I once saw a farmer plowing his field with a camel and a donkey. It was almost ludicrous to watch. The camel was three times the height of the donkey, and his legs were three times as long. He was striding along at a rather slow pace, but the little donkey was running as fast as he could to keep up. The farmer kept beating him all the time trying to get him to keep up. It was cruel. Both animals were obviously miserable; they hated being tied together like that.

It is a cruel thing to yoke together two animals with incompatible natures. Paul is saying, of course, that certain associations Christians have with unbelievers constitute a yoke, and these associations are a sure cause for misery and shame in a Christian's life. We are to avoid them. They will hinder us, limit us, bind us and keep us from enjoying the fullness God has in mind for us. Like trying to mix oil and water, they are impossible.

First, he says, "What partnership have righteousness and iniquity?" Literally, the term is "lawlessness." What partnership can a right-loving person have with someone who does not care anything about rightness? What partnership can a heart that loves fairness and justice have with someone who cares nothing for truth, who refuses all authority and does what he pleases? That is a formula for certain heartache.

Then Paul says, "Or what friendship has light and darkness?" Those are the two most opposite things we know anything about. Christians are said to be light. Unbelievers are in darkness. It is not anything superior about the Christian that gives him light. It is simply the fact that he, as an unbeliever living in darkness, came to the light, and now he is "light in the Lord," as Paul puts it in Ephesians.

Light is always a symbol of understanding in Scripture, of an awareness of true reality. Now imagine someone who sees life clearly, who understands what is happening, joining himself or herself to someone who lives in ignorance of life, who lives in illusion, fantasy and blind selfishness? That is a formula for disaster, for much pain, suffering and heartache, isn't it?

Then the apostle goes further: "What accord has Christ with Belial?" Belial is another name for Satan, a word meaning "worthlessness," referring to Satan and his activities. What he does is always worthless, with no enduring value; it disappears; it is a froth, it is gone in an instant. Here then are the two great captains of the opposing philosophies of life, Jesus Christ and Satan or Belial.

I remember reading in the history of the Civil War several instances where brothers found themselves on opposite sides in the conflict. In every case they were fearful lest they should run into each other and be forced to face the possibility of having to kill each other. Similarly, a Christian joined in a yoke to a non-Christian lives in fear that some day their ultimate loyalties must clash headlong; sooner or later they are going to have to face a showdown in these areas.

Finally, Paul says, "What agreement has the temple of God with idols? For we are the temple of the living God; as God said, 'I will live in them and move among them, and I will be their God, and they shall be my people' " (2 Cor. 6:16). Some years ago a theological conflict came into prominence called, "The Death of God Movement." Certain theologians were teaching that God had actually died. But that movement did not last long. God had not died, of course; these men had simply lost his address. They did not realize that God lives in his people. The glory of Christianity is the revelation that our bodies are the temples of God, and since he lives in that temple, we are to be guided by his principles in worship and in service.

Imagine a person who, as the temple of God, is joined to another person who is the temple of an idol. If you do not worship the true God you worship a false god, and behind the false idols of any generation, Paul told us in 1 Corinthians, are demons. Therefore, you are trying to link together the worship of God and the worship of demons. But this is an absolutely impossible thing. That is why Christians everywhere are warned against certain associations, yokes.

The great unanswered question is, "What is a yoke?" Is a business partnership a yoke? Is union membership a yoke? Is marriage a yoke? Is a date with a non-Christian a yoke? We have to be careful here, because this verse has been pushed way too far in both directions. Some have taken it to justify a withdrawal from the world, from contact with non-Christians, building a wholly Christian life from the womb to the tomb without making any friends or even contacts with non-Christians.

That is a violation of other verses. Paul in this very letter has told us we are "ambassadors for Christ." We are to be in touch with the world. We are to be contacting them with friendship and openness and love so that they are ready to receive our word: "Be reconciled unto God." You cannot do that over a chasm. You have to move in close to people. It was Jesus himself who told us, "Behold, I send you forth as sheep in the midst of wolves" (Matt. 10:16). We are not to withdraw from the world.

A Yoke Is Permanent

What constitutes the yoke we are to avoid? Clearly, not all associations are yokes, but yokes have two characteristics by which we can always identify them. The first one is that a yoke is not easily broken. It is a kind of permanent relationship. When you yoke two animals together they are bound together; they do not have any choice. Uncomfortable as it may be, they must do things together.

The church has always taken this passage to refer to marriage in particular. Marriage is that kind of a yoke, a relationship which cannot be easily broken. The law, the state, society is involved in marriage. That "little piece of paper," spoken of so condescendingly today, rightfully introduces all the rights of society into a relationship between a man and a wife.

In 1 Corinthians 7 Paul tells us that marriage is to be "in the Lord" and warns against forming wrong marriage relationships with nonbelievers. Now he recognizes that some are already in that kind of relationship for one reason or another. If they are in it they are not to break it. A way of living with a "yoked" relationship, rises above it by faith so that the Christian can walk in godliness. But the wording of this verse here is "Stop forming yokes. Don't continue to enter into relationships like this." And marriage is clearly a permanent yoke that is not easily broken.

I know that it is easy to be drawn into these relationships. Often we are attracted to people as people, and we tend to discount the dangers and to feel that everything is going to work out all right. Because of love and feelings of affection, young people are especially tempted to enter into a yoke of marriage that is wrong. They sometimes rationalize themselves into it. But Paul is warning about something that is a deadly danger to faith.

Some years ago I read a prayer addressed to God that a young woman had written in her diary on her wedding day:

> Dear God, I can hardly believe that this is my wedding day. I know I haven't been able to spend much time with you lately with all the rush of getting ready for today, and I'm sorry. I guess, too, I feel a little guilty when I try to pray about all this, since Larry still isn't a Christian. But, oh! Father, I love him so much. What else can I do? I just couldn't give him up. Oh! You must save him some way, somehow. You know how much I have prayed for him and the way we've discussed the gospel together. I've tried not to appear too religious, I know, but that's because I didn't want to scare him off. Yet he isn't antagonistic, and I don't understand why he hasn't responded. Oh! If only he were a Christian. Dear Father, please bless our marriage. I don't want to disobey you, but I do love him, and I want to be his wife. So please be with us, and please don't spoil my wedding day.

It was a sincere prayer, but it was a sadly mistaken prayer. Though she did not realize it, what she was really praying was something like this:

> Dear Father, I don't want to disobey you, but I must have my own way at all costs. For I love what you do not love, and I want what you do

> not want. So please be a good God and deny yourself and move off your throne and let me take over. If you don't like this, all I ask is that you bite your lip and say nothing and don't spoil my wedding day. Let me have my evil.

That is really what she is praying, isn't it? And I am sure she went on to discover, as thousands and thousands of others have, the wisdom of the apostle's words here, "Stop being mismated with unbelievers."

A Yoke Constrains

Now the second mark of a yoke is that it constrains someone. Because it does not permit independent action, it forces you to comply with what the other person wants to do, whether you like it or not. Any kind of relationship that does not permit a believer to follow his Lord in all things is a yoke. Even a friendship can be a yoke. A possessive friendship in which you feel you cannot do what God wants you to do because you will offend your friend is a yoke—and it must be broken.

God must have first place. We are his temple and he longs to bless us, as these words go on to show us. Paul here gathers together a group of texts from various parts of Scripture and quotes them:

> Therefore come out from them,
> and be separated from them, says the Lord, (Isa. 52:11)
> and touch nothing unclean:
>
> then I will welcome you, (Ezek. 20:41)
> and I will be a father to you,
> and you shall be my sons and daughters,
> says the Lord Almighty (2 Sam. 7:14)

We are back again to this reciprocity of love. God's love is saying to us, "Look, I am here to enrich you. I want to make you my royal son and daughter. I want to be a Father to you, a tender, loving, careful, concerned, powerful Father to you, but I can't do it while you are still giving all your affection and all your ties to something else." Therefore, break the yoke, in order that you might experience the richness of God.

As we have already seen, to be enjoyed, love must be responded to, but you cannot respond if you are clinging to an association that is going in another direction. Though God's love is waiting to bless us, we cannot feel it and enjoy it until we turn from the yokes that bind us.

A Final Appeal

> Since we have these promises, beloved (Hear the endearment of that word. He is not speaking roughly, harshly, but in a loving exhortation), let us cleanse ourselves from every defilement of body and spirit, and make holiness perfect in the fear of God (2 Cor. 7:1).

Who is it up to? Cleanse *yourself.* God cannot do this. Love cannot constrain you to love back. It can only plead, beg and entreat. You have to make that decision; you must break that yoke. If you are tied with some friendship or relationship that is dragging you down, then you have to break that; you must decide to give it up. God will not take it away from you. You have to decide that, and if you do, you make holiness perfect.

Now do not misread the passage. Many people have. They think this means that if you turn away from all the unclean things in your life and give up the ugly, dirty things you may have stumbled into then you are making yourself holy. You never do that. Holiness is a gift God gives you right at the beginning of your Christian life. As Romans 12:1 tells us, "Present your bodies a living sacrifice, (already) holy, acceptable unto God" (KJV). God made it that way. You are not trying to be holy; you are holy, that is the point. But the holiness is perfected, it is made visible by acting like the one you have become, someone who is himself, herself, the dwelling place of God.

That is the appeal the apostle makes here. What a loving appeal it is, that we free ourselves from all these limiting, restricting, binding relationships to be the men and women God has called us to be. That is what this world is waiting to see.

14

How to Bring about Repentance

Everybody needs to repent. Whenever we hurt someone else, when we ourselves are hurt by our own actions, whenever we break a law, whenever we tell a lie, whenever we steal someone else's property or name, or whenever we smear some other person's reputation, we need to repent. Repentance means a change of mind, a change of attitude.

This section of 2 Corinthians, beginning with verse 2 of chapter 7, is a marvelous study on how to heal and restore instead of making things worse, as many of us do when we try to bring about repentance.

The opening paragraph gives the right approach, the right attitude, if you want to bring about repentance in another. Paul says:

> Open your hearts to us; we have wronged no one, we have corrupted no one, we have taken advantage of no one. I do not say this to condemn you, for I said before that you are in our hearts, to die together and to live together. I have great confidence in you; I have great pride in you; I am filled with comfort. With all our affliction, I am overjoyed (2 Cor. 7:2–4).

Notice the positive approach here. The apostle does not attack, does not condemn, does not accuse. As you know, this letter was written after the Corinthians had repented of a problem that Paul had been addressing for a long time. He himself had gone to Corinth to try to clear up the matter described in Corinthians, but had only made it worse, seemingly. Then he sent Titus there to help. While Titus was on his trip, Paul grew even more disturbed by the conditions in Corinth.

But now Titus has returned and has given him the good news that they have, indeed, changed their minds. There are still some things to work out, and Paul is writing now toward that end.

A Clear Conscience

Since these Corinthians had already repented, Paul traces the path they followed, involving three things. First, he himself has a clear conscience. He says,

> we have wronged no one, we have corrupted no one, we have taken advantage of no one.

Obviously he does not mean throughout his whole lifetime, because he had been a persecutor of the church and he had done a lot of wrong things. He means that as an apostle at Corinth he had not injured anyone or corrupted anyone or taken advantage of anyone. Undoubtedly some accusations were made about him in these regards. He is simply stating now that, as far as his conscience is concerned, he is blameless before the Lord: he has not done these things!

At times you or I cannot say that. Sometimes we have been wrong in a broken relationship we are trying to heal, so we cannot start out on that note. We have to start out by admitting that we were wrong. Jesus' words, "First take the log out of your own eye, and then you will see clearly to take the speck out of your brother's eye" (Matt. 7:5) makes this clear. Unless we start with a clear conscience there is no use trying to go on. But in this case Paul could say, "I did not hurt anybody while I was there." It is a wonderful claim on his part.

Without Condemnation

Then, second, he says,

> I do not say this to condemn you.

Oftentimes when we try to help somebody admit his wrong, we start out with a harsh condemnation. We rip into him, we let him have a piece of our mind. We are telling the truth, we say. Perhaps it is the truth, but it is the truth without love. There is no underlying reaffirmation of acceptance.

Paul is careful here to point out that he loves these people, regardless of how they behave. He says, "I said before that you are in our hearts, to die together and to live together. Live or die, I love you. I am going to be for you and behind you to support you. I am not going to abandon you or write you off, but I have some things to point out to you. They are not meant to wipe you out. I'm not condemning you."

In fact, he encourages them.

> I have great confidence in you; I have great pride in you; I am filled with comfort. With all our affliction, I am overjoyed.

What a marvelous note of encouragement! The matter is not fully settled yet—Paul has more to say later in the letter—but they have taken a step in the right direction, his pride in them is undiminished, his confidence in them is still strong and supportive, and he encourages them to go further.

When you must talk with someone about a wrong, begin with something right. Encourage him and affirm to him that you love him and that you are coming with that supportive purpose.

The apostle goes on to remind them how he shared their hurt; he identified with them:

> For even when we came into Macedonia, our bodies had no rest but were afflicted at every turn—fighting without and fear within. But God, who comforts the downcast, comforted us by the coming of Titus, and not only by his coming, but also by the comfort with which he was comforted in you, as he told us of your longing, your mourning, your zeal for me, so that I rejoiced still more (2 Cor. 7:5–7).

Here we have a flashback to our study of chapter 2, where we saw Paul so concerned for news from Corinth that he could not wait for Titus in Troas, but went to Macedonia to meet him. He finally ran into him there and learned the good news that things had worked out in Corinth.

We do not know exactly what Paul means when he says, "fighting without and fear within." Perhaps there was some difficulty in Macedonia. He had been imprisoned once in Philippi; perhaps enemies there were making it difficult for him. In any event he was distressed and anxious about Corinth, so there were "fighting without and fear within."

Comfort for the Downcast

"But God, who comforts the downcast, comforted us by the coming of Titus." The one thing that helps us bear these burdens, these pressures, is to remember that God knows about them. They are not accidents. He put us there and is carefully adjusting the water's temperature so that though we may be in hot water, it will never be too hot. This is his promise: "God is faithful, who will not suffer you to be tempted above that which you are able" (1 Cor. 10:13 KJV). Now do not misread that. It is not, "above that which you think you are able to bear." God knows how much we can bear better than we do. He is the God who comforts the discouraged.

Recently my wife had a burden of concern in prayer for a certain individual. She had been praying for him all week and the burden just seemed to get heavier, reaching the point where it seemed she could hardly bear it. Then the phone rang, and this man was calling to share an experience he had had with the Lord that encouraged her tremendously. Thus we saw again that God is the "God who comforts the discouraged, the downcast."

Now we come to the heart of repentance. Paul analyzes the actual process of bringing someone to repentance, beginning with loving confrontation:

> For even if I made you sorry with my letter, I do not regret it (though I did regret it), for I see that that letter grieved you, though only for awhile (2 Cor. 7:8).

Some scholars feel this "severe letter" is our 1 Corinthians. Others, including myself, think it is a letter that we no longer have. In any case it was a severe letter, containing some straightforward, faithful words to these people. He knew it would hurt them when he wrote it, and when he sent it he was distressed.

> For I wrote you out of much affliction and anguish of heart and with many tears, not to cause you pain but to let you know the abundant love that I have for you (2 Cor. 2:4).

What a loving admonition from so human an apostle! After he sent it he had second thoughts about having written it. He said, "I don't regret it now, but I did regret it. After I wrote it I wondered if I should have said it."

Have you ever felt that way? Have you ever mailed a letter like that? You knew it would cause pain and wondered if it was too much or could ever be repaired. Paul felt that way. He had second thoughts. He sometimes wished he had not written it, but sometimes he was glad he did. He knew it would hurt, but he knew that the grief and the hurt were necessary.

We do not show love to someone by withholding the truth. We often let people go on and on, saying we love them too much to hurt them, but few statements are more self-deceptive. It is true that we do not want to hurt someone, but that someone is usually us. We know that if we say these things to this individual he is going to get angry at us and this will hurt us. When we say, "Well, I just love him too much to hurt him," we are really kidding ourselves and saying we do not want to hurt ourselves.

When you love a person and tell him the truth in a loving, affirmative way, you help him see that you really love him. If you are willing to risk his friendship to tell him the truth, you must really love him. Usually that message comes through, though he may not admit it at first.

I can remember something I did as a freshman in college, a flamboyant, out-of-line action, simply trying to get some attention. Everybody either laughed or sneered at it, but one person loved me enough to come and tell me it was wrong. He took me aside and said, "What did you do a thing like that for? You knew it was wrong. I hate to see you act that way." That cemented a friendship that has continued to this day. I knew he loved me because he told me so, and I have had a high regard for him ever since.

So Paul faithfully confronts these people with what is wrong, and that is the beginning of repentance.

Now, Paul describes the next stage:

> As it is, I rejoice, not because you were grieved, but because you were grieved into repenting; for you felt a godly grief, so that you suffered no loss through us. For godly grief produces a repentance that leads to salvation and brings no regret, but worldly grief produces death (2 Cor. 7:9, 10).

Whenever somebody tells you the truth about yourself, it hurts. It can produce one of two reactions, either "godly grief," or "worldly grief." Grief is a word for "hurt" here. We all feel hurt, but is it godly hurt or is it worldly hurt? Here is the difference, as the apostle points out.

Godly Grief

Godly grief is the pain of suddenly becoming aware of something about yourself that has been hidden to you, creating in you a sense of anger, defensiveness, injury, and often tears. It is the moment of self-awareness, a "moment of truth."

Have you ever had that happen to you? You were tooling along, thinking you were doing OK, when someone came along and told you something about yourself. Even as he said it, there was a stab in your heart that said, "That's right, isn't it?" You may be defensive, you may argue, you may fight back, but deep inside you know that is true. It hurts, but if it is godly hurt it leads to repentance. It makes you change. You alter your behavior.

Jesus told a story about a man who had two sons. He said to the first one, "Go and work in the field." The boy answered, "I will not." But later he repented; he changed his mind and did go. Then the father said to the other son, "Go and work in the field." The boy said, "All right, sir, I'm going," but he did not go. Jesus asked the question, "Which of those two boys did the will of his father?" The answer, of course, is the first one (Matt. 21:28–31).

Repentance is thus an action that you take. Some people think that if you feel sorry for what you have done, this is repentance. No, it is not. The feeling sorry is the hurt, but if it is godly hurt it leads to a change of action, which is repentance. Repentance means to turn around. As Isaiah put it: "Let the wicked forsake his way, and the unrighteous man his thoughts; and let him return unto the Lord, and he will abundantly pardon" (Isa. 55:7).

This is repentance, or "salvation" as Paul calls it, and that, in turn, leads on to freedom. He is not talking about salvation from sin here because these people were already Christians. He is talking about salvation from self, the sense of freedom and deliverance.

I well remember many years ago as a young Christian having a great struggle with touchiness, sensitivity to people. I had such a poor self-image that I was dependent upon people's thoughts about me for good feelings about myself. Consequently, if they did not always say nice things and treat me well, I was very hurt and upset. You could send me into a morass of self-pity for days by merely making an offhand remark about me that cut me down.

One day I had my moment of truth. In a conversation about another matter, a Christian woman said something that struck like an arrow into my heart. She said, "I've learned that sensitivity is nothing but selfishness." I did not like that. I wrestled with it, did not want to admit it, but I knew it was true. I knew I really wanted to be the center of attention and have everybody watching out and ministering to me and taking care of me.

I had been hurt so much, so long, that I was fed up with it and I decided I would act on the basis of her insight. But it was one thing to say, another to actually do it when the moment came. Finally, after one of these hurts, I said at last, "That's not his fault. He didn't intend that. It is I who am feeling it. I'm taking it wrong." I did this a number of times, and after several such experiences I began to feel a marvelous freedom. The tiger was off my back, and I was free to enjoy things much more than I ever had before. I will never forget the sense of deliverance, of liberation that came when I acknowledged the truth that somebody had unwittingly said to me. Godly grief acknowledges truth, changes its behavior, and that in turn leads to a sense of freedom and deliverance.

Worldly Hurt

Worldly grief is quite different. Again, it starts with hurt, but it is a mixture of anger and self-pity. It makes you either want to run and hide and lick your wounds, or fight and strike back to get revenge. Someone told me of a married woman who was asked, "In your many years of marriage did you ever consider divorce?" "No," she said. "Homicide, perhaps, but never divorce." There are times when we all feel like this.

In fact, I believe that many of today's shocking news stories result from this process. Someone has been hurt by hearing the truth, bluntly or perhaps even lovingly spoken. He will not listen, he will not receive it, but retaliates with anger and revenge, even to the degree of killing children, wife, and himself. Confrontations in truth may produce such worldly hurt, even to the point of physical death. What a profound psychology is found in the Scriptures!

Worldly grief, of course, produces no repentance. There may be a temporary change until the tumult dies down, but no real change, no sense of being wrong, but rather a defensiveness that produces death. If it is not actual, physical death, it will at least be further bondage, further imprisonment to ourselves, further restriction.

Godly Eagerness

Paul now resumes his description of "godly grief" with further detail of its effects:

> For see what earnestness this godly grief has produced in you, what eagerness to clear yourselves, what indignation, what alarm, what longing, what zeal, what punishment! At every point you have proved yourselves guiltless in the matter (2 Cor. 7:11).

Here are clear-cut indications of whether your hurt is a godly or a worldly grief. How do you react? These Corinthians reacted first with a reversal of their behavior. How "earnestly," Paul says, they wanted to be free from guilt to face the whole problem in their lives; how "eager" they were to be completely clear to clean up all areas of wrong-doing.

When he says, "what eagerness to clear yourselves," he does not mean vindicate or justify themselves. He means they had an eagerness to get the whole thing out. Often when people are hurt like this, even though they may admit that they are wrong, their response, if it is worldly grief, is, "Well, let's drop the matter. I don't want to talk about it anymore. I've admitted it was wrong. Now let's forget it."

But not here. These people are saying to Paul, "Tell us the whole story. Is there anything you haven't mentioned? We want to be clear on this. We want the whole thing out."

Indignant toward Ignorance

Furthermore, they were angry at their own stupidity and failure. "What indignation," Paul says. They were upset that they had ever fallen into such tactics. In Psalm 73, the psalmist suddenly realizes that all his complaints before God are really a problem of his own blindness. He says,

> When my soul was embittered,
> when I was pricked in heart,
> I was stupid and ignorant,
> I was like a beast toward thee (Ps. 75:21, 22).

Have you ever felt that way toward God? We blame God and accuse him, but later we see the truth and we realize how foolish we have been. That is a mark of godly grief.

Vigilance toward the Future

The third mark is a carefulness for the future. "What alarm" that they will not do this again. "What longing," what a yearning to have their behavior right; and "what zeal" and what self-discipline (the actual sense of the word translated here is "punishment") is awakened here. How determined they are not to get into this kind of a state again. "At every point," he says, "you have proved yourselves guiltless in the matter."

In contrast, those who are suffering from worldly grief are unwilling to face the whole matter. They want you to "drop it," and if you do not forgive them immediately they get upset and angry. They say, "I confessed that. What's the matter? Why don't you forgive me?" They often end up putting the blame on other people. They say, "You made me do that. If you hadn't been like this, I would have behaved differently."

That betrays a worldly grief that has no repentance in it. In 1 John we read, "If we confess our sin . . . we have an advocate with the Father, Jesus Christ the righteous." When we stop justifying ourselves, he stands up and begins to justify us. But if we do not confess our sin, if we justify it, then we are left on our own before the One to whom all things are open and naked, and he sees us exactly as we are.

Renewed Identity

The final section here describes the joy of recovery, the final product when godly grief has led to repentance, and hurt has accomplished something with us.

> So although I wrote to you, it was not on account of the one who did the wrong, nor on account of the one who suffered the wrong, but in order that your zeal for us might be revealed to you in the sight of God. Therefore we are comforted (2 Cor. 7:12–13).

That may be a little difficult to understand, but what he is saying is, "The real reason I wrote was not to straighten out this problem so much as to instruct." He is implying, "The reason you let this matter go unjudged in your midst was because you forgot who you were. You forgot that you are sons of God, children of light, that you have understanding of life that others do not have; and that you have power to act that others do not possess."

"I wrote to you to show you who you are; basic to your heart, is an obedience of commitment to the Lord himself. I knew when you saw that again your whole behavior would change. That has happened, I rejoice, therefore, I am comforted," Paul says.

So that is the first thing. They began to recover a sense of their own identity, and Paul helped them to recover that.

Confidence Vindicated

> And besides our own comfort we rejoiced still more at the joy of Titus, because his mind has been set at rest by you all. For if I have expressed to him some pride in you, I was not put to shame; but just as everything we said to you was true, so our boasting before Titus has proved true (2 Cor. 7:13, 14).

Secondly, all Paul had felt about them and had even said about them to Titus was vindicated by their action. The joyful thing about repentance is it enables people to have confidence again in what they had always felt about you. When you treat repentance in this godly, scriptural way, it renews that sense of confidence—not only in Paul, but also in Titus. This is the third point: it awakens the respect of others, for he says,

> And his heart goes out all the more to you, as he remembers the obedience of you all, and the fear and trembling with which you received him (2 Cor. 7:15).

Titus was impressed by the Corinthians in their repentance. Their blindness did not impress him, but their change of heart did.

A few weeks ago I happened to be with a group of men, discussing some very significant matters involving human relationships. I became aware that one of those men was judging another from a spirit of self-righteousness, not facing the possibility of his own involvement in the same kind of sin, but being harsh and somewhat condemnatory.

In the midst of that group, as delicately as I could, as lovingly as I could, I nevertheless pointed out to him what I felt was behind his harsh accusation. I could see the hurt it caused. His face blanched, he became silent, and he did not say anything for a little while. After a bit he interrupted, looked me right in the eye, and said, "Ray, I want to thank you for those personal remarks you made to me. You were right."

My esteem for that man went up like a skyrocket. I had always admired him and felt him to be a godly man, but I was tremendously impressed with the godliness of a man who in those circumstances could openly and publicly say, "Yes, you're right. I had a wrong attitude."

When we handle a "moment of truth" in a godly way—without fighting back, getting angry, defensive—when we acknowledge it and change our behavior, respect increases on every side.

Joy Abounding

Paul closes this account with the fourth thing: increased joy.

> I rejoice because I have perfect confidence in you.

The end of all God's dealings with us is that it increases our joy, it increases everybody's joy. That is the purpose for which the Spirit of God is at work in these kinds of matters.

15

Guidelines on Giving

Chapters 8 and 9 of 2 Corinthians are all about Christian giving—not tight-fisted, miserly, grudging giving, or wild, spendthrift, careless giving, but true, generous, abundant giving—what Paul calls "hilarious" giving. The amazing thing is that Paul does this all in two chapters without once mentioning money! So we are not going to talk about money, but giving.

He begins chapter 8 with an example of giving encountered when he was in Macedonia:

> We want you to know, brethren, about the grace of God which has been shown in the churches of Macedonia, for in a severe test of affliction, their endurance of joy and their extreme poverty have overflowed in a wealth of liberality on their part. For they gave according to their means, as I can testify, and beyond their means, of their own free will, begging us earnestly for the favor of taking part in the relief of the saints—and this, not as we expected, but first they gave themselves to the Lord and to us by the will of God (2 Cor. 8:1–5).

A great famine struck the land of Palestine (reported also in 1 Corinthians), and many people were deprived of their livelihood. A great drought, much as we had in California a few years ago, produced the famine, and many of the Jerusalem Christians suffered prolonged hunger.

When word of this came to Paul, he sought the aid of all the Gentile churches for the relief of the Jewish Christians. He thought it a marvelous way to express oneness in the body of Christ, breaking down the wall between the Jews and the Gentiles, so wherever he went he told about the need in Jerusalem. When he mentioned it to these Macedonian churches (the churches of Philipi and Thessalonica and Berea), the response was tremendous, and he was greatly encouraged, as he tells the Corinthians.

In this Macedonian response we have a wonderful example of the true way to give. I am delighted that we have these two chapters because I find that most Christians today, and I mean *most,* do not understand how to give properly. Many are giving for wrong reasons, giving in wrong ways, or are not giving at all; we desperately need some teaching in this area, and the apostle himself will instruct us here.

The first note the apostle strikes is that true giving always originates with the grace of God:

> We want you to know, brethren, about the grace of God which has been shown in the churches of Macedonia (2 Cor. 8:1).

The only true motive for giving is the grace of God, the goodness of God to you. If God has not done anything for you, then, for goodness' sake, do not give him a dime. But if he has, then pour it out according to the measure you have received. That is always the argument of Scripture.

In the New Testament giving is never legislated upon us. It is not laid on us as a duty that we have to do in order to pay expenses in the church. It is given to us, rather, as a privilege to express the gratitude of our hearts for the grace that God has already given.

Wrong Motives

There are many reasons why people give. Some people give as a tax write-off so that they will not have to give it to the government, but if that is your only motive for giving it is not a proper one. A tax write-off is just not enough, because it is not going to help you any. Giving is not something you do for others so much as it is something you do for yourself. Giving has a tremendous effect upon your own life. A tax write-off does not accomplish that.

Some people give to gain a reputation for giving. It is striking that the very first death recorded in the church occurred when a couple, Ananias and Sapphira, decided they would gain a reputation for giving even though they did not deserve it. In Acts 5 we read that other people were giving property to the church, and this couple thought they would get in on the honor given those who gave generously, so they gave some property. But they pretended that they gave all of it when they really did not. When the Holy Spirit dealt with that hypocritical kind of giving he dealt with it very severely.

God is very concerned about motives. I know some people who have given because they were afraid of dying and they wanted to earn favor with God. I have known men to give hundreds of thousands of dollars because they felt it would help them in their standing before God at the judgment seat. But they were not giving to help the cause of God. They had no more use for the work of God than a hog has for hip pockets. They gave to gain a reputation for giving. All these are wrong motives.

Right Motives

These Macedonians gave because their hearts were moved by the grace of God. They ignored all the possible excuses for not giving. They were suffering "a severe test of affliction," i.e. they were being persecuted. That could have made them hang onto their property or money, because they did not know what they might need.

At the same time they were suffering "extreme poverty," possibly because of the persecution. What an excuse they would have had to say to Paul, "Don't talk to us about the saints in Jerusalem. We are about to starve to death ourselves. We can't send anything." But they had been touched by the grace of God. Paul says that their severe test of affliction and their extreme poverty, instead of being a cause for not giving, actually became an additional cause for giving. They understood what people feel like who are going through severe poverty.

They had been so blessed that they wanted to give and give abundantly. They not only gave "according to their means," they gave "beyond their means." I heard of a man who was asked to give to an offering and he said, "Well, I think I could give $10 and not feel it." The usher said, "Why don't you give $20 and feel it?" It is only when you feel it that the blessing of giving comes.

The Macedonians gave beyond their means. They dug deep, and they asked for the privilege of doing so. That is the amazing example here. Evidently Paul was reluctant to tell them about this need in Jerusalem because he did not think they could respond. But when they heard about it they asked him if he would not let them take up a collection to give to the needy people in Jerusalem.

Privileged Giving

One of the surest marks that a heart has truly been touched by the grace of God is this: it counts giving as a privilege. We had a woman in our church for many years who loved to give. She used to come to me and give me a check every now and then—sometimes a large check. Tears would come to her eyes as she would hand it to me, and she would say, "Oh, Mr. Stedman, I was 62 years old before I ever understood the grace of the Lord Jesus, even though I had been a church member all my life. I count it a great privilege to give in his name." And she meant every word of it.

That was the way the Macedonians acted. They asked for the privilege of giving. And they had the right priority in doing so. Paul says, "They first gave themselves to the Lord." That is a tremendous key to a giving heart. How you think about your possessions is very revealing. These Macedonians understood that everything they had belonged to God. They first gave themselves—and when you give yourself you have given everything you have as well.

Have you ever noticed that there is no tithe laid upon Christians in the New Testament? Never once in the epistles do you ever read of Christians being asked to tithe. Many Christians today are taught to tithe, but I am always sorry to hear it, because that is not New Testament teaching.

The tithe was a tax levied upon people for the purpose of supporting a priesthood, a separate body of people who did religious things. When you come into the New Testament you find the priesthood has, in a sense, been eliminated. Now, every Christian is a priest. We are a royal kingdom of priests, the epistles tell us, and there is no special collection or tax to support it.

God's Percentage

It is laid upon us to give voluntarily, as our hearts are stirred and moved by the grace of God, as these Macedonians did. They understood that once you have given yourself it is easy to give anything else. That is the key.

The proper Christian attitude toward possessions is reflected in William W. How's familiar hymn:

> We give Thee but Thine own,
> What e'er the gift may be:
> All that we have is Thine alone,
> A trust, O Lord, from Thee.

You do not take 10 percent and give it to the Lord and the 90 percent remains yours. That is not Christian giving. One hundred percent of it belongs to God. The true Christian attitude is, "It is all yours, Lord. You do what you want with it. Whatever you tell me to do with it, I'll do, because it belongs to you, not to me. I am merely a steward, a trustee of it, responsible to distribute it for your name's sake." That is what these Macedonians had seen, and having given themselves, they freely followed up with everything they had.

This is also Jesus' teaching. Once he was asked whether people should pay taxes or not. He asked for a coin, and, holding it up, he said, "Whose image is on this coin?" They answered, "Caesar's." Jesus' words in answer have never been forgotten: "Give to Caesar the things that have Caesar's picture on them, but give to God the things that have the image of God upon them."

Who bears the image of God? You do, don't you? You are made in his image; you bear the imprint of his image. Give yourself to God then. That is what he wants. When you give that, everything else will follow. You will hold things in trust to be used whenever he lets you know that a need exists for them. That is proper Christian giving.

So these Macedonians became a model for other churches, Paul goes on to say,

> Accordingly we have urged Titus that as he has already made a beginning, he should also complete among you this gracious work. Now as you (Corinthians) excel in everything—in faith, in utterance, in knowledge, in all earnestness, and in your love for us—see that you excel in this gracious work also. I say this not as a command, but to prove by the earnestness of others that your love also is genuine (2 Cor. 8:6–8).

Notice how carefully Paul avoids pressure. He does not say they have to give and lay a guilt trip on them. He does not say, "Now see if you can't outdo the Macedonians. We are going to have two thermometers set up when I get to Corinth. One will show what the Macedonians gave and the other will show what you give, and you had better try to do at least as well as they did." No, "I don't say this as a command," he says. His argument is this, "The Macedonians gave because their love was genuine. They were moved by the grace of God. If you give on that basis, you too can demonstrate that your love is as genuine as theirs." Without pressure, he exhorts them to consider what giving is—a manifestation of a heart that has been touched by the love and grace of God.

The Greatest Giver

That, of course, leads to the highest example of all, the supreme example of giving, the giving of Jesus:

> For you know the grace of our Lord Jesus Christ, that though he was rich, yet for your sake he became poor, so that by his poverty you might become rich (2 Cor. 8:9).

This little gem of a verse defies exposition. It states the case so perfectly. Once again grace is at the heart of giving: "You know the grace of our Lord Jesus Christ." We sing William R. Newell's hymn,

> Oh, the love that drew salvation's plan,
> Oh, the grace that brought it down to man.
> Oh, the mighty gulf that God did span,
> At Calvary.

That is Paul's supreme example of what it means to give.

There was a time when Jesus was rich. You can search the gospels but you will not find it there. He was not rich on earth, though he sometimes stayed with rich people. He had friends and neighbors who were rich; some who followed him were rich, but he himself had nothing at all.

But once he was rich, according to this verse. When was that? Do you remember in the Upper Room discourse, in the prayer of Jesus recorded in John 17, he prays to the Father and says, "Glorify me with the glory which I had with you before the world was"?

Jesus knew there was a time when he was rich, when everything in the universe belonged to him. All the hosts of heaven bowed down in continuous worship of his name, and hundreds of thousands were ready to run at his bidding. He owned it all, everything was his, but he gave it up voluntarily, he deliberately impoverished himself. As Paul put it in Philippians, "he humbled himself," and he became a man, just a poor man.

The Poorest Man

Remember how he constantly borrowed everything? We may reverently say that he was the greatest scrounger of history. He was always borrowing. He had nothing of his own. He borrowed food, he borrowed clothing, he borrowed a coin to give an illustration, a donkey to enter into the city of Jerusalem, and he finally had to borrow a tomb in which to be laid. On one occasion the disciples all went to their own homes, but he went to the Mount of Olives. He had no home to go to, no place to lay his head. Isn't that amazing?

Why did he become poor? Paul reminds us that it is in order that we might be rich. Have you been thinking about how rich the Lord has made you? Just the other day, in the midst of all the tumult that we see reported on the international scene, I was thinking how terrible it would be to have to live today without the Lord.

Would you like to do that, now that you have known him? Would you like to give up all the joy, all the peace, all the sense of forgiveness, all the lifting of the load of guilt, to give up the sense of his presence? Would you to like to give up the source of power available to you for whatever you need to do, of a continual supply of joy and gladness and restoration: all that enriching of your life?

Not long ago I watched on television a tribute to a popular entertainer, one of the wealthiest men of our generation and an idol of millions all over the world. As I watched, I said to myself, "I wouldn't trade places with that man for a thousand tributes like that." He is poverty-stricken and he is heading to utter poverty, while I have nothing but increasing joy and riches awaiting me. I would not trade, would you?

How rich Jesus has made us. He became poor that we might be rich. When you think about that, how wrong it seems to withhold our gifts from those who are in need around us. How can we clutch our affluence to ourselves when our brothers and sisters are in need?

Years ago, our church began to publish a "Need Sheet" page in our Sunday bulletin. I commend this idea to you highly. A random sample shows we need not to go to Jerusalem to find needy saints! "Foster home desperately needed for 14-year-old boy." Here is a chance to change the life of a young adolescent boy forever. "Seeking someone to care for 4-year-old boy on Thursday evenings from 7–9:00 while mother attends a much-needed Bible study. Can't afford to pay." This is a need a desperate young mother has. Surely our hearts ought to respond to needs like that. "Needed: a ride on Monday, Wednesday, and Thursday to Medical Center. I am spending four hours a day on buses." Whatever we can do to meet these needs is what manifests a heart that has been touched by the grace of God.

The apostle now turns to practical matters at Corinth and instructs these Corinthians to just what God expects of an awakened heart. In this passage we have some wonderful principles of giving:

> And in this matter I give my advice: it is best for you now to complete what a year ago you began not only to do but to desire so that your

> readiness in desiring it may be matched by your completing it out of what you have. For if the readiness is there, it is acceptable according to what a man has, not according to what he has not (2 Cor. 8:10–12).

Evidently, when Titus first visited Corinth he announced the needs of Jerusalem saints. Many had promised to give to that need, but no collection was actually taken. Now, a year later, Paul is reminding them of their commitment.

There is a hint here that some Corinthians were indicating a present inability to give the amount they had promised before. They were now waiting until they got it all together before they gave it. (They may have been troubled by the law, which demanded that if you vow something to God you must pay it. The law warns that if you make a vow to God, do not ignore it because he heard that vow and he expects you to fulfill it.)

But Paul says, "Don't delay. Give what you can, for (as he puts it in verse 12) if the readiness is there, it is acceptable according to what a man has, not according to what he has not. So when the need exists, give what you can. If it is not as much as you said you would give, God understands. He knows your heart and he is not requiring what you do not have. He delights in one who gives all that he can."

Later on he will say, "God loves a cheerful giver." He means God loves one who feels that whatever the gift can do is far more important than the value of the gift. A great principle of giving is: according to what you have. Do not worry if it is not as much as you would like it to be or even as much as you said it would be.

Real Equality

The next section introduces another important principle, one often severely misinterpreted:

> I do not mean that others should be eased and you burdened, but that as a matter of equality your abundance at the present time should supply their want, so that their abundance may supply your want, that there may be equality. As it is written, "He who gathered much had nothing over, and he who gathered little had no lack" (2 Cor. 8:13–15).

Some have taken the word "equality" here as a call for Christian socialism, some system devised to redistribute wealth so that everyone has an "equality," everyone has the same amount.

But that is misreading the passage completely. Paul is not arguing for an equality of *amount.* He is arguing for an equality of *response:*

"Now is your time to give because it may turn out very shortly that you may lose all you have and then it will be your turn to receive."

He is not saying, I want you to work so the other guy can play. "I do not mean that others should be eased and you burdened." Nor does he mean, "I want you to give to me, and I (like the government) will take 80 percent of it for my expenses and deliver 20 percent of it to Jerusalem." As far as Paul was concerned the whole amount was going to go to Jerusalem.

What he is saying is, "Now it turns out that you have more than you need and they have less, so that you might give to those who have less." He supports that with this quotation from the Book of Exodus: "It is written, 'He who gathered much had nothing over, and he who gathered little had no lack' " (16:18).

The quote refers to the story of the manna falling in the wilderness to feed this great crowd of almost 2,000,000 people. (They did not know what it was so they called it "manna," which means "What is it?" Can you imagine eating "What is it?" for forty years?) When they went out to gather it, some were able to gather more than others. Perhaps they had larger pots or they worked faster; for various reasons some gathered much and some gathered little.

But, according to the story of Exodus, an amazing thing happened. When they got it all together in the camp and started dishing it out, those who had more than they needed gave to those who had less so that it came out exactly even; everybody had exactly what he needed. Paul holds that up as a parable. He says, "That's what God intends. God is behind what you have."

I hear people boasting about how they are self-made men, taking credit for the fact that they have so much because they were careful, or very astute in their investments. Such statements have only a limited validity, because you and I know people who do not have any wisdom at all, who are very careless, yet they have all they can spend and a lot more besides.

Why are there inequalities in possessions? The answer is, God does it. God gives to some more than they need in order that they might have the joy of giving to somebody who has less. Perhaps on another occasion he will take it all away from them so that they can know what it feels like to receive as well. God determines it all.

Dr. Donald Grey Barnhouse, the great Bible expositor, for years was pastor of the Tenth Presbyterian Church in Philadelphia. He used to have a kind of a forum after the message on Sunday mornings, when people could ask him questions. In one of these question hours one rather skeptical person said, "Dr. Barnhouse, what explanation do you give for the fact that almost 2,000,000 people could live in a total desert for forty years? How do you explain that kind of a thing?" Dr. Barnhouse answered with one word, "God! Next question, please."

Yes, God. God gives you what you have. God gave you the opportunity to make money. You did not achieve that by your own smartness. There are people ten times smarter than you who have tried very hard but they could not put it together. God gives these opportunities in order that we might learn the joy of sharing with those who have needs around us. Paul brings these Corinthian Christians to a recognition of that.

> For you know the grace of our Lord Jesus Christ, that though he was rich, yet for your sake he became poor, so that by his poverty you might become rich (2 Cor. 8:9).

16

Giving Joyfully

We have examined great examples of giving in chapter 8 of 2 Corinthians. Poverty-stricken Macedonians gave beyond their means, out of their deep, desperate poverty. Then there was the incredibly rich giving of Jesus, who gave up everything and became poor that we might be rendered incredibly rich. What wonderful examples of giving from two ends of the scale—from the poor who had nothing to give and yet gave, and from the very richest of all who gave all he had that we might be rich.

Then we began to look at some of the principles of giving that guide us. I do not know any area of the church life more in need of teaching than this. The three biggest religious broadcasters of this country receive more than $163,000,000 in contributions every year. The combined amount of Christian giving in the United States alone has been estimated at well over a half billion dollars a year.

That is a lot of money, and yet much of it is wasted. Much is given to causes that ought not to be supported, or given in ways that are foolish and spendthrift. Much of it goes to line people's pockets, to be used for the enrichment of a few and the exploitation of many. We desperately need to be helped in our giving, learning to give responsibly with intelligence and care, so that the money goes to the right purposes and is used in the right way.

Now not all of this money is wasted, by any means; giving is certainly a very right and proper Christian exercise. But the very purpose of these chapters of 2 Corinthians is to help us in our understanding of how to give. In the preceding chapter, we looked at some of the principles, God's principles for correct giving. We saw, first, that our motive is more important than the amount. God is interested less in how much you give, more in why you give. He reads the heart. A number of passages from the Lord himself underscore this. In one, he talked about the widow who cast two mites into the treasury. That was all she had, and she gave it all. Jesus, observing her, said, "She has given more than all the rest combined." Her gift was more useful to God and more delightful to him than all the rest that was given. So it is not the amount that is important, it is the heart. As Paul puts it here, if there is a "readiness" to give, "it is acceptable according to what a man has, not according to what he has not." God sees, not the amount of your income tax deduction, but why you gave that money.

Equal in Response

Secondly, our opportunities to give are arranged by God. God gives more to some and less to others in order that those who have more might give to those who have less. It is not that we might spend it on our own self-indulgence, or that we might have an increasingly higher standard of living than others. This does not mean, as we saw in the last chapter, that we are to all seek the same level of living. That is never taught in Scripture. But we are taught that God does give to some certain excess. The reason is that they might give to others. That can be reversed, too. What you have now in excess can all be taken away; overnight it can disappear, and you may be the one who needs to be given to. God himself determines that. Paul illustrated this truth by the manna in the wilderness all of which came from God. Those who gathered much were expected to give to those who had less, so that there might be an equality of response.

Not in One Hand

Now we come to the third principle concerning responsibility in our giving:

> But thanks be to God who puts the same earnest care for you into the heart of Titus. For he not only accepted our appeal, but being himself very earnest he is going to you of his own accord. With him we are sending the brother who is famous among all the churches for his preaching of the gospel; and not only that, but he has been appointed by the churches

> to travel with us in this gracious work which we are carrying on, for the glory of the Lord and to show our good will (2 Cor. 8:16–19).

(We skip over the next two verses, 20 and 21, for a moment. We will return to them after understanding a third principle involved in the kind of men he is sending to Corinth.)

> And with them we are sending our brother whom we have often tested and found earnest in many matters, but who is now more earnest than ever because of his great confidence in you. As for Titus, he is my partner and fellow worker in your service; and as for our brethren, they are messengers of the churches (*literally, apostles of the churches*), the glory of Christ. So give proof, before the churches, of your love and of our boasting about you to these men (2 Cor. 8:22–24).

The third principle of giving requires that the conveyance of a certain amount of money be vested in several individuals, not in merely one. Paul clearly urges the churches to appoint other men to go with Titus to Corinth to take up this collection for the famine-stricken Jerusalem saints. He is careful to see that the control of this fund not be placed in any single hand.

And not just anyone was appointed. These were men who were tested and proven, men of responsibility the churches themselves had selected because they were trustworthy.

There were three of them. Titus we know already. He has been prominent in this letter. He is the one who went down to Corinth and brought word back to Paul. He travels back and forth as a courier and as an associate of the apostle, and now he has been asked to go back again and take up this collection before Paul arrives. And "with him," Paul says, "we are sending the brother who is famous among all the churches for his preaching of the gospel." From these clues, most of the scholars have deduced that this is probably our old friend, Dr. Luke, the beloved physician, a traveling companion of the apostle's. Since we have "The Gospel according to Luke," it seems likely that he was known for his preaching of the gospel. With them was another brother, whose name is not given to us, whom Paul identifies as "our brother whom we have often tested and found earnest in many matters, but who is now more earnest than ever because of his great confidence in you."

We cannot be certain of this man's identity. Frankly, I think Paul, who is probably about sixty years old, is suffering one of the problems common to all of us who have been young for a long time: a lapse of memory! He cannot think of the brother's name. Paul is dictating this letter, and he cannot quite get it out: "What is that fellow's name?" So he describes him: "He's the one whom we've proven and tested." The Corinthians, of course, will know him when he arrives. So we will just call him, "Old What's-his-name." Titus, Luke, and What's-his-name went down to Corinth to be welcomed because they were trustworthy and responsible men. So Paul is careful to see that this responsibility is shared among several.

Actual Accountability

Let us now come back to the verses we skipped:

> We intend that no one should blame us about this liberal gift which we are administering, for we aim at what is honorable not only in the Lord's sight but also in the sight of men (2 Cor. 8:20, 21).

What a tremendous thing to say, and how different from what we often hear today. In these days, if someone responsible for funds is asked for an accounting, he says, "What's the matter? Don't you trust me?" Then it is very difficult to examine accounts because it appears you are questioning his integrity. But Paul would never allow himself to get into that situation. He says, "We know in our own hearts that we are doing right, but that's not enough. It must be obvious to everybody that we are doing right. It must also be open in the sight of men."

When I was a young Christian I was a member of a church where the pastor took all the offerings, depositing them in an account under his name. He even owned the church building. It was not surprising, though it was grievous to me as a young Christian, that after a couple of years of operation he became suspect in his handling of funds. It became apparent that he was appropriating a great deal for his own personal use. Eventually it split the church, and the congregation went several ways because of his failure to handle responsibly the money that the people of God gave. Now this is an important principle.

Paul is careful to arrange that control is shared to avoid any criticism. This helpful guideline shows us how and where we are to give our money. Personally, I would never give to a Christian organization that is headed by a single individual, no matter how responsible he may seem to be. It is just not wise to trust an individual with the administration of sums of money. We ought to check that our giving is to organizations and individuals who are responsible to a group of men, a board. Most Christian organizations do provide a board. But we should also take care that such boards are not "padded" with several members of the same family. It is a common thing in Christian service to have a family group constitute the board—the man who started it, his wife, and several of his children, perhaps. But that is no different from giving to the individual himself, and it is not a responsible handling of funds. Paul would never have allowed it. These three men were not related to him. In fact, he did not even choose the majority. He sent Titus, but the other two were chosen by the churches; he had nothing to do with who they were.

I personally think it is a good idea to give only to those groups which are willing to publish an audit or make known in some way how they handled their money. One of the practices that has kept the Billy Graham Crusades' money from being mishandled and misused through these thirty years has been the publishing of a full newspaper page in every crusade city, giving an accounting of their funds. That has helped relieve the normal tendency of many to feel that funds have been misused.

Furthermore, in this regard, it is an excellent practice to require two signatures on every check disbursed from Christian funds. We do that at Peninsula Bible Church. From time to time, someone may suggest this is awkward, forcing a check writer to run around to find a co-signer. But it is impossible in this church for any one person to write a check to his own name without somebody knowing about it, and it is well to preserve that protection.

We need to be very careful about our giving. Money is given to us as a trust from God. We are responsible to see that it is handled rightly, not committing it to anyone who might use it in ways we have no knowledge of and for which we have no accounting.

Not from Pressure

Now the apostle goes on and points out another reason for sending these brothers:

> Now it is superfluous for me to write to you about the offering for the saints, for I know your readiness, of which I boast about you to the people of Macedonia, saying that Achaia (*that is Greece, where Corinth was capital*) has been ready since last year; and your zeal has stirred up most of them. But I am sending the brethren so that our boasting about you may not prove vain in this case, so that you may be ready, as I said you would be; lest if some Macedonians come with me and find that you are not ready,

> we be humiliated—to say nothing of you—for being so confident. So I thought it necessary to urge the brethren to go on to you before me, and arrange in advance for this gift you have promised, so that it may be ready not as an exaction but as a willing gift (2 Cor. 9:1–5).

There is another very important principle in giving. Giving must not come from pressure. Paul says, "I sent these brothers to you so that you would not be embarrassed if, at the last minute, obstacles had interrupted your collection. I sent them so that the whole matter can be taken care of before I come."

Secondly, as we have seen in Corinthians, "I want it done before I come because I don't want my presence to be the reason why you give." What a contrast to many Christian leaders, evangelists and others today who insist that you wait until they come before any offering is taken. They want to put the squeeze on, to tell emotional stories of deathbed experiences, to hold up pictures of crying children to twist your heart, to use competitiveness and rivalry as a means of extracting more funds. This is a terrible thing. It scorns the spirit of grace in a congregation. So this helpful guideline says, do not give to organizations or people who habitually rely on emotional appeals to get you to give.

I am sure you receive, as I do, dozens of letters every week appealing for funds. Oftentimes they are blatantly emotional. They include pictures of starving children and terrible stories of people suffering. Now we ought to hear needs, but habitual appeals on that basis are wrong, because it is the wrong basis on which to give. The knowledge of the need is all right, but to try to use it as an emotional vise to extract more funds is absolutely wrong.

Some time ago the well-known institution in Nebraska, "Boy's Town," was severely excoriated in the public press because it was discovered that appeals for orphan boys concealed millions of dollars in the bank, enough to carry on the work for years without any additional giving at all. Now this is an irresponsible appeal, and there are organizations making that kind of appeal today.

In Poland, I was told of organizations that were actually stockpiling Bibles in warehouses because they could not get them into the Soviet Union. But they were still making appeals to people to give for more Bible purchasing when they actually had warehouses full that they could not move. That is the wrong kind of appeal. When we learn of something like that we should stop giving, because we are responsible for what we do.

True Bounty

Finally, the apostle turns to the possibilities of giving:

> The point is this: he who sows sparingly will also reap sparingly, and he who sows bountifully will also reap bountifully (2 Cor. 9:6).

The closest analogy to giving that we have in life is the farmer going out to sow his crop. Giving is more than distributing your funds or resources, it is a process that will return something to you as well, like a farmer who sows seeds in the spring. He scatters seed out upon the ground, and he cannot gather it up again. It looks as though it is lost to him, and it is. He actually has to give up control of it and the use of it. He throws it away into the ground where it deteriorates, rots, and is seemingly lost.

But it is not lost; it is not gone. Let it fulfill its appointed process and the farmer will have it back again and much more besides. That is what God designed. The return is proportionate to the sowing. If a farmer sows a little amount of seed, that is what he will get back, a small and niggardly harvest. If he sows bountifully and scatters prodigally, he will receive a prodigal harvest in return. The analogy is clear. If you give just a little bit, then what you get will be a little bit, too. But if you give abundantly, what you get will be abundant also.

Freely Give

Paul gives a brief summary of how to give in the words that follow. He first stresses again that giving must be voluntary:

> Each one must do as he has made up his mind, not reluctantly or under compulsion, for God loves a cheerful giver (2 Cor. 9:7).

I do not know about you, but I always cringe at meetings where tremendous emphasis is put on the offering. Sometimes it turns into a kind of three-ring circus. People are stationed with an adding machine, the ushers are running up and down the aisle, the thermometers are up there, and people are being exhorted to give. A sense of competitiveness and rivalry obtains where people are trying to see if they can outgive others in order to drive the thermometer up; and if there is not enough, you just keep taking the offering until there is enough.

I think that is a shame, frankly, but I know a lot of money is given that way, enabling people to boast about the amount. They can feel comfortable because they belong to such a missionary-minded church.

But I deplore that kind of giving, and I think the apostle Paul would also. No, giving must come from a desire to give to meet the need, not a desire to gain a reputation as a church which gives a lot of money. Jesus warned about that. He said, "If you give to be seen of men, you've got your reward" (Matt. 6:1–4). You were seen of men. That's it; don't expect any more. But if you give because you know you have received and you want to share in the blessing that God is carrying out, then "each one must do as he has made up his mind, not reluctantly or under compulsion (pressure), for God loves a cheerful giver."

Then the second principle is, true giving must be expectant giving. You are dealing with God, and he is able to give back. Many people get nervous about this, feeling such a motive is selfish. Certainly, as we have already seen, our giving can turn selfish, but the Word everywhere points to the benefits of giving, so recognizing them cannot be wrong. If you do not give, something happens to you. You become narrow, rigid; the boundaries of your experience are narrowed and reduced and you become a tight, stingy, Scroogelike person.

Those who learn to give for right reasons become generous, gracious, godly minded people. That is what Paul is talking about here. God is able to give back. It is not wrong for you to give with that recognition in mind, for everything we have ultimately comes from him. When you eat a loaf of bread you ought to remember that, "Back of the bread is the flour, / and back of the flour the mill, / and back of the mill is the field of wheat, / the rain, and the Father's will." Therefore, everything comes from his hand.

> And God is able to provide you with every blessing in abundance, so that you may always have enough of everything and may provide in abundance for every good work (2 Cor. 9:8).

So give and it shall be given to you again, Jesus said. Men will pour a return into your treasury as you learn to give—pressed down and running over.

> As it is written, "He scatters abroad, he gives to the poor; his righteousness endures for ever." He who supplies seed to the sower and bread for food will supply and multiply your resources and increase the harvest of your righteousness (2 Cor 9:9).

That is not wrong. If you give in order that you might have more to give, you are right in line with God's program. That is exactly what he wants. Now that is not to spend on yourself. Here again the motive comes in to guide us. If you give in order to have more for you to enjoy, then you are giving for wrong reasons. Many Christians are being taught that today.

Recently a woman told me about her brother, a graduate of a Christian university in this land. He was told by the leader of the school that if he would give God would give back to him so he would never have a material lack in his life. The boy had asked God for $50,000. He did not get it, and his faith was beginning to waver because of that. He had been taught that it is wrong for a Christian to be poor, that if you keep giving, God will make you rich. Such is a twisted and distorted application of this passage.

A friend of mine replied to a letter in which he was told, "You can't outgive God. We have figured it out, therefore, if you and everybody else who hears our program send $67 to us, we'll have all the money we want and God will give it back to you five times over." He wrote back and said, "I believe that. I believe that you can't outgive God. But I tell you what: You give me the $67 and God will give it back to you five times over. Then you get the bigger amount!" For some reason they took him off the mailing list!

God delights to give, but his return is not always, by any means, material return. That is what the next verses proceed to show us:

> You will be enriched in every way for great generosity, which through us will produce thanksgiving to God; for the rendering of this service not only supplies the wants of the saints but also overflows in many thanksgivings to God. Under the test of this service, you will glorify God by your obedience in acknowledging the gospel of Christ, and by the generosity of your contribution for them and for all others; while they long for you and pray for you, because of the surpassing grace of God in you (2 Cor. 9:11–14).

Do you understand what he is saying? If you give according to the law of harvest, God will give back. And this is the form it will take: First, it will awaken gratitude in those to whom you give. We have had the joy on many occasions with our congregation of having people stand up and publicly give thanks, sometimes with tears running down their faces, for the response that people have made to a physical or material lack of theirs. Many times I have been proud of our congregation for the response to an appeal. I do not know any need that has ever been expressed, without some people (and often a lot of people), responding generously. I am delighted at that. It is a wonderful repayment for our giving to see people moved and touched and blessed and helped and giving thanks. We are richly repaid already when we see something like that.

But that is not all. According to the apostle Paul, not only does it awaken gratitude in people's hearts, it also stimulates them to pray for you. You who gave become the object of other people's prayers: "While they long for you and pray for you, because of the surpassing grace of God in you." And when people pray for you, you become the beneficiary of the blessing of God in ways that you, perhaps, will never fully know until you get to glory. Heaven begins to open up and pour blessings in ways that you could never identify or even suspect, because people are praying for you.

Finally, giving glorifies God with the thanksgiving of many. How it delights God to see his people generously respond to needs. "Pure religion and undefiled before . . . the Father," says James, "is this, that you visit the widow and the orphans in their affliction" (James 1:27).

Paul winds this whole thing up on that note. He says in one brief sentence:

> Thanks be to God for his inexpressible gift!

Giving is godlike, and we are everywhere in Scripture reminded that we are to give because we have been given to. Therefore, we are encouraged by a passage like this to sow with a prodigal hand, to give generously, to realize we have affluence, we have additional money beyond our own needs for the very reason that we might have something to give to those who have less. Take advantage of it. Jesus put it as beautifully and as simply as it could ever be put: "Freely you have received, freely give." That is God's basis and motive for encouraging Christian giving.

17

Our Secret Weapons

This last section of 2 Corinthians includes some of Paul's strongest language against the Corinthians. Because of its severity, and its contrast with earlier passages that express joy over the Corinthians' repentance, many scholars have felt this is a fragment of another letter, somehow tacked onto 2 Corinthians. Some have thought it may be the "severe letter" Paul mentions earlier which is now lost to us. We ought to remember, however, that when he wrote this he was traveling about from place to place. He would dictate his letters at night and a letter could have taken several evenings, perhaps separated by days, to complete. This may explain some of the sudden changes of subject we encounter from time to time.

Here in chapter 10 he does, indeed, change the subject very abruptly. But when we note that the sharp words are addressed, not against the church as a whole but against a special group of false teachers, we can understand why this might well conclude this letter.

This section is a helpful passage because we too have many false teachers in the church today. Some are blatant and easy to recognize. Every congregation has some member influenced by false teachers, such as Sun Myung Moon. This Korean "Messiah" is capturing the attention of many young people and inspiring them with the hope that he is the Messiah who will deliver the nations. Then there are the Mormons, going from door to door trying to convince people that the Book of Mormon is authentic history. They teach strange doctrines that have no correspondence with Scripture, yet try to hide under the guise of being evangelical Christians. There is also the Krishna group. They meet you in the airport, pin a nice flower in your buttonhole, and seek to engage you in conversation on spiritual matters in order to set forth their teaching. There are also the Scientologists, and the followers of est, and many other groups today.

The Wolves in Our Midst

Some are more subtle, coming from within the church itself, espousing transcendental meditation and various other self-improvement movements. There are the "Christian homosexuals," as they call themselves, forming churches that teach homosexuality as an acceptable life style among Christians. There are many who are teaching legalism, spiritual elitism, or pushing some special experience as a shortcut to spiritual power. So these passages in 2 Corinthians are relevant to us. Especially in these days, we can understand the apostle's concern about this kind of thing in the church at Corinth.

Now all these false teachers have one thing in common. Whether they know it or not, the devil is using them as a tool to derail the church, if he can, and to rob individual Christians of their liberty and joy in the Lord. He seeks to oppose and defeat the gospel in its powerful ministry of deliverance within a community or a nation. So the apostle writes with considerable feeling about this:

> I, Paul, myself entreat you, by the meekness and gentleness of Christ—I who am humble when face to face with you, but bold to you when I am away!—I beg of you that when I am present I may not have to show boldness with such confidence as I count on showing against some who suspect us of acting in worldly fashion. For though we live in the world we are not carrying on a worldly war, for the weapons of our warfare are not worldly, but have divine power to destroy strongholds. We destroy arguments and every proud obstacle to the knowledge of God, and take every thought captive to obey Christ, being ready to punish every disobedience, when your obedience is complete (2 Cor. 10:1–6).

Clearly, these are the words of a faithful shepherd who sees his sheep under attack from wolves in sheep's clothing. Appearing as Christians among Christians, these wolves are teaching destructive heresies. Paul does not normally speak sharply or severely. In fact, he acknowledges his enemies' description of him: "I who am humble when face to face with you, but bold to you when I am away!" These teachers were saying, "Don't pay any attention to Paul. He's just a paper tiger. He sounds very impressive when he writes, but when he comes he is meek and inconsequential." Paul says, "That is what they are saying about me, but . . .," he links these qualities with the meekness and gentleness of Christ.

Our Lord was indeed meek and gentle, but he spoke very severely at times. When he drove the moneychangers out of the temple his eyes were blazing and his arm was lifted up in violent action against those who were destroying the people of God. Paul says, "When I come, I will behave that way as well. I am fully prepared to employ all the weapons at my command."

The great question, of course, is, what are those weapons? What can Christians use to counteract the cults around us? How do we respond when we see a loved one, or a whole community of believers, threatened by error, by a false idea which may take over a church, a community, or even a whole nation? Perhaps we are being faced with a powerful threat from the homosexual community to impose, by law, an unrighteous life style upon our young people in schools and in public institutions. Christians are rightly asking, "How can we oppose this? What weapons can we employ?"

In the broader context outside the church we are also harassed and bombarded daily. For example, sexual themes in the media imply that any form of sexuality is acceptable. We are constantly assaulted by crude and offensive slogans on bumpers, billboards and television commercials. Drug pushers do their best to hook our young people on narcotics. Pornographers push their wares at us at every newsstand. Teachers openly espouse Marxism and revolution in our classrooms. Inflation depletes the value of our dollar every day, while politicians continue mouthing empty words and doing nothing about it. Do you ever feel, as I do sometimes, a great sense of frustration, an increasing sense of desperation at being so helpless? I am sure you do. How do we stem this downward slide into national disaster? Well, listen again to these words.

> For though we live in the world we are not carrying on a worldly war, for the weapons of our warfare are not worldly, but have a divine power to destroy strongholds.

The Revised Standard translators substituted the words "world" for "flesh" here. The text does not say, "We are not carrying on a 'worldly' war." It really says, "We are not carrying on a 'fleshly' war, for the weapons of our warfare are not 'fleshly.'" The "flesh" is inherited selfishness, that self-centeredness of life which all of us have without exception, impelling us to pursue our own interests at the expense of everybody else's. Now when a lot of self-centered individuals come together to work and plan together you get a flesh-governed society. That is what the Bible calls "the world," a society committed to the advance of its own interests, to protecting its own rights, and thus inevitably engaged in eternal conflict. That is "the world" and what the translators apparently had in mind when they used the term "world" here.

Weapons of Flesh

So Paul says we do not employ the weapons of the flesh. What are those weapons? What does the world use to try to solve the problems it recognizes in society? We all know them: coercion, manipulation, legislation, pressure groups, compromises, and demonstrations that ultimately result in raised voices, clenched fists and outbreaks of conflict—boycotts, pickets and strikes—all attempts to pressure people into doing what others want. These are the weapons of the world. It does not have any others so it is understandable why those governed by the flesh would employ fleshly weapons to get things done. But the universal testimony of history is, these do not work. We still have the same problems we have had for centuries. We never will get rid of them. We only rearrange them by these methods so that they seem to take another form for a little while. But soon we are right back with the same problems, if not worse, and that has been the unbroken experience of history which no one can deny.

Weapons of Faith

What, then, are our weapons? Paul makes it clear that Christians are not to use coercion, manipulation, pressure groups, compromises and conflict to oppose the evil in our midst. We have other weapons, he says. They are mighty and powerful—they accomplish something. They will "destroy strongholds" of evil, he says. But when you ask yourself, "What are these weapons?" no answers emerge in this passage. The apostle clearly assumes that the Corinthians know the weapons, since he has referred to them in other letters. We find them scattered all through Scripture so we must go to other passages to understand what he is talking about here.

Scripture gives first place to the weapon of truth. The Christian is given an insight into life and reality that others do not have. We know what is behind the forces at work in our society. As Paul put it in Ephesians, "We do not wrestle against flesh and blood." Our problem is not people, though we, like the world around us, may fool ourselves to the contrary. Scripture says, no, it is not people, but rather, "principalities, powers and wicked spirits in high places, the world rulers of this present darkness" (Eph. 6:12). We wrestle with spiritual powers behind the scenes. We need to understand that.

Such truth is realism. The wonderful thing about the Word of God is that it describes life the way it really is. I do not know anything more valuable than that we understand the Scriptures, refresh our minds with them all the time, for in this constant bombardment with illusion and error it is easy to drift back into thinking as the world around us thinks. Unless our minds are renewed by the Spirit, refreshed by the truth about life and what it is we really are up against, we will find ourselves acting just like everybody else. So the first and greatest weapon is "the truth as it is in Jesus."

When we read the gospels we see that Jesus is a man who understands life. He does not act like anybody else because he really sees what is happening. He ignores much of the visible symptoms and strikes right at the heart of problems to the direct cause of events. If we are going to follow him we will not adopt fleshly weapons and fall heir to fatal approaches to problems. We will begin to see things differently.

Secondly, the Word of God always links truth with love, "speaking the truth in love." When you begin to treat people with courtesy instead of anger, to accept them as people with feelings like yours, struggling with difficulties and seeing things out of focus as you yourself often do; when you begin to treat them as people in trouble who need help—then you confront the problem with the powerful weapon of love.

This is why Christians must be very careful as they approach the homosexual community today. These desperate, damaged people have been greatly hurt by factors that they think are right but which actually destroy them. We need to understand this and treat them tenderly and courteously even though we oppose the convictions they are trying to impress and impose upon us. Love is a mighty force. We pay lip service to it, quoting 1 Corinthians 13, but how often do we put it into practice?

The third weapon is faith, the recognition that God is active in history. He has not left us alone to stumble on our own way. God is at work. The Lord Jesus sits in control of all the nations of earth. "He opens and no man shuts. He shuts and no man opens" (Rev. 3:7). Faith believes that and expects him to do something. In Hebrews 11 we have the record of plain, ordinary men and women like you and me who found, by faith, that they could stop the mouths of lions, open the doors of prisons, and change the course of history. Faith is not a religious entity merely for churchgoing people. Faith lays hold of ordinary, human events and changes the course of history through them.

Linked to faith is the weapon of prayer. Everywhere in Scripture, we are exhorted to expose our situations to the prayers of believing people, both individually and corporately, praying together that God would move in and change things. Again and again the record testifies that events have been drastically altered by Christians who pray.

With prayer we would also link loving service. Scripture says, "Do good to those who hate you; pray for those who despitefully use you"; and minister to those who treat you wrongly or misuse you. Do something good back. When is the last time you did that? When Christians act differently they change history. You will never find non-Christians acting differently. Their response to evil is to get even, to demand justice. Christians are to remember that if we had justice all of us would be in hell. Only Christ's mercy can return good for evil, but this is a fifth potent weapon we can employ.

Paul uses a vivid word to describe the errors we are attacking. He calls them "strongholds," a word taken out of the military life of the time, used only here in the Scriptures. It describes a castle with its moats, walls, turrets and towers, defended by a handful of determined men. History records many times when a castle like that could hold out for weeks and months and even years against an attacking force because it was so difficult to dislodge its defenders. This word vividly describes some of the evils we are talking about here. Why is it so difficult to bridge the moat to deal effectively with the homosexual issue today? Why do we find it so hard to get hold of this matter? The break-up of the home and the rising divorce rate seem like impenetrable dungeons of evil. Drug traffic is another. What can we do against these things?

Paul now describes some of the things that lend strength to these powers of evil:

> We destroy arguments and every proud obstacle to the knowledge of God, and take every thought captive to obey Christ (2 Cor. 10:5).

Wrong Reasonings

Arguments ("reasonings" is literally the word) support these evils with rationalizations that powerfully defend the error. Have you ever noticed that when you get upset about certain matters and decide to do something about them, you are soon confronted with almost unassailable arguments which the other side uses to defend itself?

Recently I saw a pamphlet put out by a homosexual community to defend their claim to public acceptance of a homosexual life style. It was headed, "Dare We Lose Our Rights to Love?" One might wonder, "What could be wrong with that? After all, don't people have a right to love?" It went on to suggest that anyone opposed to a homosexual life style is a narrowminded, bitter bigot who wants to deprive other people of a beautiful and wonderful thing.

But Paul describes what truth, love, prayer, and faith will do. They will reveal that these arguments rest on vain suppositions, unrealistic assumptions that are not true. Homosexuality, for instance, is not really love. Honest homosexuals will often admit they are not satisfied, that their lives are not enriched by this life style. Rather, they find themselves hopelessly launched on a search for something they can never find, experiencing increasing depression and disappointment as they pursue it.

A Christian with a loving touch and a truthful word can point out that this is the case. When Jesus met the Samaritan woman at the well, he dealt directly with her unending search for happiness in marriage. He showed her that she was on a wild-goose chase which would never end in anything but utter frustration. He knew he had the true gift of satisfaction, which could be hers if she would only receive it. That is the Christian approach. It outflanks and destroys these arguments, these reasonings.

Proud Obstacles

The second thing Paul mentions is, "proud obstacles to the knowledge of God." If you read the writings that defend the errors of our day, you are likely to encounter arrogant descriptions of man's ability. You will read claims that men are brilliant, understand life, can handle all their problems and do not need any help. Paul is referring here to this strange insanity that makes men think they can handle the world and life without any wisdom beyond their own. Only truth, love, faith and prayer can surmount these high walls of pride.

Secret Thoughts

Paul now points out a final wall against good. It is the very personal matter of thoughts which come into our own minds and hearts, the imaginings of our minds. These refer to fantasies which we indulge in, endless day-dreams of power and accomplishment, lustings by which we attempt to satisfy inward sexual desires by feeding upon pornography, mentally, if not openly. You will never win the battle against sin as long as you allow yourself to indulge in these kinds of fantasies. That is why the apostle, with all realism, faces us with the fact that we must bring these things captive unto Christ and no longer permit them to engage our minds and hearts. They, too, can be conquered by truth, by love, by faith, by righteousness, by prayer and service, the weapons of our warfare.

Now once these imaginings are conquered, once we really face up to them and no longer permit them to govern our lives, because of the truth that God has shown us, then we must be quick and alert to deal with the return of any of them.

> Being ready to punish every disobedience, when your obedience is complete (2 Cor. 10:6).

Once you have been delivered from the inner strongholds that render you weak in the spiritual warfare of our day ("when your obedience is complete"), then you must maintain an alertness to deal promptly with any return to these things. I do not know anything more practical than this. Many people struggle for years against weaknesses in their lives and wonder why they get nowhere. But they are trying to stop an act, not the inward thought that precipitates it. They permit themselves an inward dalliance with ugly and hurtful things; with ambitious projects where they see themselves as the hero on the white horse, always riding out to deliver the damsel from distress, winning the attention of all the multitudes around; or giving way to lust and replaying the whole movie on the silver screen of the mind. Then they wonder why they are so weak when an opportunity comes to indulge in the act. The battleground is our thought life—that is what Paul is telling us. When we win that battle then we must be careful to punish every disobedience after our obedience has been made complete, after we have learned what it takes to walk with God.

The problem of history is not the world. It is the church. It is we who do not use the weapons at our disposal. Instead, we give way and go along with worldly approaches, using pressure-group tactics and petitions to seek to overcome with legislation the wrongs of our day. May God help us to understand the nature of spiritual warfare. The weapons of our warfare are not those worldly tactics. But, our weapons are mighty. They will destroy strongholds and bring into captivity every thought to the obedience of Christ.

The cause is not hopeless. We are not helpless; there is much we can do. Let a Christian act along the lines of the revelation of Scripture in this regard and things will begin to change. Any one of us can change things, in our lives individually, in our homes, in our communities, where we work, in our nation itself. Let us begin to learn the truth about life from the Scriptures—to act in love instead of in rivalry and competition, to trust God that he will work as we work in faith; to pray and to join others in prayer that he will do so. Let us begin to live righteously ourselves; let us maintain integrity in the midst of these deviations and lovingly serve those who are opposing us. We will find tremendous changes beginning to occur quickly as God uses these weapons to destroy the strongholds of darkness and evil around us.

Do you know anything more challenging for our day and time than that? God has placed in our hands the opportunity to change our nation, our communities, our homes, wherever we are. May God grant that we will do it. You are the salt of the earth. You are the light of the world.

18

How to Spot a Phony

Recently I pondered the reaction if, while I was away on vacation, some visiting speaker came in and began to suggest to our congregation that I was a religious phony. He might imply that I had been teaching false doctrine all of these thirty years—that I had introduced some rather strange and unbiblical ideas to the congregation. He could accuse me of trying to feather my own nest. Some would say, "We knew that all along! We're just surprised to hear you admit it like that!" Others, perhaps, would say, "Let's give him a chance, at least, to answer these charges." On the other hand, I hope some might say, "Well, let's check the Scriptures and see if these charges are true."

I am painting a faint picture of the situation that existed in Corinth when Paul wrote this letter. I am not trying to compare myself with Paul. The more I read these letters from his hand the more humbled I feel, the more unworthy I am to even loosen the latchets of his shoes. But I confess that if something like this occurred in our church I would have a hard time trying to answer it. I would feel uncomfortable about defending myself. I would have difficulty believing that people I had worked with, loved, and lived with all these many years, would fall prey to this kind of an approach.

Yet that is what Paul must have felt as he was writing to these Christians in Corinth. A small band of men had come down from Jerusalem and were charging the apostle with various errors. They were claiming, for one thing, that he was a self-appointed apostle, that because he was not one of the original twelve, he had perhaps concocted the whole story about encountering Christ on the Damascus Road. They were suggesting that his teachings were not in line with the other apostles, therefore he was not to be believed. Furthermore, they suggested he was a moral coward; that he could write tremendous letters which could scare them, but in person he was as meek as a lamb. They suggested that he taught a frightening kind of message which set Christians free from any obligation to keep rules or guidelines of behavior. They added plausibility to their charges by pointing out that Paul evidently had trouble getting churches to support him. Unlike these "super apostles" from Jerusalem, he did not have the support of churches but had to make tents for a living. This was proof, they said, that Paul was not really a validated apostle.

True Credentials

In Paul's answers to these charges, a clear picture emerges of what a true servant of Christ ought to be. Since all of us who belong to Christ are called to be his servants, and each one has a ministry given us by the Lord himself, it will be helpful to recognize a truly God-authenticated ministry and, contrariwise, the marks of a counterfeit ministry.

When false teaching appears, when we encounter wrong philosophies and claims to truth not in line with Scripture, how do we answer them? In the preceding chapter we looked at the weapons which we are to employ. We saw that we are not given the usual weapons of the world to use. We are not to use pressure tactics, coercion, or manipulation. Rather, we are given spiritual weapons: faith, love, truth, righteousness, prayer, and so on.

Now here in this section we see the credentials we require in order to use these weapons in a proper way:

> Look at what is before your eyes. If any one is confident that he is Christ's, let him remind himself that as he is Christ's, so are we. For even if I boast a little too much of our authority, which the Lord gave for building you up and not for destroying you, I shall not be put to shame. I would seem to be frightening you with letters. For they say, "His letters are weighty and strong, but his bodily presence is weak, and his speech of no account." Let such people understand that what we say by letter when absent, we do when present (2 Cor. 10:7–11).

Paul is asking these Corinthians to examine the situation, and not simply to believe these men without checking up on them. I submit that this is one of the greatest needs of our day. Many Christians turn on the television and, because some colorful personality is using the Bible and speaking in the name of Christ, they blindly follow. When they are asked to send in money they do so, sometimes sending huge sums without asking any questions. They will even forsake meeting with other Christians to follow these programs, creating some difficult problems in the local church today. But Paul says, "Look at what is right in front of you. Here are certain visible marks of authentic Christian ministry."

In Christ—Now

The first credential, obviously, is that one must belong to Christ. As he says here, "If any one is confident that he is Christ's, let him remind himself that as he is Christ's, so are we." That is absolutely fundamental. You cannot be a Christian minister without having *much* to say about Jesus Christ, revealing a relationship with him. Now if that seems self-evident, let us realize that there are teachers in the churches today who set aside the ministry and work of Christ. They talk about "God," and what "God" will do. They claim to be led by "God"; they talk much about doctrinal understanding and insight which they get from "God." But one of the sure signs of a phony is that he does not say much about Jesus.

Now these men in Corinth were talking about Christ. Perhaps they claimed to have known him in the days of his flesh, claiming a superiority on the ground that Paul had not known Christ then. But, as the apostle told us earlier in this letter, the important thing is not whether you knew Jesus in the days of his flesh, but, "if any man *be* in Christ he is a new creature: old things are passed away; all things are become new" (2 Cor. 5:17 KJV). So the first requirement of genuine ministry is that people truly be "in Christ," and for that fact to be clearly evident in what they have to say. Paul does not challenge these men's relationship to Christ, for in the final analysis only God, who knows the heart, knows the answer. But he does insist on his own relationship; obviously he was "in Christ," and these Corinthians ought to be the first to know it.

Recognizing Real Authority

The second credential mentioned is a true authority. Paul speaks of his authority. "Even if I boast a little more about the authority which the Lord gave me, I shall not be put to shame," i.e., he would not be exaggerating because his authority is genuine. This is one of the questions we must ask today: By what authority do these television teachers, these radio broadcasters, and these traveling evangelists speak? They all claim to be authoritative spokesmen for God. How can you tell if it is a true or a false authority?

Notice that the apostle gives us a very helpful clue here. He says, "Look at the results." Jesus had said this: "By their fruits you will know them." Paul is saying, "What is happening to those who listen to these people? Are they being set free? Are they growing into a wholesome, happy, loving people? Are they obviously being helped, strengthened, released and delivered? Or are they being turned into critical, narrow-minded bigots, or fearful, anxious neurotics, or perhaps, calloused, indifferent, carnal libertines?" What is happening? Look at the fruits and see what kind of ministry these people have. Are people being helped by their leadership, set free and encouraged, or are they being attacked and destroyed, intimidated and limited by those in authority within the congregation?

When my wife was a teenager, and a new Christian, she was in a church where she fell under the attack of the pastor. He became upset with her because she was listening to some radio broadcasts teaching a viewpoint toward the Bible different from his own. He called a church trial and threw her out of the church. The scars of that experience are still tender in her memory. Paul's question is sharply to the point: What kind of leadership is being displayed?

Paul's authority was from Christ, who commissioned him to deliver what he calls, "a secret and hidden wisdom of God, which before the ages God ordained for our glorification" (1 Cor. 2:7). That marvelous verse says that though we (mankind) certainly are to live for the glory of God, yet the amazing declaration of Scripture is that God lives for the glory of man! Has this great truth dawned on you? He ordained certain truth to result in *our* glorification, to bring us to where God intended us to be, to set us free to rule and reign in all the affairs we touch. Man can do that only when he learns to be a servant, because it is only the servant who can rule as king. God is intent on teaching us this great fact, the exact opposite of "Defend your own rights, stand up for yourself and insist on what you have coming." To reign and rule by means of serving, loving and responding is, "the secret and hidden wisdom of God." Paul was commissioned to deliver that, and that, he says, was his authority.

Such authority is clearly not the right to tell people what to do. Earlier in this letter he says, "We are not lords over your faith"; we have not come in as your bosses to tell you how to behave. But rather, he says, "we are helpers of your joy" (2 Cor. 1:24). We stand alongside of you to encourage, strengthen and teach you the reality God sees so that you might be set free. True authority is not for tearing you down, he says, it is for building you up. Therefore, when you watch the ministry of any spiritual leader, ask yourself what is happening to the people who are listening to him? Are they being set free or are they being destroyed?

I know of churches on the West Coast today where men have assumed a certain prerogative of office. They call themselves "elders," sometimes even "apostles." They claim authority to regulate all the affairs of the congregation to the point of determining what kind of work members can do, whom they can marry, where they should live, and what income they may earn. That is a false authority. Those who are exercising that kind of authority in the church in any age are what Paul calls "tools of Satan," destroying, not building people up. The church is full of such people today, making these passages tremendously helpful to us.

The Only Commendation

There is a third credential here: beginning with verse 12:

> Not that we venture to class or compare ourselves with some of those who commend themselves. But when they measure themselves by one another, and compare themselves with one another, they are without understanding. But we will not boast beyond limit, but will keep to the limits God has apportioned us, to reach even to you. For we are not overextending ourselves, as though we did not reach you; we were the first to come all the way to you with the gospel of Christ. We do not boast beyond limit, in other men's labors; but our hope is that as your faith increases, our field among you may be greatly enlarged, so that we may preach the gospel in lands beyond you, without boasting of work already done in another's field. "Let him who boasts, boast of the Lord." For it is not the man who commends himself that is accepted, but the man whom the Lord commends (2 Cor. 10:12–18).

That rather extensive paragraph is summarized by a little phrase in verse 13, "the limits God has apportioned us." What Paul is saying is, "It is God who gives us a ministry." Jesus said to his disciples, "You did not choose me, but I chose you and appointed you (the word means, "strategically placed you") that you might go and bring forth fruit and that your fruit should abide" (John 15:16).

Jesus is the head of the body, and it is his business to place people in the body where he wants them. We have been learning through these Corinthian epistles that all of us who belong to Christ have been given gifts of the Spirit, equipping us for the ministry God has given us. Christ has already set you where he wants you to exercise that ministry—in your home, among your family, among those who work with you, in the contacts you have throughout your life. He has given you the equipment and he is teaching you the resources and the power by which you are to work. Therefore, do not object; do not wait for some other circumstance to come your way. This is where he put you. Paul recognizes that about himself. He says, "How did I get to Corinth? Well, God led me there."

Four things in this paragraph mark the ministry authenticated by God. The first insists, it is not to be a self-commending ministry. Whenever you hear someone boasting and bragging about what he has done for Christ, be careful, beware. A great pile of promotional material for a certain ministry crosses my desk almost every week. When I look at it I discover that it was sent out by the man himself. Surely he would not be crass enough to come to me and boast about himself, but he allows extravagant phrases to be mailed out to a large group. That is what Paul says he would not do: "Nor that we venture to class or compare ourselves with some of those who commend themselves. But when they measure themselves by one another, and compare themselves with one another, they are without understanding." They are utter fools, he says. Yet Christians today must endure floods of literature in which someone commends himself. We should regret the frequency of these terms: "dynamic speaker," "world-renowned preacher," "internationally known," "universally acclaimed." To me it is a mark that a man does not realize his ministry is given to him by God, and only God's commendation counts.

A number of years ago I was at a great meeting in St. Louis, Missouri, where Dr. Oswald Hoffman, the speaker on the "Lutheran Hour" was introduced. The man who did so gave him a rather flowery introduction, which he concluded by saying, "And now I gave you the famous Dr. Oswald Hoffman." Dr. Hoffman stood at the pulpit for a moment, then he said, "I'm not the great Dr. Oswald Hoffman. I'm a nobody . . . just like you." It was refreshing to hear someone take that approach to his ministry.

You cannot help what other people say about you. It is not wrong if praise and commendation comes from them, but to sanction literature that commends you is deadly; men who commend themselves, the apostle says, are lacking in understanding.

Now information and promotion differ: information simply identifies who you are, what your name is, what you are coming to do, or something like that. But to promote something, to propagandize and to blow it up in extravagant terms is absolutely out of order for a God-authenticated ministry. As some man once said in response to an overblown introduction, "There are no great preachers. There is only a great God."

Doors Already Opened

Secondly, a genuine ministry enters the doors which God has opened. To trace Paul's path to Corinth in the Book of Acts makes this clear. Paul had a vision one night from a man in Macedonia saying, "Come across into Europe and help us." In response to that Paul landed in Philippi. There he got into trouble and ended up in jail. When he got out he went to the next city, Thessalonica. Again, his preaching of the Word aroused opposition and he was driven out of town. Next he went to Berea, and once again there was trouble and a riot. He had to leave there by night and was taken down to Athens, fifty miles to the east of Corinth, where he preached on Mars Hill, but they did not receive his message. Finally he arrived in Corinth, all alone in the dust of the road, armed with nothing but the power of the Spirit of God, and began to preach the gospel throughout this city. Out of this came the Corinthian church.

Knowing this background we understand Paul when he says, "We are not overextending ourselves as though we did not reach you." God had marked out Corinth for Paul and had sent him there. This was clearly evident to all these people. He did not go around and manipulate extravagant openings. Contrast this with the practice of many today who arrange elaborately contrived "invitations" by their team of advance publicists. Paul would have had nothing to do with that. He was simply entering doors that God had opened to him.

Reaching Out

Then a third mark of authenticity is found in verses 15 and 16: a genuine ministry always seeks to reach out to the unreached: "We do not boast beyond limit, in other men's labors; but our hope is that as your faith increases, our field among you may be greatly enlarged, so that we may preach the gospel in lands beyond you, without boasting of work already done in another's field." As these Corinthians learn the truth, as their faith increases and they begin to bear a more open, obvious witness for what Christ has done in their lives, the whole church will be strengthened. This will enable Paul to leave that place and go on to another place that has not been touched yet, perhaps supported by the ministry that has been brought into being in Corinth.

I am always distressed by squabbles that arise between churches over what they call "sheep stealing." One Christian may leave one church and go to another and the first pastor gets upset and accuses the other of "stealing his sheep." Such anxiety seems pointless, when thousands of unreached people all around us would come if we were reaching out to them.

An authenticated ministry is always reaching out, never content with merely having its own private flock, but hungry, with the hunger of the Spirit of God himself, to touch the lives of those around who are hurting and dying and being destroyed by enemy forces at work in their lives.

The final mark is found in verses 17 and 18. Whenever anybody boasts, Paul says, it is to be in what the Lord has done: " 'Let him who boasts, boast of the Lord.' For it is not the man who commends himself that is accepted, but the man whom the Lord commends." How that wipes out with one stroke all men's proud evaluations of their own ministries. You never hear anything like that from Paul. In the next section he is distressed by being forced to talk about himself and his ministry. He only does it to defeat the kind of argument used by these false teachers.

The following section is similar to Paul's brief description of his ministry in 1 Corinthians 15:10:

> By the grace of God I am what I am, and his grace toward me was not in vain. On the contrary, I worked harder than any of them, ("Well," you say, "that certainly sounds like boasting, doesn't it?" But notice what he says) though it was not I, but the grace of God which is with me.

Paul everywhere recognized that only what Christ does in him matters, not what he does for Christ. I have sometimes seen on the wall of Christian homes a little plaque that says, "Only one life, 'twill soon be past./Only what's done for Christ will last." That sounds very pious, and it has certainly a germ of truth about it, but it always bothers me because I do not think it is very accurately expressed. What I would like to see is, "Only one life, 'twill soon be past./Only what Christ does through me will last." Though the meter may be wrong, the theology is right: it is not what I do for him that makes any difference at all. That can be utterly wasted time, in God's estimation. It is what he does through me; what I expect him to do and what he promises to do, that counts. Therefore, the true evaluation of a ministry is to look back and say, "Well, thank God for what happened. But I didn't do it. God did it through me. I am grateful for the privilege of having the opportunity to be an instrument in his hands." That is true evaluation.

So how do we spot the phonies who are all around us? They commend themselves, for the most part. They are always boasting of their accomplishment, printing it and spreading it around so you can see. They do not let others speak for them, but they talk about it themselves. And they are not concerned about reaching the unreached. They are concerned only with having a little group of their own supporters, and building that to the highest number, but paying little attention to the lost around. They manipulate and try to set up various open doors instead of following those which God opens for them. Most of all, when they boast they make it clear that God is mighty lucky to have them on his side. That is the mark of a counterfeit. He may not be a counterfeit Christian, but he has a counterfeit ministry.

I trust that God will help us evaluate our own ministries in the light of this, and help us withdraw from any spiritual beauty contests, competing for the best-looking ministry around.

19

Keep It Simple

In the final chapters of 2 Corinthians the apostle Paul confronts Satan's most powerful tool, his most dangerous threat to the church: infiltration from within by teachers who veer from the truth.

Be assured that this is still the most dangerous threat to a church today. In any American city, church buildings stand on almost every corner. Christianity would seem the dominant faith of our land, the church a powerful moving force in our society. Yet, as you well know, many of those buildings are empty; many have a mere handful of people coming to services that are prosaic and devoid of real vitality. The churches represented by those buildings have long since become an ineffective force in our society. What happened? Most were destroyed from within by a satanic process of infiltration, by people who came in and began to teach a deviate gospel. That was happening at Corinth, and is also threatening many of our churches today.

In the two preceding chapters we noted the weapons that counteract the evil strongholds and arguments in our midst, and the personal credentials we must have to be effective in this battle. In this chapter we will examine the tactics tha apostle employs to counteract this threat to the Corinthian church, tactics we may use today. Many are falling for some form of theological error. What do you do about it? What kind of tactics can you use? Let us look at what Paul did.

A Good Jealousy

The first note struck is a striking one: Paul reveals to the Corinthians the jealousy of his heart:

> I wish you would bear with me in a little foolishness. Do bear with me! I feel a divine jealousy for you, for I betrothed you to Christ to present you as a pure bride to her one husband. But I am afraid that as the serpent deceived Eve by his cunning, your thoughts will be led astray from a sincere and pure devotion to Christ (2 Cor. 11:1–3).

Jealousy is an angry, powerful emotion which refuses to tolerate a rival. It can become a powerful motivator to aggressive action, and is one of the most frequent causes for broken homes, broken hearts and broken bodies in the world today. Yet, amazingly, God declares in the Book of Exodus, "I the Lord your God am a jealous God" (20:5). All through the Scriptures God reveals his jealousy.

Now if jealousy is bad, why is God jealous? Paul says that he feels "divine jealousy," a godly jealousy, for these people. If jealousy can be both good and bad, then when you feel jealous of someone you must ask yourself, "Is my jealousy right, or is it false?" The distinction is clearly made: false jealousy is always selfish, concerned about *my* feelings. It is possessive, dominating, even cruel and tyrannical. It usurps the rights of others and insists on its own way, imposing upon someone else whether he likes it or not. Because it is so vicious in its cruelty and its tyranny, jealousy is perhaps the most destructive force in the world today.

A true jealousy, a godly jealousy, on the other hand, which Paul felt for the Corinthians, arises from a deep concern for the welfare of another. It is careless of self, and always manifested in a tender and thoughtful concern about someone else. It is powerful and may not cease, for it borrows its constancy from God.

Paul likens his jealousy to that of a father who has betrothed his daughter to a young bridegroom. Every father (I speak from experience) longs to be able to present his daughter to her chosen young man as a chaste and lovely virgin. This may seem an ironic metaphor to use of these Corinthians, because Paul has already told us that some were adulterers, immoral people, homosexuals, thieves, drunkards, robbers and cut-throats. "Such were some of you," he said (1 Cor. 6:11). Yet now he says, "I have presented you as a chaste virgin to Christ."

That is a wonderful commentary on the reality of forgiveness of sins. I have often used this passage with many who struggle to believe that God can forgive their past. Not long ago I sat down with someone who told me his life story and he said, "I don't believe God can forgive me. The things I have done have been too vicious and too hurtful to others. I have been so cruel, so selfish." I turned to this very passage and said, "Do you see what Paul said about these Corinthians who came from a sordid and ugly background? God has cleansed them so they are like a chaste and lovely virgin, and Paul longs to present them to Christ in that way."

The Simple Truth

But now Paul sees a threat to this: "I fear lest you be led astray in your thoughts as the serpent deceived Eve by his cunning, that your thoughts will be led astray from a sincere and pure devotion to Christ." (Literally it is, "from the simplicity and purity which is in Christ." Some manuscripts even leave out the word "purity," so it becomes basically, "that you might be led astray from the simplicity that is in Christ.") This is one of the most important phrases of the Bible for nothing is more important than to maintain the simplicity that is in Christ. At the heart and center of your life there is to be the "simplicity that is in Christ."

I have noticed over many years of observation that when religion becomes complicated it is because it is drifting away from the centralities of faith. The world around us becomes increasingly complex because it is drifting farther and farther from God. But look at the world of nature and you will see the simplicity of God's design everywhere. He divides the year into four seasons which repeat themselves endlessly without fail. Yet that simple pattern of four seasons contains within it all possible variations of weather. Look at a flower and see the simple pattern of its makeup, and yet what an infinite variety God produces in a field of flowers. If we know how to see we will find God's simplicity everywhere around us. Thus, when religion becomes complex it is a sign that it is departing from Christ.

The old medieval saint, Thomas à Kempis, has expressed this same idea: "By two wings man is lifted from the things of the earth—simplicity and purity."

Dr. Martyn Lloyd-Jones says:

> As life in general becomes more and more complex, so religion tends to be affected in the same way. It seems to be assumed that if the affairs of men are so difficult and complicated, the affairs of God should be still

> more complicated, because they are still greater. Hence there comes a tendency to increase ceremony and ritual, and to multiply organizations and activities . . . the argument is that it is ridiculous to assert that the vast problems of life today can be solved in an apparently simple manner suggested by those who preach the gospel in the old evangelical manner. . . . The fact is, that as we get further away from God life becomes more complicated and involved. We see this not only in the Bible, but also in subsequent history. The Protestant Reformation simplified not only religion, but the whole of life and living in general. . . . The truly religious life is always the simple life.

When you ask yourself what simplicity Paul is talking about, the answer from everywhere in the Word of God is: the daily companionship of the Lord Jesus. Do you believe that Christ is yours all day long? Do you reckon upon that, think about that, live out of that relationship, out of that sense of the expectation of his presence? We often say, and rightly so, that Christianity is not a creed, it is a relationship; it is living with a Person. This is the simplicity that is in Christ. The danger we constantly face, even in a church where the Word of God is taught, is that we become involved in things *about* Christ and fail to live in a relationship *with* Christ. That is why Paul is jealous to maintain "the simplicity that is in Christ." First Corinthians expresses the same truth;

> God is faithful who has called us into the fellowship of his Son Jesus Christ our Lord (1 Cor. 1:9).

"But Life Is So Complex"

When your Christianity begins to cool and you find yourself getting complicated it is a definite sign that your relationship with the Lord Jesus is being threatened. He is a living Lord; he is not dead. He is not for Sundays only. He is for all the moments of life. In Philippians Paul says: "To me to live is Christ"—he fills all moments. Though Paul lived one of the busiest lives ever recorded, the heart of it was this quiet reckoning upon the presence of the living Lord, the realization that Jesus was with him to do everything that was to be done. That is the simplicity he is talking about.

Karl Barth, who has gained a reputation as a great theologian was once asked, "What is the greatest theological thought that has ever crossed your mind?" Some very complicated answer was expected, but his answer was: "Jesus loves me, this I know, for the Bible tells me so." This is the simplicity of Christ.

It is easy to lose that simplicity. It can be lost in the midst of Christian activity. You can lose it in Bible study. You can become so involved in fascinating aspects of Scripture that you can lose "the simplicity that is in Christ." I once sat with a prominent theologian who is known all over the world and we talked about his teaching experiences in various seminaries. He told me how most of the seminaries he knew were filled with men who had world-wide reputations for scholarship but whose personal lives were dull and dead (and deadening) because they had lost the simplicity that is in Christ.

It can be lost in the pressures of daily living. It is possible to become so busy, worried and anxious about yourself and the things that are happening to you that you lose the sense of Christ's presence with you and that he is adequate. These Corinthians were troubled with teachers who had caught their attention, but they were drifting from the central point. Caught up with fascinating philosophies based on the Word of God, these teachers went off on sidetracks and rabbit paths of thought; certain ego-appealing experiences made them feel great, wonderful, and God-possessed (like many today who seek to explore strange and wonderful mysteries involved with Christian faith) but which tended to move them from the simplicity that is in Christ.

Looking for a Different Gospel?

And so Paul lovingly but firmly warns:

> For if someone comes and preaches another Jesus than the one we preached, or if you receive a different spirit from the one received, or if you accept a different gospel from the one you accepted, you submit to it readily enough (1 Cor. 11:4).

What he is saying is, "If you believe without questioning, all the things that these people are teaching you, how much more ought you to listen to me? I have brought you the truth. You submit to those teachers, now submit to me and listen to me."

Then Paul uses a tactic he seldom employs in his letters. It is what we call "irony." Irony is a gentle form of sarcasm. The difference between sarcasm and irony is that sarcasm hurts people. Sarcasm pretends to agree, yet, through subtle tone or attitude, conveys a sharp disagreement, and is usually designed to hurt. Irony, on the other hand, sounds similar but is designed not to hurt but to help. Irony is a play-back, helping others hear their words in such a way that their foolishness is gently revealed. Here is Paul's irony:

> I think that I am not in the least inferior to these superlative apostles. Even if I am unskilled in speaking, I am not in knowledge; in every way we have made this plain to you in all things (2 Cor. 11:5, 6).

Here he is using the language of his adversaries in Corinth. He is saying, "You call me unskilled in speaking and maybe you are right." He freely admits it because he says in another place that he did not employ the normal, flowery oratory of that period, or use a "stained-glass" voice. He says, "I may not be a very good speaker, but what is important is not style, but content. Look at what we have told you. What do these other men know? They titillate your senses, they capture you with flowery words, and so on, but what do they know?"

In the realm of knowledge Paul was absolutely superb. His writings have for twenty centuries unveiled truth that men have never heard before, and can be found in no other place. He was sent to unveil reality, to tell us how life really is, to speak the truth. It is universally agreed by all who study the Word of God that no apostle writes more penetratingly, more perceptively, more aware of the nature of reality and of human life than the apostle Paul. His writings are marvelous studies in human psychology, in basic sociology—in all the realities of life as we know them, because of the vast knowledge that was given to him. Paul wrestles with the tough, hard questions of life and gives us answers that satisfy the mind and set the heart at peace.

A Gospel Free of Charge

Now in a further use of irony he deals with the charge that he did not love the Corinthians enough to even let them support him:

> Did I commit a sin by abasing myself so that you might be exalted, because I preached God's gospel without cost to you? I robbed other churches by accepting support from them in order to serve you. And when I was with you and was in want, I did not burden anyone, for my needs were supplied by the brethren who came from Macedonia. So I refrained and will refrain from burdening you in any way. As the truth of Christ is in me, this boast of mine shall not be silenced in the regions of Achaia. And why? Because I do not love you? God knows I do! And what I do I will continue to do, in order to undermine the claim of those who would like to claim that in their boasted mission they work on the same terms as we do (2 Cor. 11:7–12).

What he is saying here is clear: he himself had taught these people the principle that he who preaches the gospel has a right to live by the gospel. He used the old law, "Thou shalt not muzzle the ox that treads the corn." Yet when he came to Corinth he would not accept support from anybody. All the time he was there he made tents to support himself, and it appears that sometimes he did not do very well. Either he did not have much time left over for that occupation or there was not a very good trade in tents. He was in want, he says, and could barely make it financially. That may encourage some of us who are struggling today with inflation. Paul could barely make it, but he said he still would not receive support from them, for the churches in Macedonia, where he had already been, were supporting him. But these teachers in Corinth were saying, "You know the reason why Paul won't accept your support? It is because he's an amateur apostle. He's not a professional like us. He didn't graduate from the right school; he doesn't have an acceptable degree. He can't get anybody to support him because nobody believes he is a true apostle."

But Paul says, "The real reason is that I wanted to show you how free the gospel is, to demonstrate in my own life that the gospel is free-of-charge. God does not ask anything from you. He offers life freely in Christ. So I determined that I would not be a burden to any of you when I came." From this we can see what Paul's practice was. He would never accept support from people to whom he was preaching the gospel for the first time. He would accept support only from those whom he had already led to Christ so that they could help him in his ministry in a new place.

"Furthermore," Paul says, "I don't intend to change because I don't intend to let these false teachers claim that they work as we do. They're leeches, they're parasites, they're not teaching you the truth. They're using up your resources, living off you people, and yet they want to turn around and claim that they live like we do. I'll never give them that advantage, so I'm not going to change just to satisfy them."

Imposters Exposed

Then, as is sometimes necessary, Paul employs a third tactic, an open frontal exposure:

> For such men are false apostles, deceitful workmen, disguising themselves as apostles of Christ. And no wonder, for even Satan disguises himself as an angel of light. So it is not strange if his servants also disguise themselves as servants of righteousness. Their end will correspond to their deeds (2 Cor. 11:13–15).

With these words, the facade is stripped away, and the false teachers can no longer hide. Paul says, "They're imposters, they're phonies, they're impersonators, masquerading as apostles of Christ. But they were not sent by Christ and they're not teaching what Christ said to teach. They're teaching attractive lies instead of the truth."

This tactic of plain-spoken exposure is missing in the churches today; many are destroyed because no one will stand up and confront false teachers. We are caught up with the world's philosophy and anything goes. We must be nice to everyone, always. But the apostles never did that, nor did Jesus. Look at the sharp language he employed on occasion with the Pharisees. Right to their faces he called them, "snakes and vipers," and "dead men's tombs, full of rotting bones," filled with an awful stench. That is not the way to win friends and influence people! Jesus set that aside and told them the truth.

Paul goes on to say these people are like their invisible master, Satan. When he comes like a roaring lion he is frightening, but not nearly as dangerous as when he comes as an angel of light. If the devil knocked on your door, took off his top hat and said, "Good morning, I'm the devil. I've come to ruin your life. I want to trip you up and destroy your relationships and fill you with hatred and violence," you would not have any trouble handling that. But when he comes and says, "Ah, good morning. I'm your friend. I've come to help you. I want to introduce you to something so alluring, so exciting, and so fulfilling that you can't afford to miss it," and then begins to set forth attractive lies, you are much more likely to welcome him, to your own destruction.

But Paul says their end is inevitable, "Their end will correspond to their deeds"; they will fall victim to their own lies. They will lose their ability to tell truth from evil, and they will fall victim of their own errors. The terrible tragedy of those who get trapped into wrong is the loss of "the simplicity that is in Christ." The way to avoid being trapped, in a world filled with delusion, is simply this: Keep close to the Shepherd. Retain the simplicity that is in Christ. Walk closely with the Son of God himself every day.

20

The Cost of Love

We come now to the famous passage where Paul details the hardships and troubles he experienced during his ministry. This list of difficulties comes from the lips of Paul himself. It sounds as though he is bragging about his exploits. There is no denying that some people are bothered by Paul. I have had people say to me, "I can't stand him: imagine telling someone, 'imitate me as I imitate Christ.' How conceited!" But Paul was not conceited. Boasting was personally repugnant to him, and in this passage he explains why he sometimes spoke this way. He did it strictly for the spiritually immature who were only impressed by outward performances, flamboyant actions and unusual abilities. That need for the dramatic undermines many Christians today as well. Many Christians feel that no one will listen to their testimony because they have never been in prison, on drugs, murdered their mother, or raped their sister.

Unfortunately, many feel that Christian testimony must arise from a sordid, lurid background before it has value in anyone's sight. That is similar to the problem Paul was facing. Many of these Corinthians had been carried away by a group of men from Jerusalem who boasted of their tremendous accomplishments as apostles for Christ. The Corinthians were in danger of following their false teachings rather than listening to the apostle who had won them to Christ, faithfully taught them, prayed for them, and loved them.

An Unpleasant Task

Thus Paul explains to the Corinthians why he finally resorts to boasting: It is the only thing that will impress them and win them back to a hearing of the truth of the gospel. So, reluctantly and with evident displeasure, Paul begins to talk about his accomplishments for Christ:

> I repeat, let no one think me foolish; but even if you do, accept me as a fool, so that I too may boast a little. (What I am saying I say not with the Lord's authority but as a fool, in this boastful confidence; since many boast of worldly things, I too will boast) (2 Cor. 11:16–18).

Clearly, Paul is repelled from this task: he says he does not have the Lord's authority to do it, i.e., it is not normally right for a Christian to do this. Now that may surprise many, for much Christian literature suggests that boasting is the normal thing to do. But Paul is talking about true Christianity. He says that it is not right for Christians to boast about themselves, but he is ready to do so because he hopes it will break the spell these false teachers have created in Corinth. Some Corinthians had so completely accepted these false teachers that they actually endured arrogance and insult from them without protest:

> For you gladly bear with fools, being wise yourselves! For you bear it if a man makes slaves of you, or preys upon you, or takes advantage of you, or puts on airs, or strikes you in the face. To my shame, I must say, we were too weak for that! (Obviously that is an ironic statement) (2 Cor. 11:19–21).

These false apostles were becoming arrogant and boastful. Anyone who depends upon boasting to gain people's attention tends, ultimately, toward arrogance. I attended a service in another state a few years ago with probably a thousand people present, most of them in their 20s and 30s. The pastor, who had a reputation as a Bible teacher, was teaching from a certain New Testament passage. I could not quite see what happened but evidently a young woman sitting in the front row reached up and patted her hair. The Bible teacher interrupted his discourse and said to her, "What are you doing? This is a Bible study, not a beauty parlor. That's the trouble with you flaky females, and flaky is a good adjective for females." He went on and just ripped into her. She sat there, red-faced and embarrassed, but uttered no protest, nor did anyone else. Then he resumed his study.

After a bit he spotted a man in the back row (sitting very close to me actually), who was thumbing through his Bible, checking a reference.

The teacher said, "There's a man back there who's not reading where we are." He said, "We're in the New Testament and if you are in this Bible study you will be in the New Testament. If you don't have time for what we're studying you can just get up and leave." Again the whole congregation sat there. Nobody said a word. Evidently this was normal fare for them. I was amazed at what arrogance and insult people would endure when they were under the spell of someone teaching falsely from the Word of God.

That is what was going on in Corinth. Paul was willing to stoop to boasting about his accomplishments if it would reveal that even on their own grounds he was more credible than the false apostles. So he reluctantly boasted of secondary matters, matters these Corinthians viewed as marks of success.

> But whatever anyone dares to boast of—I am speaking as a fool—(Notice how he keeps interjecting this so his readers will not understand that this is something right.) I also dare to boast of that (2 Cor. 11:21).

Then he takes up in detail some of the things the false teachers were bragging about. First, there was their ancestry:

> Are they Hebrews? So am I. Are they Israelites? So am I. Are they descendants of Abraham? So am I (2 Cor. 11:22).

It is incredible how much importance some people put upon their pedigree. I have never been able to understand why some seem to feel they are better than others simply because their ancestors happened to come over on the *Mayflower.* (From what I have been told about mine, they probably met the *Mayflower* when it docked!) Clubs have been formed, such as The Daughters of the American Revolution, as though there was some prestige to be descended from those who fought in the American Revolution. But that does not say a thing about the worth of the individual involved.

At once Paul recognizes the foolishness of this kind of thing, and yet he himself does it. He says, "If you think that those things are important, then you must accept what I am saying to you because I outshine them even in these categories. Are they Hebrews? Do they claim to be part of the chosen nation and be able to speak the chosen language? Well, so can I. Are they Israelites? Are they descendants of Abraham? Well, so am I," he says. Yet it is clear he thinks this has no real importance whatsoever.

I know Christians who boast about their spiritual pedigree, although they perhaps would not say anything about their natural pedigree. Some Christians flaunt the schools they have graduated from, or the number of degrees they have after their name, or whether they have been to the right places, what churches they were members of, and so on. Some people have even assumed they belonged to a spiritual aristocracy because they have attended Peninsula Bible Church. But that does not impart any value in itself. We ought to beware of this tendency to value outward circumstances that really say nothing about the individual.

Paul goes on now to speak of his activities:

> Are they servants of Christ? I am a better one—I am talking like a madman—(That is what you are when you boast about what you have done for Christ) with far greater labors, far more imprisonments, with countless beatings, and often near death (2 Cor. 11:23).

Unfortunately, men still travel about getting a hearing because they have endured persecution for Christ. Certainly, in this category, Paul can outshine the false teachers:

> Five times I have received at the hands of the Jews the forty lashes less one.

That was a purely Jewish form of punishment. The law of Moses prescribed for certain offenses a public whipping of forty lashes. But it also required, according to the Jewish rabbis, that if more than forty were inflicted the man who did the whipping must receive forty lashes. So they were careful not to go over forty; they made it thirty-nine lashes, "forty less one." Since the law also prescribed that death resulting from such a whipping would be blamed on the man handling the whip, we may be sure it was not so severe it could take one's life. But incredible as it sounds (and we have no record of it other than this), Paul had endured that terrible beating five times!

Paul continues:

> Three times I have been beaten with rods.

That was a Roman punishment, and although Paul was a Roman citizen and Roman law decreed that no citizen should be beaten with rods, yet he had been so beaten on three different occasions. (In the Book of Acts there is another incident of that nature which comes later than this.) Because of angry mobs and weak judges the law was sometimes disregarded and thus this form of punishment had already been inflicted on the apostle three times.

> once I was stoned.

We must interpret this today—it was with rocks, not by drugs. This incident is recorded in the Book of Acts. In the city of Lystra, where he met young Timothy on his first missionary journey, Paul was actually stoned by a mob and dragged out of the city and left for dead. But God restored him and brought him back to life and to his ministry again. Then he goes on:

> Three times I have been shipwrecked; a night and a day I have been adrift at sea; (There is an account in Acts of a shipwreck but that comes after this, so that four different times, at least, the apostle was shipwrecked) on frequent journeys, in danger from rivers, danger from robbers, danger from my own people, danger from Gentiles, danger in the city, danger in the wilderness, danger at sea, danger from false brethren; in toil and hardship, through many a sleepless night, in hunger and thirst, often without food, in cold and exposure (2 Cor. 11:25–27).

When I read this list I ask myself, "What have I ever endured for Christ's sake?" It makes me feel two things—first, grateful that God has never asked me to endure such things. He could have, he could have asked us all to, but he did not. And second, I wonder if my life has not been overprotected. I wonder if I would react as the apostle did if I were called to endure such a thing. One cannot read this passage without being impressed with what Paul endured for Christ's sake.

Then there is the question of anxiety,

> And, apart from other things, there is the daily pressure upon me of my anxiety for all the churches. Who is weak, and I am not weak? Who is made to fall, and I am not indignant? (2 Cor. 11:28).

In the more than thirty years that I have been a pastor, I have been privileged to hear the burdens, sorrows, pain, heartache and tears of many. I confess that it is sometimes a great strain. I have not always done very well with it. It makes me even more impressed at this mighty apostle who bears the burdens of dozens of churches that he founded, remaining open to their needs and praying for them daily. He had never even been to Colossae, and did not start the church there, but he prayed for them and upheld them before God every day. What a tremendous ministry of intercession this man had! What empathy he shows. What ability to respond to the emotional heart-cries of people! I shake my head in wonder.

The Cost of Love

To read a list like this raises the question: Why would anyone put up with this kind of life? What made this man willing to go through these terrible hardships, pressures, trials, and dangers? What motivated him? The only answer I can find is the one he himself gives us in chapter 5 of this letter: "the love of Christ constrains me" (vs. 14). It was his sense of gratitude to the risen Lord who not only had forgiven him, filled him, and restored him, but who went with him through these trials and sustained him in every one of them, turning them into experiences of joy rather than hardship. That love flowed through Paul, reaching out to minister to those around him.

In the letter to the Thessalonians he says, "We were willing to have imparted unto you, not only the gospel of God only, but also our own souls because ye were dear unto us" (1 Thess. 2:8 KJV). It is beautiful to see the love of this man's heart. I have often said to young people, "As you go on in life you are going to find a lot of people who want to be your friends. Many of them will like you and you will be drawn to them, but some of them will be false friends. You can always tell the difference by this: whether they are willing to keep on loving you when things do not go well with you, whether they are willing to suffer with you and stand by you, even when you offend them. Trust the ones who are willing to suffer for you." This is the mark of love.

Paul has proven to these Corinthians that he genuinely loved them. None of these false apostles would put up with rejection. As Jesus himself said, "When the wolf comes, the hireling runs away but the true shepherd will lay down his life for his sheep." Now Paul is forced to bring this out so that the Corinthians may see where the truth lies and hear the voice they can trust in this conflict of voices.

True Boasting

Now at this point he turns to the things that a Christian can truly boast about. We are not to boast about what we have accomplished or even how much we have had to bear for Christ's sake. But there are some things we can boast of:

> If I must boast, I will boast of the things that show my weakness. The God and Father of the Lord Jesus, he who is blessed forever, knows that I do not lie. At Damascus, the governor under King Aretas guarded the city of Damascus in order to seize me, but I was let down in a basket through a window in the wall, and escaped his hands (2 Cor. 11:30–33).

Paul reaches twenty years into the past to a rather remarkable incident that occurred shortly after his conversion. He says, "If I must boast, this is the kind of thing I am going to boast of." What is it? Well, as he puts it, "It's the things that show our weakness." That is what we may truly boast about, the times when we did not look good, the times when we fell on our faces. This is so incredible that he takes a solemn oath he is telling the truth: "The God and Father of the Lord Jesus, he who is blessed forever, knows that I do not lie." "As I look back on my past life, one incident comes to mind more than anything else. It was a time when I was a complete failure at what I was trying to do. That is what I boast in, because that is when I began to learn the most important lesson of my life."

If Paul were alive today and was living like many Christians do today, he would have had a list of things that he endured printed up and published everywhere. You would be reading, "Come and hear the man who was beaten five times for Christ and endured tremendous hardships and dangers. Come and hear the man who has been stoned for his faith, who has been in shipwrecks, night and day, and so on." Paul dismisses all this with a wave of his hand and says, "The thing that I want to be known for is the time I was let down over the wall in a basket."

The Turning Point

The account in Acts tells us that after his conversion Paul went into the wilderness of Arabia for awhile. There he undoubtedly studied through the Scriptures to try to understand how he had missed seeing who Jesus was, because he had regarded him as an imposter and a phony. But as he searched he found Christ on every page. He must especially have seen him in Isaiah 53 and in Psalm 22, in the sacrifices of the Old Testament, in the arrangement of the tabernacle; everything pointed to Jesus. When he came back from that experience he had two burning convictions in his heart. First, the Old Testament proved that Jesus of Nazareth was the Messiah. He went into the synagogues and began to prove this to the Jews from their own Scriptures.

The second thing experience taught him was that God had chosen him to be the apostle to Israel, to reach this nation of Jews for Christ. And he tried! He did his level best with his brilliant mind, his great knowledge of Scripture, all his Hebrew qualifications (he lists them for us in Philippians 3) a Hebrew of the Hebrews, circumcised on the eighth day, born of the tribe of Benjamin, a Pharisee (the strictest sect of his religion), zealous according to the law, blameless in his outer life. He had it all, and so he started out to reach the Jews for Christ. But things kept falling apart until they reached such a terrible state that one night the governor, at the instigation of the Jews in Damascus, tried to find him to seize him and put him to death. On hearing about it his friends took him out to one of those houses built on the wall of Damascus, and through a window in the dark of the night they let him down in a basket. So Paul says, "The night I became 'a basket case,' that is the event I boast about."

Isn't that interesting? Looking back he says, "That was it. As I walked away from the city of Damascus, with all my plans and dreams of glory for Christ collapsed around my feet, that was the night I began to learn a great truth: my natural gifts are not what qualify me as a servant of Christ."

Oh, that I could teach this to all of Christendom today! We are being bombarded with the philosophy that natural abilities are what make us usable as Christians—a strong personality, an outgoing, optimistic outlook, gifts of leadership, handsome frame and body, musical ability, speaking ability—all these are the things that God will use. Paul says, "That is a mistake. I had to learn that my natural gifts did not help, that Christ working in me is the only thing that God accepts." Anyone who is a Christian has Christ, and if you learn to reckon on Jesus at work within, ready to work through you as you choose to do things, he will work alongside you and make your labor meaningful and valuable in God's sight and ultimately in man's. That is the great secret that Paul learned. That is why he says, "I look back on that incident on the Damascus wall as the greatest event of my career." In Philippians 3 he tells us that those things he once counted gain he now counts as nothing but a pile of barnyard manure in contrast to what he has learned Christ can become to him.

True Greatness

I do not know any truth that God wants us to learn which is greater than this. Yet it is the hardest truth we ever learn. Recently, I talked to a young man, 21 years old, a good athlete with a strong body, an attractive Christian who loves the Lord and who wants to serve him. But he was struggling with an opportunity that had been opened to him. It would put him in a well-known, fashionable church and give him a name immediately, plenty of money. It would lead him into a ministry that would very likely have much fame attached to it. He was facing the choice of that or whether he was willing to become obscure and lose himself, trusting God to lead and Christ to use him, even though he was never heard of publicly again. That is a struggle we must all go through in one way or another. Do you remember how Jesus put it? "He who saves his life will lose it, but he who loses his life for my sake will save it." That is where Paul was at Damascus. So Paul says he will boast about the things that show his weakness, because, "when I am weak, then I am strong" (2 Cor. 12:10b). In successive chapters of this study, we will see further illustration of this "boasting."

Paul stresses and underscores this one great truth that made all the difference in his life. If he had never learned that great lesson we would never have heard of him today. He would have been just another flashy figure out of the first century who shot up like a rocket on the horizon for awhile and then disappeared. Nobody would have heard of him since. Instead, he became the mighty apostle who has shaken the world for Christ in every generation for twenty centuries since, because he learned the secret that Jesus taught his disciples, "without me *you* can do nothing." That is what we too must learn. May God help us to learn it.

21

The Ecstasy and the Agony

As Paul concludes this letter, he is, as we have seen, caught up in a game of one-upmanship. He does not want to play, but he is forced into it. Recently I participated in three pastors' conferences on two different continents and noticed that no matter where in the world you gather a group of pastors together, they start playing one-upmanship. One pastor will say to another, "How are things going with your church this year?" The other will say, "Well, we've had a pretty good year." (It is apparent they are feeling each other out to see how far they can go.) One of them will ask, "How many converts did you have?" (If they are Baptists they will ask, "How many baptisms did you have?") The other will say, "Well, we've had two or three a month. The first man then changes the subject because that is more than he had. He will say, "Our choir did very well this year." The other one will say, "Our missionary budget is better than ever before." So they go on, playing "Can you top this?" games.

That is what was happening in Corinth. Some false apostles had come there boasting about their exploits, how faithful and how tremendously dedicated they were, hypnotizing these Corinthians into believing that they were true apostles of Christ, but teaching them false things. To regain the Corinthians' attention, Paul has had to compare notes with them, in a sense, and boast of his exploits.

But what remarkable boasts he makes, with not a word of what we might expect, not a word of what many preachers boast about today. He does not display an impressive list of scholastic degrees.

He does not mention any of his famous converts. He does not make any claims about the great crowds or the remarkable miracles that accompanied his ministry. He does not say anything about being internationally known. All of these things were true, but Paul did not say one word about them, in sharp contrast with many who are preaching today. Rather, he boasted about an incredible list of hardships—beatings, fastings, imprisonments, stoning, shipwrecks, dangers from every side. Then he concludes with the embarrassing story about the night he had to be let down over a wall in a basket to escape a plot to take his life. That does not sound like much to boast about for it represented a collapse of all his dreams and plans.

But when we come to chapter 12, Paul describes an experience that finally sounds like something well worth boasting about. In this chapter we have the story of his being caught up into Paradise, and an accompanying account about a thorn in the flesh that was given to him. He introduces this with a suggestion that this vision of Paradise is only one of many he had:

> I must boast; there is nothing to be gained by it, but I will go on to visions and revelations of the Lord (2 Cor. 12:1).

These visions of the Lord were the basis of his claim to be an apostle. Luke tells us that apostles were those who had seen the risen Lord after his resurrection. Paul, of course, was not one of the original twelve, but he had seen Christ on the Damascus road. Now he tells us there were many occasions when he had visions of the Lord. That does not mean a fantasy, something he saw only in his mind. He actually saw the Lord; the Lord appeared to him and taught him. Jesus himself had taught Paul all he had learned, the truths of the gospel he preached. We must remember this whenever we hear Paul's authority challenged in our own day; we must remember that it was the Lord who taught him these things. After many years of ministering Paul had a chance one day to compare notes with the original apostles, Peter, James, John, and others, and he tells us in Galatians that they could add nothing to what he had learned from the Lord himself. So here is the basis of this great apostle's teaching; it came directly from the Lord in personal appearances.

Caught Up into Paradise

Now Paul goes on to give us one of the most dramatic of these occasions:

> I know a man in Christ who fourteen years ago was caught up to the third heaven—whether in the body or out of the body I do not know, God knows. And I know that this man was caught up into Paradise—whether in the body or out of the body I do not know, God knows—and he heard things that cannot be told, which man may not utter (2 Cor. 12:2–4).

Perhaps the strangest thing about this account is that Paul puts it in the third person, as though it happened to someone else. I am not sure why that is since later, in verse 7, he makes it clear that this happened to him. Here, however, he sounds as though it occurred to somebody he had once known. He does not tell us very much; there is not much detail given about life beyond. (I have always wished I could interview him about this.)

But several things are clear from what he says. One is that it was obviously an experience where he went beyond this present life; he entered, he says, "the third heaven." (He also calls it "Paradise.") Now the "third heaven" was a reference to the Jewish belief about the structure of the universe. There were three heavens, they believed. The first was the atmosphere around the earth, the clouds, and so on. Beyond that they could see a second heaven where the stars, the sun and moon were. The third heaven was the invisible realm where God's throne was; therefore it was called Paradise. All through the Scriptures, whenever someone appeared out of or went into heaven, this invisible dimension of reality is in view. It does not mean that heaven is way out in space somewhere; it means that it is not visible to our present senses. It constitutes a kind of fourth dimension of life. It is there, into this realm, that the apostle was taken. If you trace back the dates, it was somewhere around the time when he came out of Tarsus back to Antioch (some ten years after his conversion). A revival broke out in Antioch, and Barnabas had gone to Tarsus and brought Paul back to help him in this work.

Secondly, it is clear Paul's body was rather unimportant in this event. If he was in the body he was not aware of it; and if he was out of the body, he did not miss it. This has always suggested to me that going to be with the Lord will not be as unique or as different an experience as we might think. Remember that in chapter 5 Paul calls it, "being at home with the Lord." After a season in a foreign land, it's such a great feeling to get home because home is the place where you relax, you feel at ease, you are not under strain or pressure, you can kick off your shoes, stretch out and feel comfortable. That is what being with the Lord was like, Paul says. It was like being home. He was not sure just how the body fit in, but clearly it was a great experience of relaxed enjoyment for him. This is perhaps one reason why he gives this account in the third person, because it was almost like it happened to someone else. He was not aware of whether his body was involved or not.

Thirdly, Paul cannot tell us what he heard. Now he must have heard some marvelous things, things which contributed greatly to his understanding of life and reality. These must have deepened his grasp of what exists and what God is doing. But he could not describe these things in earthly words. When you read the Old Testament prophets, and some of the New Testament prophets, you notice that those who had visions of the Lord, visions of heaven, were never able to quite accurately describe what they saw. They had to put it in symbols—Ezekiel's wheels within wheels and strange animals with four faces. Daniel's descriptions are somewhat similar; so are John's in Revelation. Not one could describe exactly what he saw because it is so far beyond what we presently know. This surely indicates that when we are with the Lord our knowledge will be vastly increased. We will know secrets we never dreamed existed, secrets that are so beyond us now they cannot be put into language.

We might expect that this, at least, is an experience Paul can boast about. We might expect him now to put down these false apostles and challenge them to come up with something greater than this. But remarkably, he does not do so. In fact, he goes on to say:

> On behalf of this man I will boast, but on my own behalf I will not boast, except of my weaknesses. Though if I wish to boast, I shall not be a fool, for I shall be speaking the truth. But I refrain from it so that no one may think more of me than he sees in me or hears from me (2 Cor. 12:5, 6).

In those words Paul is admitting this way a very unusual experience; and if he did boast about it at least he would be telling the truth. But he does not boast because he does not want people to look at him in any way different from what they could see for themselves. In other words, he does not desire status beyond what a personal acquaintance would ascribe. "What you see is what you get" is the apostle's motto. He is not making any claims about anything unusual in his ministry.

That is very remarkable, especially in these days when we have a rash of books appearing, all telling us of some unusual, fantastic experience of people who supposedly died, went to heaven, and came back into the body. All describe what the writers saw, but not one of them would have waited fourteen years before rushing into print. These people immediately arrange lecture tours, television interviews, and welcome a celebrity status. You do not see anything like this with the apostle Paul. In fact, he says, "I haven't spoken of this for 14 years, and I do so reluctantly now. I don't want to boast about it. In fact, what I want to boast about I haven't even come to yet. This vision of Paradise is the introduction to what I have to say."

The Thorn in the Flesh

> And to keep me from being too elated by the abundance of revelation, a thorn was given me in the flesh, a messenger of Satan, to harass me, to keep me from being too elated (2 Cor. 12:7).

"That," Paul says, "is my point of boasting—boasting about my weaknesses. Out of that experience of tremendous revelation and glory came the most annoying, irritating agony of my life"—what he calls, "a thorn in the flesh." Everyone wants to know what this "thorn" was and there are many guesses. Some commentators think it was a disease, perhaps malaria, and frequent spells of the fever laid him low. Others suggest that it was epilepsy, and claim this explains some of his strange utterances and what happened on the Damascus road. Some felt that perhaps Paul had bad eyesight, owing to the passage in Galatians where he commends his readers for their willingness to tear out their very eyes and give them to him. In that letter he also says, "You see with what large letters I have written to you with my own hand." (When I traveled with Dr. H. A. Ironside he was suffering from cataracts, and he used to write me with large letters. I often thought of those words of Paul as I read his letters.) I personally think it may well have been some eye problem that repeatedly bothered him and perhaps even made him rather repulsive at times. Some commentators feel he may have had a speech impediment because he mentions having difficulty uttering things as he wanted to. Some have even suggested that he was married once and had known a nagging wife. That would indeed be a thorn in the flesh! I do not think there is much evidence for that, although there is some evidence that Paul was once married. Whatever it was, we know one thing: it was in the flesh, i.e., it was probably something physical that was bothering him.

Behind the Thorn

According to Paul's word here, both Satan and the Lord were involved in giving this to him. He calls it, "the messenger of Satan," which came to harass him, to annoy him, to keep constantly digging at him like a thorn embedded in the flesh that he could not get hold of to pull out. And yet, he says, it was given to him "to humble him to keep him from being too elated" about the revelations he had. Obviously, this was from the Lord.

Notice that both the Lord and Satan are involved in this together. Satan is the instrument the Lord uses. There is a similar scene at the beginning of the Book of Job, when Satan has to appear before the Lord to get permission to afflict Job and bring about the terrible sessions with boils. Yet at the end of the Book God appears alone and says to Job, basically, "I'm responsible, Job. Any questions?" There is always this combination of these two forces. Satan's purpose was to destroy and harass Paul, to make life miserable for him, as is his purpose in the trials that we have. But God's purpose was to strengthen him, to humble him and to keep him usable in his hands. I have never seen a trial or so-called tragedy come to Christians that did not have both of these elements in it.

When in Poland I talked with a pastor there who was going through a tremendous personal struggle. He had been involved in an incident that had resulted in very severe criticism of him (which I do not think he rightly deserved). It was tearing him apart emotionally. He could not sleep or eat; his family was upset by it; he was tormented with terrible thoughts of ugly, evil things, suicidal impulses, and so on, which kept coming into his mind. He was wretched, worn out, exhausted, and physically trembling because of the pressure. It was clear that he was undergoing an attack of the devil. Satan was getting at him and tremendously assaulting him. But it was also true, as I had the privilege of pointing out to him, that God was involved too. If he would stand against the devil and resist him with the weapons of spiritual warfare, God would win a great victory by this, and he himself would emerge from it strengthened, helped and more usable in the hands of God. This is the secret behind all our trials.

The Point of the Thorn

Now whatever this thorn in the flesh was, Paul did not like it. He went to the Lord about it, he tells us:

> Three times I besought the Lord about this, that it should leave me; but he said to me, "My grace is sufficient for you, for my power is made perfect in weakness" (2 Cor. 12:8, 9).

Paul was a mighty man of prayer, so it was natural for him to ask that the Lord would take this away. I am sure that the first time he prayed he expected immediate relief. But none came; the thorn in the flesh kept nagging away at him. Once again he asked, perhaps a bit puzzled by the fact that he had received no positive answer. Still there was no answer. So once more he came before the Lord and asked to have it removed. At last, after some considerable length of time the answer came, and it was very clear. Whether it was in a vision or some inner conviction of his mind, I do not know, but the answer was clear: "My grace is sufficient for you, for my strength is made perfect in weakness." If that principle is true of life, and God knows it to be true, what do you think he is busy doing with us? Making us weak, isn't he? And what makes us feel weak? Well, it is being under attack, feeling inadequate to handle the pressures and the problems that we have. So if you feel this way it is not only the devil who makes you feel that way, it is God, too. God allows us to feel this to keep us from that which could render us useless in the work of spreading his kingdom. Paul knew that the worst thing he could do was to become arrogant and conceited about his revelations. It was evidently more important to God to keep him humble than it was to make him comfortable, so he allowed the thing to go on.

The most dangerous threat to any servant of Christ is spiritual pride. I confess that this is the thing I fear most in my own ministry. So many nice things are said to me, I get so many strokes, so many boosts to my ego that I fear lest I begin to believe some of these compliments! I was at a conference some time ago speaking with its director about another leader who was asked if he would send one of his organization's top speakers for a series of special meetings. This man drew himself up and said, "Well, I am the top speaker of our group. I'm Number 1." It was not surprising to me to hear a short time later that this man's ministry was beginning to crumble and fall apart; soon he was removed from his leadership position by his own organization. I have seen many fall because they grew arrogant and boastful about what God was doing through them.

The Time to Boast

So Paul comes to this conclusion:

> I will all the more gladly boast of my weaknesses, that the power of Christ may rest upon me. For the sake of Christ, then, I am content with weak-

nesses, insults, hardships, persecutions, and calamities; for when I am weak, then I am strong (2 Cor. 12:9, 10).

Paul learned two things from this lesson. One is that he would never permit himself to brag about what he was doing. If he found himself wanting to boast, he would find some area of weakness and boast about it. He was going to do so deliberately in order that he might not succumb to the temptation to be proud. But on the other hand, notice that he did not invite these Corinthians to work at keeping him humble. Many people today feel it is their business to keep others humble. They never encourage or say something nice about them because they are afraid it will go to their heads. But no one is ever given that responsibility. In fact, you cannot help somebody by not encouraging him; each individual must handle this problem of pride in his own life. In other words, only he can keep himself humble. It depends on how he looks at what he does, whom he sees behind it, whether he sees his resources coming from God or himself. That is what will keep him humble. Paul says, "I'm going to remind myself who I really am and what I really can do, by boasting only in my weaknesses, the times of apparent failures, the times when I don't do very well. That is what I want to boast about."

How to Know When You're Winning

Second, Paul learned whenever trouble comes to be content. "I don't want to gripe or complain or feel sorry for myself. I want to recognize that this is the best setting for God to work in my life. For when I am weak, then I am strong." This underscores the spiritual battle we are involved in. When is the devil being beaten? Not when we feel great and confident, when it looks like wonderful things are happening, when the ministry is going well. (And I speak to all of us, because we are all in the ministry. We all have an area of responsibility given to us by God.) No. The devil is being defeated when we are feeling attacked and under the gun, when we feel weak and helpless and do not know what to do, when we are not sure how to respond, when, in our perplexities and sense of weakness, we come before the Lord and plead with him for strength to go on one more day, and for grace to help us stand. That is when we are winning and when the kingdom of God is being spread more abundantly than ever before.

Some years ago I ran across a letter from a missionary out in New

Guinea. He was writing home to his supporters, sharing with them some of the struggles he was going through. This is what he wrote.

> Man, it's great to be in the thick of the fight and to draw the old devil's heaviest guns, to have him at you with depression and discouragement, slander and disease! He doesn't waste time on a lukewarm bunch; he hits good and hard when a fellow is hitting him. You can always measure the weight of your blow by the one you get back. When you're on your back with fever and at your last ounce of strength, when some of your converts backslide, when you learn that your most promising enquirers are fooling, when your mail gets held up and some don't bother to answer your letters, is that time to put on mourning? No sir! That's the time to pull out the stops and shout hallelujah! The old fellow's getting it in the neck and hitting back. Heaven is leaning over the battlements and watching. Will he stick it? And as they see Who is with us, as they see the unlimited reserves, the boundless resources, as they see the impossibility of failure, how disgusted and sad they must be when we run away. Glory to God! We're not going to run away!

That captures the spirit of what Paul is writing. "When I am weak, then I am strong." God knows this is true. That is why when we get through one battle there is another one waiting for us. We want to throw up our hands and say, "Lord, what are you doing to me? I thought life was a Sunday school picnic where I could drift through and have a great time eating my Wheaties and doing OK." But God puts us right under the gun. Trouble comes, difficulties hit us, three or four at a time on occasions. But they are not times for complaining; they are opportunities to fight and to win.

22

The Marks of a True Apostle

In a famous and often-quoted remark, Mark Twain said, "When I was a boy of fourteen I thought my father was the most ignorant man in the world, but when I was twenty-four I was amazed at how much the old man had learned in ten years." That is somewhat analogous to the situation in Corinth. Paul founded this church. He was the Corinthians' spiritual father, having taught them how to live as Christians. But after he had left some itinerant teachers came in, so smooth, so flowery and so impressive that after a bit the Corinthians began to look on Paul as an ignorant rustic who did not know very much, and couldn't even express well what he did know. Paul was forced, as we have seen, to compare his record with that of these false apostles, and in every way he outshone them.

The apostle now concludes this section with what I like to designate as "The Marks of a True Apostle," that we might compare them. We, too, have many false apostles around us today, on television and in print, getting a following everywhere. In this passage we will see four marks by which we can identify a true apostle of Christ. (I suggest you clip these and put them up on your refrigerator and compare them with what you see on television or read in books today.)

> I have been a fool! You forced me to it, for I ought to have been commended by you. For I am not at all inferior to these superlative apostles, even though I am nothing. The signs of a true apostle were performed among you in all patience, with signs and wonders and mighty works. For in

> what were you less favored than the rest of the churches, except that I myself did not burden you? Forgive me this wrong! (2 Cor. 12:11–13).

Signs of an Apostle

In this brief paragraph Paul indicates certain signs of a true apostle which he had performed before these people in Corinth. He expresses surprise that they did not defend him when these phony apostles showed up. After all, they had seen the marks of a true apostle, and should have recognized phonies and come to his defense. What are the signs of a true apostle? The apostle Paul calls them here "signs," i.e., they have symbolic meaning; they signify something; they represent something. And they are called "wonders," i.e., they are striking demonstrations of the power of God. They make people's eyes open up. They are also called "mighty works." It is evident that only God could do them. Man cannot act in this realm. Paul has made amazingly slim reference to any signs in his ministry. He does not talk about any of the miracles that occurred. (The Book of Acts refers to several of them but Paul calls no attention to them himself.) Nevertheless, they were there, and it is my personal belief that these link up with the signs mentioned in the sixteenth chapter of Mark's gospel.

In this somewhat debatable passage, Jesus said that certain signs would follow those who believed. Unfortunately, some people have misunderstood this passage, assuming these signs were to follow everyone who believed in the gospel. But if you carefully read that passage in Mark 16, what our Lord indicates is that these signs would follow those among the apostles who believed in his resurrection. Jesus had just rebuked them because they did not believe in his resurrection, even though they had ample evidence of it. Though he himself was standing before them as a resurrected being, still some of them had doubts. He rebuked them for it and said that these signs would follow those who believe: they would cast out demons; they would speak in other tongues; they would take up serpents and would not be harmed; they would drink any deadly thing and no harm would come to them; they would lay hands on the sick and they would recover.

Now almost all of these signs are recorded in the Book of Acts as having occurred in the ministry of the apostle Paul, therefore the signs of a true apostle had been done among the people. We must understand these as authenticating signs to indicate that the original apostles were genuinely from the Lord himself. Remember, the passage in Mark closes with these words:

> And *they* went forth, and preached every where, the Lord working with *them*, confirming the word with signs following (Mark 16:20 KJV).

. . . So these are the signs of an apostle that Paul refers to here. He had done these, evidently, at Corinth, but still they were questioning his apostleship.

Another identification mark, not pointed out by Paul, is hidden in verse 11, a remarkable paradox which is possible only to those who are true servants of Christ. Notice how he puts it: "I was not at all inferior," he says; and then in the next phrase, "yet I am nothing." Now one statement is, "I am the equal of anybody; I am not inferior at all to these superlative apostles; I have everything they have and more," while at the same time he can say, "yet I am nothing." That is the mark of a true servant of Christ: the ability to say both of those things and for both of them to be equally true. When Paul says, "I am not inferior," he means, "Everything I am in Christ, everything that Christ can do through me, makes me equal to anything they can do."

Every Christian's attitude toward himself ought to be: "I can do all things through Christ who strengthens me." If God tells me to do something I can do it. I can obey his Word. I can follow his precepts. I can do what he asks. There is to be a ringing note of confidence because you are not relying on yourself but on Christ. At the same time the apostle could add, "Yet by myself I am nothing. All my abilities, my gifts, my natural talents won't get me anywhere in God's sight. They are impressive to other people, and I could fool a lot of people this way, but they are not at all impressive in the eyes of God." I wish I could get more Christians talking this way today, willing to say, "If Christ tells me something to do or something to be, then there is no limit to my ability to do it because he will provide the power. But in myself, trying to do anything depending on my gifts, I will accomplish nothing of any value in God's sight." This is the mark of a true servant of Christ.

One of the ways you can test the false apostles of our day is to listen carefully to what they say about themselves. Do they claim anything is coming from them? Do they claim to be remarkable people of remarkable ability, or are they talking about the power coming from Christ? That is the big difference. By this Paul should have been recognized by these Corinthians. Now he does add this verse: "Did you reject all this only because I failed to let you support me? I'm sorry," he says, "I should have let you do that. Forgive me that wrong."

This is a reference, of course, to all the emphasis they had put upon the fact that he supported himself when he was with them instead of living, like the false apostles, off the fat of the congregation. Well, that is the first mark of a true apostle: there are certain authenticating signs, performed humbly without ostentation.

Now I personally believe there are no successors to the apostles in the fullest sense of the term, due to the fact that these men are still with us. We have been listening to the apostle Paul in the chapters of this book. We can hear John, Peter, James, and other apostles, too. They laid the foundations back at the beginning of the Christian era, but they are still speaking to us through their letters and their words. There is no need for other apostles to come. As you hear voices around today claiming to be new apostles, to have new revelations of the mind of God beyond Scripture, ask yourself, where are the authenticating signs? The signs of a true apostle must appear or there is no reason to accept them.

No Demands

In the next paragraph we have a second mark of true apostleship:

> Here for the third time I am ready to come to you. And I will not be a burden, for I seek not what is yours but you; for children ought not to lay up for their parents, but parents for their children. I will most gladly spend and be spent for your souls. If I love you the more, am I to be loved the less? (2 Cor. 12:14, 15).

An important principle is stated very plainly here. Paul gives himself in selfless love because he is the parent and they are the children; he had led them to Christ. It is the responsibility of parents to provide for the children, not to expect the children, while they are yet children, to support their parents. New parents lay aside money to be used for children's education years down the road. That is because a parent's heart's desire is to provide for the welfare and the future of children. God has made parents that way. One of the great marks of a true servant of Christ, a true apostle, is that he gives himself without restraint to those to whom he is ministering. He does not ask for anything back from them. What a contrast that is with false apostles. How upset they get if you do not minister in return to them.

But notice what Paul's attitude is. He says, "I will most gladly spend and be spent for your souls. If I love you the more, am I to be loved the less?" That is, these Corinthians were not responding with love. The normal response of a child to his parents' care is to love them. But even if the Corinthians do not, Paul says, "I am still going to pour out everything for you."

And he indicates that his love is an unqualified form of love. I remember years ago reading a story of a mother who went down to breakfast one morning and found a bill from her son lying beside her plate. He had written it out for her.

Mowing the lawn	$ 2.00
Drying the dishes	1.00
Raking leaves	3.00
Cleaning garage	4.00
Total	$10.00 owed

She did not say anything, but went about her work. When the boy came home from school for lunch that day he found a bill lying beside his plate. It said:

Ironing clothes	nothing
Mending socks	nothing
Cooking meals	nothing
Bandaging cuts	nothing
Baking cookies	nothing
	Love, Mother

That is the apostle's attitude, isn't it? He does not expect and does not demand anything in return. It would be nice if he got it back, but even if he does not, this fact is not going to stop him. That kind of selfless, unqualified love is the mark of a true servant of Christ. You can use it to test the claims of many voices today as to whether they are the servants of Christ or not, because it is the invariable mark of those who genuinely love that they love without demanding something in return. This is the second mark of the genuine apostle.

No Advantage Taken

They are so suspicious of him, however (though it is hard to believe), they actually press this even further:

> But granting that I myself did not burden you, I was crafty, you say, and got the better of you by guile (2 Cor. 12:16).

Although they could not find fault with what he did, they said, "Well, he is only doing it because he wants to allay our suspicions. When he gets us eating out of his hand, then he is going to take advantage of us." Paul responds "Just name one time when I did that":

> Did I take advantage of you through any of those whom I sent to you? I urged Titus to go, and sent the brother with him. Did Titus take advantage of you? Did we not act in the same spirit? Did we not take the same steps? (2 Cor. 12:17).

What a beautiful, selfless attitude the apostle demonstrates here. He challenges them to name even one time when he took advantage of his relationship, expecting them to give something back to him for what he had been pouring out to them. I am sure this effectively silenced the opposition in Corinth in that regard.

Standing before No Jury

Then beginning with verse 19, we have still a third mark of a true apostle of Christ, for the apostle says:

> Have you been thinking all along that we have been defending ourselves before you? It is in the sight of God that we have been speaking in Christ, and all for your upbuilding, beloved. For I fear that perhaps I may come and find you not what I wish, and that you may find me not what you wish; that perhaps there may be quarreling, jealousy, anger, selfishness, slander, gossip, conceit, and disorder. I fear that when I come again my God may humble me before you, and I may have to mourn over many of those who sinned before and have not repented of the impurity, immorality, and licentiousness which they have practiced. This is the third time I am coming to you. Any charge must be sustained by the evidence of two or three witnesses (2 Cor. 12:19–13:1).

Paul is saying clearly here that a true apostle is answerable only to God, not to the congregation. As a true servant of Christ, Paul does not always need to justify himself before the people to whom he ministers. It is nice to have their approval, but it is not necessary when he comes among them again: he will deal with the reality of what he finds, what is actually going on in the congregation.

Clear Dealings

Evidently that is not a pleasant picture. He anticipates he will find certain wrong attitudes, i.e., "quarreling, jealousy, anger, selfishness, slander, gossip, conceit, and disorder." Dr. William Barclay calls those, "marks of an unchristian church." I wish I could tell you there are few churches like this, but I have to admit, unfortunately, that as I travel about I find these conditions very common in many, many churches. It is always a shameful thing that churches should be divided; quarreling, filled with jealousy, anger and selfishness. The cause is always simply the failure to obey what Scripture tells us to do with regard to one another. One reason many Christians are having to go to psychologists and secular counselors for help with their problems is that they have neglected what Scripture says to do to one another. Instead of going to someone and telling him the fault privately, they start gossiping to others about it, complaining, feeling bitter and refusing to talk to the other party. These are the kinds of things that destroy the witness and testimony of a congregation. Paul says, "When I come I will deal with these because I do not require your approval of me, therefore I can deal honestly with what I see to be there."

Not only were there wrong attitudes, but there was wrong conduct there. Paul speaks of "impurity," "immorality," and "licentiousness." These are actions that have to do with the whole realm of sexuality and its purposes. I am impressed by these Corinthian letters. How faithfully the apostle dealt with these matters of sexual impurity in a place and time where they were widely accepted as being normal. (We are coming to these conditions rapidly in our own day.) The apostle persists in this, dealing with these conditions over a period of months, even years. He sent others, went himself, wrote four letters, all to try to help the Corinthians deal honestly and openly with the things that are wrong in public life. He labored to show them how to refuse to go along with the trend of the times, yielding to what everybody is doing. If there is anything a Christian is called on to do, it is not to do what everyone else is doing. It is to be different, because Christ has made the difference in our lives. The apostle deals with this and says that he will come again and deal honestly with it. He is free to do so because as a true apostle he is answerable only to God and not to the congregation.

But he is going to handle it in an orderly way. Any charge must be sustained by the evidence of two or three witnesses. Things are going to be opened up; nothing is going to be hidden after he arrives; all is going to be brought out into the open. And then what? How will it be handled? That is what the next paragraph brings before us, and it constitutes the fourth mark of a true apostle.

Who Effects the Work of God?

> I warned those who sinned before and all the others, and I warn them now while absent, as I did when present on my second visit, that if I come again I will not spare them—since you desire proof that Christ is speaking in me. He is not weak in dealing with you, but is powerful in you. For he was crucified in weakness, but lives by the power of God. For we are weak in him, but in dealing with you we shall live with him by the power of God (2 Cor. 13:2–4).

Twice in that paragraph Paul speaks of the "power of God." That is what a true servant of Christ relies upon. Many of the commentators picture the apostle in this section as going back to Corinth and sitting as a judge. He will bring all these cases before him, and as a kind of bishop over the whole church, pronounce judgments and then mobilize the congregation to put economic and social pressure upon the dissenting individuals to boycott or excommunicate them.

But I do not find anything like that in Scripture. These are men's ideas brought in. Paul is not stooping to some kind of social pressure brought to bear to bring an evildoer to heel. He is talking about the ability of God to act inside people's consciences and hearts and change them by pressure, trouble, perhaps even disaster, whatever God's judgment may choose. Paul's reliance is not on the congregation to execute this judgment but on God, on Christ, and that is quite different from what we often think of in this regard.

Paul is probably referring to the fact that he would take the last step in the discipline of a church and church members mentioned in Matthew 18:15–20. Discipline begins by going to someone and quietly telling him his fault, between you and him alone. Then if he will not hear you, take one or two more and tell them and talk it over among yourselves. But if he will not hear them, then there comes a time when it is to be told to the church. When Paul comes, all he will do is simply make public what he has known privately up to now. He will tell it to the whole church and then the church will seek to try to reach this individual and bring him to repentance. If he will not hear the church, then the Lord says, "let him be unto you as a publican and sinner," i.e., regard him no longer as a Christian: let him go his way. But nothing further is required, for God will begin to work. As Paul says, "He was crucified in weakness but lives by the power of God. He is not weak in dealing with you, but he is powerful in you. When we come, though we are weak in him, in dealing with you we shall live with him by the power of God." He relies on the fact that God will bring about the result.

I want to share what I regard as an outstanding example of this very experience. Several years ago we had to take an action in our church, very painful at the time, with regard to a brother Christian. He was involved with certain acts of homosexuality, resisted counsel and refused to acknowledge wrong, and eventually we had to take the step of telling it to the church. It was a very painful and a very grievous time because we loved him deeply. Years passed, and then I received this letter from him, and it is reprinted here with his full permission:

My fellow Christians,

Several years ago the congregation of PBC and South Hills Community Church took public action against me in accordance with Matthew 18: 15–20. The charges against me were true.

I cannot reverse history and relive the events that led to my downfall. I have harmed many people and brought ruin to myself. Because I was an outspoken, prominent member of the Christian community my sins have been all the more deplorable and horrendous.

After I became a Christian some 18 years ago I failed to deal thoroughly with lust, covetousness and masturbation. In time I became self-deceived, proud and arrogant. Moreover, eventually God shouted upon the housetops that which I had tried desperately to keep hidden. God finally let me go into alcoholism and sexual immorality, both of which were worse than I experienced before my conversion. Twice I went through the horror and hell of manic-depressive psychoses (as Nebuchadnezzar did) that I might learn that God resists the proud but gives grace to the humble.

I am very fortunate to be alive. I came very close to suicide and should have died in ignominy and disgrace except for the scripture which says, "Dost thou work wonders for the dead? Do the shades rise up to praise thee? Is thy steadfast love declared in the grave, or thy faithfulness in Abaddon?"

I am in need of your forgiveness for I have wronged you all. I earnestly desire your prayers for wholeness and complete deliverance from homosexuality. The church widely believes today that there is no cure for homosexuality beyond arrested development as a celibate. I am certain that God can do much more than he has already done for me and for countless others in this area who are afflicted with this crippling disease.

It is impossible for me to retrace my footsteps and right every wrong, however, I welcome the opportunity to meet and pray with any individuals who have something against me that needs resolution. I am looking and waiting for the further grace and mercy of God in this matter. What

> you have bound on earth has been bound in heaven, and I now know your actions were done in love for my own good and that of the Body.

Immediately, a number of us who had been closely associated with this man asked him to join us in a "welcome home" dinner. We killed the fatted calf. (We had barbecued veal. This was the first time veal steaks have ever been barbecued, I think!) Then we asked him to stand up and we welcomed him back as one who had been dead, but was alive again. We called out to bring a gold ring to put upon his finger. We bought him a new sport coat and put it on his back and welcomed him home as the prodigal son. He felt so welcomed and forgiven that he sat down afterward to tell us what God had taken him through in these intervening years, how God had dealt with him in ways that were ruthless and yet loving, and what a hell he had experienced. He said, "I've come to know the full meaning of the words, 'It is a fearful thing to fall into the hands of the living God'." But it was a joyful time of restoration and renewing our love and fellowship. We rejoice, as I am sure the angels in heaven are rejoicing, that God has effected this discipline not by human pressures, but by the power of God at work in an individual heart in obedience to the Word of the living God. This is what the apostle is talking about.

Here again are the marks of a true apostle:

- Certain authenticating signs that only the original apostles had;
- A selfless spirit that loves and does not demand anything in return;
- A sense of accountability to God alone and not ultimately to the congregation or any man;
- A reliance upon the power of God to carry out the work of God on earth.

If we base our faith on men with these qualifications we will find ourselves standing firmly, in spite of all the shaking that is going on in our day. I urge that upon you in this time.

23

Who Am I—Really?

We come now to the close of this Corinthian letter. Paul has said about all that he can say. Most of the church has repented and changed its attitude toward him and he has rejoiced over that. But there is a handful of people there who are still following the false teachers who had come in, and there are still some who are living in licentiousness and open immorality. The apostle has already told them that there is nothing left except public exposure and when he comes, he says, he is going to do this with them.

Examine Yourself

Now before he does come he faces them with one final question which he hopes will change their attitude and make them clear up their difficulties:

> Examine yourselves, to see whether you are holding to your faith. Test yourselves. Do you not realize that Jesus Christ is in you?—unless indeed you fail to meet the test! (2 Cor. 13:5).

Is Jesus Christ in you? Paul exhorts every individual in the church to ask himself that question. All wrong behavior leads at last to that question. Somewhere, somehow, when we are out-of-line with Christian standards we have to ask ourselves, "Am I a true Christian or am I a counterfeit? Have I been born again or am I only putting up a front?" Those of us who are Christians ought to ask ourselves that occasionally. It is a good idea to examine yourself, especially if there is any kind of wrong behavior involved.

Now the very fact that the apostle could ask such a question indicates what marks true Christianity. A Christian, of course, is not simply one who joins a Christian church. Many people feel that this is the criterion, but it is not; there are millions of church members in this country today who are not Christians. Nor does adhering to a certain moral standard in your life, or the fact that you consistently read the Bible make you a Christian. A true Christian is someone in whom Christ dwells. And the person in whom Christ dwells will have certain inescapable evidence of that fact given to him or her. That is what Paul is suggesting we ask ourselves. Do we have the evidence that Jesus Christ lives in us? Has a fundamental change occurred at the very depths of our being? Actually the question is, "Are you really born again?" That term is being misused these days; people who merely change their actions for a little while are said to be "born again." But this is the question that Paul is asking, "Are you truly and permanently different because Jesus Christ has come to live within you?"

Inner Witness

You may be asking, how can I know that? The answer is found in several places in Scripture. For instance, Scripture speaks of an "inner" witness. In Romans Paul says, "God's Spirit bears witness with our spirit that we are the children of God" (Rom. 8:16). There is an inner testimony, a feeling, a sense within, produced by the Spirit of God who dwells within that you are part of the great family of God. If we are really born again this will be a mark that we have occasionally borne to our hearts, the "witness of the Spirit that we are the children of God." Scripture suggests that this will sometimes take the form of a sense of identity with God as a Father. Our spirits will occasionally want to cry out, "Abba, Father," an intimate term for father. We no longer see God as our judge waiting to condemn us, we see him as a loving Father who is concerned for us, whose arms are around us and who loves us deeply.

I had the joy of pointing my barber to Christ some time ago. Recently while I was having my hair cut he was telling me about the changes that have occurred in his life because he has become a Christian. (One of the great changes is that he gives me free haircuts! That is an almost infallible mark that he has been born again, especially when haircuts are running $7.00 or $8.00 today!) He told me how confident he feels within, and that many of his friends have been noticing this. They have been telling him, "You are so confident. Where do you get that feeling?" (Some of them have actually been accusing him of conceit because of his sense of confidence.) He told me, "They don't understand what I feel within, but I'm confident because" (and this is the way he put it) "I have a deep sense that Daddy is with me all the time." That is the witness of the Spirit. One of the chief marks that we are Christians is that we belong to the Father.

Inner Peace

Scripture also speaks of a sense of "inner peace." In Romans 5 the apostle says, "Having been justified by faith, we have peace with God through our Lord Jesus Christ" (Rom. 5:1 NKJV). The sense of conflict with God is ended; the war is over, we are conscious that the problem of our evil, our sin, no longer troubles God. The work of Christ has satisfied his justice, therefore we have a sense of peace. We also have a sense of destiny. We are going to go to heaven when we die. That is settled and sure not because of anything we have done, but because of what Christ has done. Now that peace is a mark of the witness of the Spirit that Jesus Christ is in us.

Scripture speaks also of new desires that are born in the heart of a new Christian. First Peter 2:2 says, "As newborn babes, desire the sincere milk of the word, that you may grow thereby" NKJV. One of the marks of born again believers is that they have a deep and sudden thirst for the Word of God, a hunger to be fed, to know the truth of God. This ought to continue all our lives for the Bible speaks with tremendous clarity of the things that are essential to our knowledge. Not long ago I saw a video tape of a Bible teacher telling the story of her conversion. Though she had been a church member all her life and had read the Bible from time to time it really was not a very interesting Book to her. But the moment she was born again she had a tremendous hunger to know the Word of God. She haunted church services everywhere, she went to every meeting she could because she could not get enough Bible study. That is one of the marks that Christ is in you. Even as a much older Christian I find that there are times in my experience when I am under pressure, feeling bored or whatever. At this point the only thing that will speak to me is to read one of the Psalms. How that ministers to my heart. Now the Spirit of God creates that hunger, and if Christ is in you this will be one of the marks of it. Because you understand that what

Christ did he did for you, a fundamental change has already occurred in your life. The Spirit of God has entered and released to you the life of Jesus so that it is literally true that Jesus Christ lives in you. That is what Paul says he wants these Corinthians to ask themselves, "Does Christ live in you? Have you been transferred from the kingdom of Satan to the kingdom of God by faith in Jesus Christ?"

Outer Witness

Now this inner change will also produce an outward change, which is not all subjective. We can answer the question, "Is Jesus Christ in you?" by observing our conduct, because the inner change will produce a different behavior. One of the striking things about new Christians is that they invariably manifest a totally different attitude toward things they once thought OK. Perhaps they had been living in sexual immorality, indulging in regular or frequent acts of fornication or sexual perversion of some sort, and had accepted these things, as they are widely accepted today, as being OK. But when they were born again, they suddenly saw these things as injurious and hateful. They no longer wanted to have a part in them. They may have struggled in that, but their desire was now different. In some of the more open and blatant forms of evil, such as attitudes about lying or drunkenness or stealing, they find immediately that their attitude is changed. That is because Christ lives in them, and light can have no part with darkness. Christ cannot have part with Belial. Even your attitude toward your own selfishness changes. You see how selfish you have been. It looks ugly and distasteful in your eyes and you want to be free from it.

It is right here that problems arise in the Christian life. There are many people who truly have been born again who, in the initial years of their Christian experience, did change. Later on, however, as Christianity became old hat to them, as it lost its newness and its freshness, they began to drift back into old patterns that are wrong. Under the pressure of their peers or their circumstances, they allowed themselves to get involved again in things that they once had forsaken as Christians. When that happens it raises the question we have been asking, "Are you really a Christian? Were you born again? Has the change occurred?" The reverse of this situation also raises the question. That is, many people think, for one reason or another, they have become Christians because they went through a certain experience or had a certain feeling at a given time, yet never really surrendered to the Lordship of Jesus, making him Lord of their lives. They, too, can get back into habits they once left; they, too, can give way. There is no difference in their behavior from somebody who is genuine Christian but has slid back into this. So the question, "Are you really a Christian?" is raised at that point. This is what Paul is doing. "Examine yourself," he says. "Others who are watching you cannot answer that question. They do not know whether something you have been doing is only temporary or if it is real with you. They cannot tell, but you can."

Here is the issue: the question you must ask yourself at this point is, how do you feel about your behavior? Are you glad to get back to it? Do you see your conversion as something that represented a kind of religious kick you were on, but you are glad to get back where you can be "normal" and live like everybody else? Or do you hate yourself for doing it? That will tell the story. How do you feel about it? Do you justify it? Do you want to go on with it or do you inwardly hate yourself and wish you were free from it? Are you sorry you went back to it and long to be freed again by the power of Jesus Christ? That is the question Paul is asking the Corinthians.

I hope every one of us will occasionally ask ourselves the same question. Are we holding to our faith? Our attitude and behavior tells the story. If we really believe what we are told to believe we are going to be different. What you think about yourself tells the story of what you are going to do; it governs how you act. We all know that instinctively. Have you ever said to yourself or to somebody else, "Who do you think you are anyhow, doing this sort of thing?" You instinctively know that it is what people think themselves to be which will govern and control their behavior. So the most important question you can ask yourself is: "Am I really a Christian? Have I been changed? Who am I—really?"

The answer to that question, Paul says, will also answer the question that these Corinthians were asking about him for they were asking, "Is Paul really an apostle? Has he failed us as an apostle of Christ? Are these other men who came in and taught us different things right? Is Paul the phony apostle?" Now Paul says, "When you answer the question about yourself you will have the answer to the one about me. If you find that you are real Christians then you will also know that I am a real apostle." Listen to the way he puts it:

> Examine yourselves, to see whether you are holding to your faith. Test yourselves. Do you not realize that Jesus Christ is in you?—unless indeed you fail to meet the test! I hope you will find out that we have not failed. But we pray God that you may not do wrong—not that we may appear to have met the test, but that you may do what is right, though we may

> seem to have failed. For we cannot do anything against the truth, but only for the truth. For we are glad when we are weak and you are strong. What we pray for is your improvement (2 Cor. 13:5–9).

Paul explains that he is not looking for an opportunity to come and demonstrate his authority by judging them; he takes no delight in flexing his apostolic muscle. He would be quite happy if they would judge themselves and stop their evil behavior, leaving nothing for him to do when he comes but to rejoice with them. In fact, he says, "I would be quite willing to let you go on thinking that I am very weak as an apostle, that I really do not amount to much, that I am only a paper tiger, as long as your behavior changes in line with who you really are." What he wants is their moral improvement, not an opportunity to personally exhibit his authority.

In verse 10 he says something which is very important:

> I write this while I am away from you, in order that when I come I may not have to be severe in my use of the authority which the Lord has given me for building up and not for tearing down.

The Right Authority

That principle is often forgotten today. The apostle makes clear that true authority in the church, even beginning with the apostles, is not intended to destroy people or tear them down; it is to build them up. In other words, apostolic power is not to boss people with. It is not given so that somebody can lord it over the brothers. Everywhere in the Word of God we are warned against that idea of leadership. Yet as I travel around I find many churches where one man is enthroned as the pastor. He sees himself as the authority in the church. He alone can pronounce on doctrine; he alone has the right to determine who is going to exercise spiritual gifts in the congregation; he alone is the final, authoritative teacher. But Scripture warns against that. It warns against "lording it over" the brethren, bossing them and regulating the intimate details of their lives. Paul makes it clear that is not the kind of authority even he as an apostle has. It is not a totalitarian control over all the details of someone's life.

Recently I heard an account of a church where certain elders have assumed commanding authority over others. These elders were concerned about a certain couple who lived in the same apartment building with them. They felt the wife was not submissive to her husband so they insisted she demonstrate submission by obtaining their written permission for a whole year to even leave the building. She said that on one occasion her mother became very ill but since she could not leave the building without permission, and none of the elders happened to be home, it created a serious emergency.

Now that kind of authority is everywhere condemned in the Word of God. Even the apostle said his authority is given to build people up, to encourage them, to support them, to restore them and renew them. If discipline is called for it is a last resort. Note how reluctant he is to exercise this discipline, how long he gives them to correct conditions. When he does move, he says, it will be in line with what the Lord has said in Matthew 18. He will move step-by-step, looking to God, not to the congregation, to bring pressure on the individual, and the discipline will cease immediately upon the person's repentance. Paul is clear about what a Christian should be; it especially depends on the answer to that all-important question, "Does Jesus Christ live in you or not?"

A Hug and More

Paul's last word appeals for mutual support among the brethren:

> Finally, brethren, farewell. Mend your ways, heed my appeal, agree with one another, live in peace, and the God of love and peace will be with you. Greet one another with a holy kiss. All the saints greet you. The grace of the Lord Jesus Christ and the love of God and the fellowship of the Holy Spirit be with you all (2 Cor. 12:11–14).

It is wonderful that this last word is a word of peace. The apostle sees beyond all the fragmentation in Corinth to the basic unity of the church. God created that unity. Even though quarreling, jealousy and division invade the assembly, still Christians belong to each other. They are part of the family of God and they ought to act that way. Beyond the rebellion he sees the grace and the power of God, able to heal these breaches and restore people even to the point where they can share a holy kiss. (That was the standard greeting of the day. Most of us have lost that custom, although in Poland I noticed it has stayed alive. For too long we have substituted a handshake and I am happy to see hugs coming back in again. Hugs are a much warmer and more accurate expression of Christian love and acceptance, one with another.)

The apostle urges these Christians: "Change your ways. If Jesus Christ is in you, you can do it." You cannot go on living like everybody else if Jesus Christ lives in you: this is the fundamental reason why there must be a difference in Christians. I was driving down the freeway the other day and a car cut in front of me, almost driving me off the road, then it cut in ahead of the car in front of me. I noticed a bumper sticker on it that said, "The difference in me is Jesus." Well, I was not much impressed, and neither is the world impressed when they look at us and see us behaving just like everyone else. We are not to behave that way in our personal lives because Christ is in us. We are not to behave in our corporate life that way because Christ is among us. We are to be friendly, loving, open, forgiving, not condemnatory, narrow and bitter. We are different because Christ is among us.

Notice how the apostle closes. What a beautiful greeting this is. It is the clearest reference to the Trinity that there is in the New Testament:

> The grace of the Lord Jesus Christ and the love of God and the fellowship (or commonality) of the Holy Spirit be with you all (2 Cor. 12:14).

What a gracious word from the great apostle as he closes this letter to the church at Corinth! History does not tell us what happened in the church there, whether it was able to recover and obey this word or not. But Paul has done his best. He has left with us a tremendous testimony as to what constitutes Christianity at work in a pagan world.

We are called to live in Corinthian conditions today. I hope and pray that these letters to the Corinthian church will mean much to us, that we too will obey the Word of the apostle and recognize that when Jesus Christ is among us we cannot be the same kind of people. This is the issue. May God grant that we will understand this more thoroughly in days to come.